D1389591

Transforming Government

General Editor: **R. A. W. Rhodes**, Professor of Politics, University of Newcastle

This important and authoritative new series arises out of the seminal ESRC Whitehall Programme and seeks to fill the enormous gaps in our knowledge of the key actors and institutions of British government. It examines the many large changes during the postwar period and puts these into comparative context by analysing the experience of the advanced industrial democracies of Europe and the nations of the Commonwealth. The series reports the results of the Whitehall Programme, a four-year project into change in British government in the postwar period, mounted by the Economic and Social Research Council.

Titles include:

Simon Bulmer, Martin Burch, Caitríona Carter, Patricia Hogwood and Andrew Scott
BRITISH DEVOLUTION AND EUROPEAN POLICY-MAKING
Transforming Britain into Multi-Level Governance

Nicholas Deakin and Richard Parry
THE TREASURY AND SOCIAL POLICY
The Contest for Control of Welfare Strategy

David Marsh, David Richards and Martin J. Smith
CHANGING PATTERNS OF GOVERNANCE IN THE UNITED KINGDOM
Reinventing Whitehall?

B. Guy Peters, R. A. W. Rhodes and Vincent Wright (*editors*)
ADMINISTERING THE SUMMIT
Administration of the Core Executive in Developed Countries

R. A. W. Rhodes (*editor*)
TRANSFORMING BRITISH GOVERNMENT
Volume One: Changing Institutions
Volume Two: Changing Roles and Relationships

Martin J. Smith
THE CORE EXECUTIVE IN BRITAIN

Kevin Theakston
LEADERSHIP IN WHITEHALL

Kevin Theakston (*editor*)
BUREAUCRATS AND LEADERSHIP

Patrick Weller, Herman Bakvis and R. A. W. Rhodes (*editors*)
THE HOLLOW CROWN
Countervailing Trends in Core Executives

Transforming Government
Series Standing Order ISBN 0–333–71580–2
(*outside North America only*)

You can receive future titles in this series as they are published by placing a standing order. Please contact your bookseller or, in case of difficulty, write to us at the address below with your name and address, the title of the series and the ISBN quoted above.

Customer Services Department, Macmillan Distribution Ltd, Houndmills, Basingstoke, Hampshire RG21 6XS, England

British Devolution and European Policy-Making

Transforming Britain into Multi-Level Governance

Simon Bulmer
Jean Monnet Professor of European Politics
University of Manchester

Martin Burch
Professor of Government
University of Manchester

Caitríona Carter
Lecturer in European Union Studies
Edinburgh Law School
University of Edinburgh

Patricia Hogwood
Lecturer in Politics
University of Glasgow

Andrew Scott
Professor of European Union Studies
Edinburgh Law School
University of Edinburgh

First published 2002 by
PALGRAVE MACMILLAN
Houndmills, Basingstoke, Hampshire RG21 6XS and
175 Fifth Avenue, New York, N.Y. 10010
Companies and representatives throughout the world

PALGRAVE MACMILLAN is the global academic imprint of the Palgrave Macmillan division of St. Martin's Press, LLC and of Palgrave Macmillan Ltd. Macmillan® is a registered trademark in the United States, United Kingdom and other countries. Palgrave is a registered trademark in the European Union and other countries.

ISBN 1–4039–0010–8

This book is printed on paper suitable for recycling and made from fully managed and sustained forest sources.

A catalogue record for this book is available from the British Library.

Library of Congress Cataloging-in-Publication Data

British devolution and European policy-making: transforming Britain into multi-level governance / Simon Bulmer ... [et al.].
    p. cm. – (Transforming government)
    Includes bibliographical references and index.
    ISBN 1–4039–0010–8
    1. Regionalism–Great Britain. 2. Decentralization in government–Great Britain. 3. Home rule–Scotland. 4. Home rule–Wales. 5. European Union–Great Britain. I. Bulmer, Simon. II. Transforming government (Palgrave Macmillan (Firm))

JN297.R44 B735 2002
320.441′049–dc21   2002075807

10   9   8   7   6   5   4   3   2   1
11   10   09   08   07   06   05   04   03   02

Printed and bound in Great Britain by
Antony Rowe Ltd, Chippenham and Eastbourne

Contents

Preface

1 July 1999 – designated 'Devolution Day' – saw a formal transfer of powers between the UK Parliament at Westminster and the newly-established Scottish Parliament in Edinburgh and the National Assembly of Wales in Cardiff. This, the first tranche of transfers within what is generally considered to be a continuing process of devolution, was accompanied by formal ceremonials, media events, street festivities, and was heralded as representing the advent of a new, inclusive type of politics for Scotland and Wales.

Devolution, it has been claimed, is the most significant constitutional reform to affect the territorial politics of the UK since the Great Reform Act of 1832 (Bogdanor 1998). Incontestably devolution has altered fundamentally the constitutional framework of the British state. At the same time, of course, the practice of delegating administrative authority (and, in the case of Northern Ireland after 1920, considerable political home rule) to territorial administrations to act on behalf of central government is a long-standing feature of UK governance (Mitchell 1999). The Scottish Office could boast a history dating back to 1885 while the Welsh Office was created more recently, in 1964. And although the Northern Ireland Office dates only from 1972 following the decision to suspend the Stormont Parliament, this was an exercise in political control being repatriated by central UK government (by establishing 'direct rule') rather than a latter-day exercise in administrative devolution.

Notwithstanding the unique historical circumstances of Northern Ireland governance, the 'devolution project' launched by the Labour government in 1997 properly can be regarded as marking the beginning of a new phase in British politics. For although distinct territorial administrations had operated in Scotland and Wales prior to 1999, the absence of elected assemblies to whom they were answerable meant that they were not *directly* accountable at the territorial level. In short, administrative devolution had no counterpart in political devolution, and it was this perceived anomaly which Labour's 'devolution project' was designed to address. Viewed in that light, devolution signalled the willingness of the newly elected Labour government to concede (as legitimate) to what were becoming increasingly vociferous demands from within Scotland and Wales for administrative authority to be matched by democratic accountability at the level at which it was exercised

(Munro 2000). The underlying problem was straightforward. In the eyes of the critics, government from the centre – from London – had failed to meet what might be termed 'common-sense' criteria of good governance. Not only had the UK government seemingly failed – at least since 1979 and arguably before – to meet the aspirations of the Scottish and Welsh publics, it had foisted upon these publics economic and social policies for which there was very little popular support. This failure of UK governance had been exploited by the nationalist political parties in Scotland and Wales and had contributed to creating a popular mood that was predominantly in favour of some measure of home rule. Such was the rationale for Labour's 'devolution project'.

Formally, of course, the rebuttal to this line of argument was equally straightforward. Although the activities of the territorial offices were not directly accountable 'locally', nonetheless these offices were departments of UK government and fully accountable as such. Both the Scottish and Welsh Offices were headed by a Secretary of State who was a member of the UK Cabinet, while specific parliamentary procedures and committees existed to ensure that matters of particular political and/or legislative relevance to Scotland and Wales were fully debated and scrutinised. Critics of devolution thus concluded that there was no democratic deficit, and no corresponding crisis of legitimacy of UK governance. Indeed, their concerns were that the devolution project itself might precipitate precisely such a crisis (or at least a confusion) of governance which, ultimately, might lead to the break-up of the United Kingdom. As one constitutional expert has noted, 'on this question, however, the jury is still out' (Munro 2000).

The devolution project

Although the implementation of the 1997 devolution programme marks a watershed in British constitutional and political arrangements, devolution is by no means a new idea. Indeed, it had been extensively debated in the UK during the 1970s and, following the Report of the Royal Commission on the Constitution (Kilbrandon 1973), the 1974–79 Labour government procured legislation for devolved governments to be established in Wales and Scotland. Ultimately these proposals were rejected under the terms set for consultative referendums held in the two territories. In the wake of the election of the Conservative government in May 1979, devolution was removed from the government's agenda. Despite the referendum defeats, devolution remained a 'live' political issue in both Scotland and Wales, forcefully so in Scotland they were to be members of these committees. The upshot is that the Assembly is a hybrid between a Westminster-Whitehall system and an arrangement resonant of a County Council structure.[2]

As already noted, the differences in the Scottish and Welsh devolution settlements are not only organisational and procedural. A crucial distinction revolves around the respective legislative competencies of the two assemblies. The Scottish Parliament may issue both primary and secondary legislation in devolved matters (i.e. it has full legislative powers, but with particular limits on competence in ss. 28–29 of the Scotland Act 1998), while the Welsh Assembly has the power to issue subordinate legislation (i.e. will exercise those ministerial functions as transferred to it by Order in Council). Moreover, the devolution legislation delegated a more extensive range of policy responsibilities to the new Scottish administration than to its Welsh counterpart – in large measure mirroring the differences in functions assigned to the Scottish and Welsh Offices of UK government respectively prior to devolution. An overview of the situation as it stands is presented in Table 0.2. One point worth noting is that the two offices of the Secretary of State for Scotland and the Secretary of State for Wales are retained. Both Secretaries of State retain membership of the UK Cabinet, albeit with only a fraction of the resources previously at their disposal (most of the staff previously employed in the 'territorial' departments having been transferred to the new assemblies and their executives). However, both have a small staff located in what were subsequently renamed the Scotland Office and the Wales Office.[3]

Leaders and events

Inevitably, the realisation of the devolution project has come to be associated with a handful of dominant political actors and key administrators and advisers. Chief amongst these were the incumbent Secretaries of State for Scotland and Wales who were charged with the task of managing the passage of the devolution legislation through the Westminster Parliament – Donald Dewar and Ron Davies respectively (see Chapter 1). Both men were firm believers in devolution – as both an integral element in Labour's package of constitutional reform measures and a political imperative. Both recognised devolution as an essential step if government was to be brought closer to the people of Scotland and Wales – indeed as a means of renewing the moral legitimacy of government in those parts of the UK.

Important as their role was in managing the devolution legislation through Westminster, both Dewar and Davies were highly influential in shaping the devolution project in their own countries. Dewar not only came to be regarded as the principal architect of Scotland's devolution, but brought to the debate a sense of calm authority and confidence without which opponents of devolution from across the political spectrum and beyond may have had greater success. Indeed, Dewar emerged from the devolution debate with his political and personal reputation hugely enhanced and found himself occupying a unique place in Scottish public life. Significantly, neither Dewar nor Davies viewed the 1998 legislation necessarily as the end of the devolution debate. Ron Davies famously described devolution as 'a process, not an event' (Davies 1998), while Donald Dewar's depiction of the Scottish Parliament as 'not an end: a means to greater ends' (Dewar 1999) could be interpreted in a similar vein.

In September, 1998 Dewar and Davies were selected as the Labour candidates for the leadership of the devolved administrations in Scotland and Wales respectively, should Labour win the respective elections – which, of course, it subsequently did. With Dewar assuming office of First Minister of the Scottish Executive, and heading a coalition executive of 11 ministers, he resigned the post of Secretary of State for Scotland and was replaced by John Reid, MP, who took over at the renamed Scotland Office. Dewar remained in office until his sudden death in October 2000 whereupon he was succeeded as First Minister by Henry McLeish.[4]

In Wales, as in Scotland, unanticipated leadership changes marked the early phase of the devolution process. Ron Davies, a popular and colourful figure, was expected to become First Secretary of the Assembly (election result permitting). However, following controversial press speculation over his personal life, on 27 October 1998 he resigned both as leader of the Welsh Labour Party (and so potential Assembly First Secretary) and Secretary of State for Wales. He was succeeded as Secretary of State by Alun Michael who, the following February in a contentious selection process, narrowly defeated Rhodri Morgan for the post of leader of the Welsh Labour Party. Michael had received strong backing in his candidacy from Prime Minister Blair, and it was he who, in May 1999, became First Secretary of the National Assembly of Wales. Like Dewar, Michael found himself leading an Assembly without an absolute majority but unlike Dewar opted to form a minority administration rather than enter into a formal coalition with the Liberal Democrats, and duly appointed a Labour executive of seven Assembly Secretaries. Controversially, Michael remained as Secretary of State for Wales in the Blair government until July, 1999 discharging the obligations of that post in tandem with his duties as Assembly First Secretary. He was succeeded as Secretary of State by Paul Murphy. However, controversy continued to dog him and, amidst mounting criticisms over his alleged subservience to the Blair government and his control of Assembly business, Michael resigned as First Secretary on 9 February 2000 shortly before the Assembly adopted a vote of no-confidence in his leadership. On 11 February Rhodri Morgan – Michael's rival in Labour's Welsh leadership battle – was elected unopposed as First Secretary and his position was formally endorsed in the Assembly plenary of 15 February. On 16 October 2000, the Labour Assembly group entered a coalition with the Liberal Democrats, who obtained two portfolios in an expanded nine-member cabinet.

It was against this political background that the initial phase of devolved governance in Scotland and Wales unfolded. In Northern Ireland, however, the devolution project was considerably more fragile and was under constant threat of being swamped by long-standing political and civil tensions. On 10 April 1998 – Good Friday – the Belfast Agreement was signed establishing a framework for power-sharing in Northern Ireland. The Agreement provided for the creation of an Assembly of 108 members that would have legislative and executive powers, and whose policy functions were broadly comparable to those of the Welsh Assembly – although certain legislative measures would require special majorities before entering into force to ensure that these commanded cross-community support. The Belfast Agreement was endorsed in referendums held in Northern Ireland and in the Republic of Ireland on 22 May 1998, and elections to the Northern Ireland Assembly followed on 25 June 1998 under the terms of the Northern Ireland (Elections) Act 1998. With the conclusion of the passage of the Northern Ireland Act through Westminster in November 1998, power was formally transferred to the Assembly on 2 December 1999. Unlike the situation in Scotland and Wales, devolution to Northern Ireland was not a free-standing political initiative. Instead, it was part of a much broader package of measures enacted simultaneously and impacting over a range of linked factors, each of which had a bearing on the complex political situation in Ireland (the new 'north–south' and 'British–Irish' agreements came into operation at the same time as devolution). However, since then the political situation has remained tense and the Northern Ireland Assembly continues to face an uncertain future.

We have already recorded Ron Davies's famous aphorism that 'devolution is a process, not an event'. Arguably it is in terms of its geographical scope rather than in its intensity that the devolution project has yet to make its most profound constitutional impact. This is because the Labour government's commitment to devolution was not confined to Scotland, Wales and Northern Ireland: the principle of devolved governance also was to extend to the English regions. Here, however, progress has been very slow reflecting, in part at least, the absence of a substantial lobby favouring devolution to the English regions. Even in those parts of England where support is strongest (e.g. the North East and North West of England), the devolution project seemingly has failed to capture the public's imagination – in short, apparently devolution is not regarded as a political priority for the average voter in England. Nonetheless, some preliminary measures have been implemented. On 1 April 1999 Regional Development Agencies were established in eight English regions, and in May–July 1999 eight corresponding Regional Chambers were designated.

In London, however, a measure of 'devolution' has occurred. In July 1997 the process to create a directly-elected mayor for London and a Greater London Assembly (GLA) began. This culminated in a local referendum held on 7 May 1998, which approved the proposals and, in November 1999, the Greater London Authority Act received Royal Assent. In London, as before in Wales, the Prime Minister, Tony Blair, became embroiled in a controversial selection contest over who should be Labour's mayoral candidate. Following his narrow defeat by Frank Dobson to be Labour's candidate in the forthcoming mayoral election, Ken Livingstone – who had been strongly opposed by Blair – decided to stand as an Independent candidate and won. Meanwhile Dobson, Labour's candidate, could only manage third place behind the Conservative candidate, Steven Norris. Labour also performed poorly in the elections for the GLA, which were held simultaneously with the mayoral election: the Conservatives matched Labour's nine seats in what had been widely tipped as a Labour-dominated race.

Behind the politics: administering devolution

Given the constitutional and political significance of the devolution project, it is hardly surprising that the personalities and politics surrounding its conception and implementation have dominated – and continue to dominate – the public consciousness. But there is more to devolution than these often highly-charged political issues. The devolution project has to be managed, and this gives the arrangement an administrative underbelly which is likely to be immensely important in shaping the ultimate consequences of this constitutional experiment.

design and inter-administration procedures rather than on broader political considerations. However, we were fully aware of these considerations, and became more so in the course of many interviews. In total we undertook more than 50 in-depth interviews, principally with senior officials working in Edinburgh, Cardiff, Whitehall, Westminster and Brussels. We interviewed a number of key participants on two occasions; once before devolution went 'live' and once in the aftermath of devolution. This provided key insights into the anticipated and – significantly – the unanticipated consequences of devolution from the perspective of the administrations. We would like to extend our sincere thanks to those who agreed to be interviewed for their invaluable assistance with the research. All interviews were conducted on a non-attributable basis, and this is reflected in the referencing method used in the report. There are a small number of senior officials who went beyond this and acted as important facilitators in the project. We cannot name them but they deserve especial thanks. We would also like to thank Lord Falconer of Thoroton, then Minister of State in the Cabinet Office, for giving the keynote speech at a project conference held in Edinburgh in February 2000. A number of other speakers contributed to that conference, including Klaus Goetz, Elisa Roller and Dermot Scott, who helped put our findings into a comparative context.

Empirical research of the type reported here necessarily is processed and filtered through an extant mindset or theoretical framework. The research interpretation we offer in the report is informed by institutionalist thinking, specifically historical institutionalism. This framework was chosen because of its concerns with continuity and/or change over time. The project was not concerned principally with advancing the analytical literature, although a number of pertinent issues arise from this project, such as how to measure institutional change. We will follow up these issues elsewhere.

There are a number of debts of gratitude to be expressed. First and foremost, we must thank the ESRC for support under award no. L327253024 for the project. We would also like to thank Ian Holliday for his help in putting together the grant application; Christine Agius for her research assistance in Manchester; Professor Colin Munro, Edinburgh Law School, Tom Brady and Andrew Jordan for reading and commenting on parts of the report. We benefited also from the support of Professor John Usher at the Europa Institute, University of Edinburgh, from Professor Chris Himsworth, Edinburgh Law School, and from support linked to Simon Bulmer's Jean Monnet Chair for presenting findings at conferences. Feedback from papers given at, *inter alia*, the UACES conference in

Budapest, March 2000, the PAC Conference in Durham, September 2000, from seminars in the Department of Government, in PREST and in the Law Faculty at Manchester has been helpful for our work. Preparation of the manuscript for publication by Palgrave Macmillan was carried out within the framework of ESRC grant L219252003. As always, we remain responsible for errors of fact or interpretation.

This book is the product of a complex division of labour but one shared equally amongst the authors. Data collection (including interviewing) and project discussions were conducted by all authors. Patricia Hogwood served as research officer prior to taking up her position at Glasgow. Each chapter had a lead-author, who was responsible for writing up the research. The lead-authors were: Chapter 1 (Martin Burch), Chapter 2 (Simon Bulmer), Chapter 3 (Andrew Scott), Chapter 4 (Caitríona Carter), Chapter 5 (Simon Bulmer), Chapter 6 (Patricia Hogwood), Chapter 7 (Martin Burch). Patricia Hogwood provided the contributions on Wales to Chapters 3 and 4; Andrew Scott provided the input on Scotland for Chapter 6. The division of labour was complex but we continue to collaborate on the same subject!

Finally, a note on citation methods. We have utilised some documents that are rather unusual in nature for referencing purposes. We have also been early users of the web-based reports of the National Assembly for Wales and the Scottish Parliament, where citation methods have not entirely stabilised hitherto. At the time of writing, citation conventions relating to official documentation of the National Assembly for Wales were under development. Verbatim reports, such as plenary sessions, written and oral questions and committee evidence sessions (especially sessions of the Audit Committee and occasionally other committees by request), are compiled as the National Assembly for Wales Record of Proceedings (NAWRP). These are also indexed by POLIS. The citation style recommended by the Assembly for such documents was: National Assembly for Wales Record of Proceedings, 22 June 1999; p. 3. It was anticipated that Volume and Part numbers might be added at a later date, as follows: National Assembly for Wales Record of Proceedings, 22 June 1999; Vol. 1, part 2, p. 3. (Page numbers are available on the pdf version of such documents accessed on the web.) Non-verbatim reports, such as those recording regular meetings of the European Affairs Committee, are not compiled under the NAWRP and as yet there is no convention for citing from them. We were advised to use a common-sense method that would allow other scholars to access the material referred to. We therefore cite material drawn from the committee meetings of the European Affairs Committee using their standard reference code, i.e.: Eur-02-99: p. 3, where 'Eur' refers to the committee; the first group of numbers to the sequence of the meeting within the year in question (here, the second meeting); the second group of numbers refers to the year in which the meeting took place (1999); and p. 3 indicates the paper referred to (paper 3).

List of Abbreviations

ADAS	Agriculture Development Advisory Service
AEC	Assembly Executive Committee (Wales; now referred to as the Cabinet)
AM	Assembly Member (Member of the National Assembly for Wales)
AMS	Additional Member System
AS	Assembly Secretary (Wales; now referred to as Assembly Minister)
BSE	Bovine Spongiform Encephalopathy
CAP	Common Agricultural Policy
CFSP	Common Foreign and Security Policy
COCS	Cabinet Office Constitution Secretariat (UK)
COES	Cabinet Office European Secretariat (UK)
COLA	Cabinet Office Legal Advisers (UK)
CoR	Committee of the Regions (EU)
COREPER	Committee of Permanent Representatives (Brussels)
COSAC	Conference of European Affairs Committees (EU)
COSLA	Convention of Scottish Local Authorities
CSG	Consultative Steering Group
DAD	Devolution Administration Department (FCO, UK)
DAFS	Department of Agriculture and Fisheries, Scotland
DCE	Departmental Committee on Europe (MAFF)
DETR	Department of the Environment, Transport and the Regions (UK)
DGN	Devolution Guidance Note (UK)
DoE	Department of the Environment
DOP	Cabinet (Ministerial) Committee on Defence and Overseas Policy (UK)
DP	Cabinet (Ministerial) Committee on Devolution Policy (UK – replaced DSWR)
DSWR	Cabinet (Ministerial) Committee on Devolution to Scotland, Wales and the English Regions (UK)
DTI	Department of Trade and Industry
EAC	European Affairs Committee (National Assembly for Wales)
EAD (NAW)	European Affairs Division (National Assembly for Wales)

EAD (SO)	European Affairs Division (Scottish Office)
EAD (WO)	European Affairs Division (Welsh Office)
EAPB	European Affairs Policy Branch (Welsh Office)
EC	European Community
ECG	European Co-ordination Group (Scottish Executive)
ECHR	European Convention on Human Rights
ECOSOC	Economic and Social Committee (EU)
(E)DOP	Cabinet (Ministerial) Sub-Committee on European Issues (UK)
EM	Explanatory Memorandum
EMU	European Monetary Union
EP	European Parliament
EPSED	Environment Protection Strategy and Europe Division (DoE)
EQ(O)	Official Cabinet Committee on European Questions (UK)
EQ(O)*	Cabinet (Senior official-level) Committee/s on European Questions (UK)
ESC	European Scrutiny Committee (House of Commons)
ESG	European Strategy Group (Wales)
ESU	European Support Unit (Scottish Office)
EU	European Union
FCO	Foreign and Commonwealth Office (UK)
FS	First Secretary (Wales; now referred to as the First Minister)
GLA	Greater London Assembly
GM	Genetically Modified
HC	House of Commons
HL	House of Lords
IDG	Inter-Departmental Group on Constitutional Reform
JHA	Justice and Home Affairs
JMC	Joint Ministerial Committee
JMC(O)EU	Officials Committee attached to JMCE
JMCE	Joint Ministerial Committee, European Issues
JOC	Joint Officials Committee (services JMC)
MAFF	Ministry of Agriculture, Fisheries and Food
MEP	Member of the European Parliament
MINECOR	Ministerial Committee for European Coordination (NB. Not a UK Cabinet committee)
MoU	Memorandum of Understanding
MP	Member of Parliament (UK)
MSP	Member of the Scottish Parliament
NAAG	National Assembly Advisory Group (Wales)

NAW	National Assembly for Wales
NAWRP	National Assembly for Wales Record of Proceedings
PES	Public Expenditure Survey
PM	Prime Minister (UK)
RIA	Regulatory Impact Assessment
SCEU	Select Committee on the European Union (House of Lords)
SCN	Scottish Cover Note
SE (Brussels)	Scottish Executive Representative Office (Brussels)
SCVO	Scottish Council of Voluntary Organisations
SE	Scottish Executive
SEB	Scottish European Brief
SEC	Scottish European Committee (Scottish Parliament)
SEL	Scotland Europa Ltd
SERAD	Scottish Executive Rural Affairs Department
SNP	Scottish National Party
SO	Scottish Office
SOAEFD	Scottish Office Agriculture, Environment and Fisheries Department
STUC	Scottish Trade Union Congress
TEU	Treaty on European Union
UK	United Kingdom
UKRep	United Kingdom Permanent Representation to the European Union (Brussels)
WCC	Wales Commercial Centre (Brussels)
WDA	Welsh Development Agency
WEC	Wales European Centre (Brussels)
WO	Welsh Office
WOAD	Welsh Office Agriculture Department

1
Introduction: Labour, Constitutional Change and European Policy

1.1 Introduction

The United Kingdom (UK) Labour government elected in May 1997 introduced a major programme of constitutional reform. This programme embraced a wide range of measures including commitment to the reform of the UK Parliament, the creation of an independent central bank, the introduction of freedom of information legislation, the incorporation of the European Convention on Human Rights (ECHR) into UK law and measures for devolution. Taken as a whole, this programme was ambitious and radical in its implication. One of the world's most ancient systems of parliamentary government, which had evolved into its contemporary characteristics over many centuries, now faced substantial restructuring on a wide front. True, reform had been undertaken in the past, but the breadth of the Labour programme made this one unique.

A key element of the reform package was the creation of devolved governments in Scotland, Wales and Northern Ireland. Clearly, the establishment of both representative elected bodies and political executives for each of these countries marked a clear departure from previous arrangements (Hazell 1999; Leicester 1999). Yet the degree and dimensions of the change involved remain matters for investigation and assessment. Just how radical is the change that has taken place and what are the implications of it for the future development of the UK state? These questions can only be addressed after careful examination of the decisions reached both during the months preceding and those following the creation of devolved governments, arguably the critical period in which new institutions emerged and became established.

Judgement on the scope and extent of change is compounded by the fact that the alteration to territorial government has not taken place through addressing and re-ordering the principles underlying UK constitutional practice. Rather these principles have been preserved intact, with the new arrangements grafted on. On the surface, this would suggest a high degree of continuity, but, given the ambiguity and flexibility of UK constitutional provisions, it should not be assumed that this will prove to be the case. In addition, the asymmetrical nature of devolved government introduces a further dimension to any assessment of change. Each of the countries has a distinctive devolutionary settlement reflecting both the pathways taken to reform and the arrangements as they existed prior to devolution. The pattern of, and prospects for, devolution are thus quite distinct in each case. That in turn raises questions about how the asymmetry is to be handled and what centripetal mechanisms are in place to consolidate, constrain and contain it.

Importantly, the manner of the emergence of the new forms of governance has been (in perhaps typically British fashion) piecemeal and accretive, beginning with White Papers followed by UK legislation. The 1997 White Papers (Scottish Office 1997; Welsh Office 1997) and the Scotland Act 1998 and the Government of Wales Act 1998 thus constitute the framework on which subsequent devolution working arrangements have been built. Yet, these only provided a broad outline of what devolved government might amount to, the legislation in particular being lacking in detail, especially by comparison with the 1979 proposals. As a matter of necessity, such primary legislation was subsequently supplemented by other documents, most notably 'concordats' and guidance notes, laying out structures, procedures, rules and understandings. Furthermore, actual practices of the devolved institutions that have emerged have now become established ways of proceeding in the early months of devolution.[5] In our view, consideration of the role of these supplementary documents, agreements and operating practices is essential to understanding and assessing the nature of the devolved settlement. Devolution must be seen as cumulative and transformative with the infrastructure of devolved government laid bit by bit, as new perspectives and priorities emerge. The substance of the constitutional settlement (to be examined) thus extends well beyond the framework legislation.

1.2   The nature and scope of the study

Our project examines the critical early stages of the process of institution building and reports on initial developments. It covers the period between the passage of the legislation in the summer of 1998 providing for the creation of the devolved governments, through the first ten months of their operation to the end of February 2000. This we see as the critical period of institution building. It is a central assumption of our analysis that this constitutive phase has set precedents that will shape the development of devolved government. During this phase, significant decisions were taken about how the devolved governments would work both individually and in a UK context. These decisions are primary ones in that they set the detailed structure within which the further evolution of the new British polity is now taking place. Our project is designed to capture and record these in this critical, initial phase of institution building.

Our approach is to concentrate on the issue of European policy-making. European Union (EU) policy is a key area in the devolution process, for although relations within the EU have been reserved to the Westminster Parliament and to central government departments in Whitehall, many of the powers that have been devolved (and transferred) to both Scotland and Wales have a substantial EU component. The handling of EU business post devolution is therefore likely to provide key insights into emergent relationships within a devolving UK state, where both the formulation and the implementation of European policy is affected. Key questions at the outset of our research, therefore, were the following:

- How would the UK government and the devolved authorities find a functioning working method to handle European policy?
- Would the UK government's reputation for having a coherent European policy, and a good record at transposing European Community (EC) law, be weakened by the need to attend to the internal dynamics of devolution?
- Would devolution lead to increased accountability of European policy through new mechanisms in the National Assembly for Wales (NAW) and the Scottish Parliament (SP)?
- Would the devolved authorities establish representations in Brussels that might undermine or compete with the established UK Permanent Representation to the EU, thus undermining the coherence of British European policy?
- What light would the experiences of an emergent multi-level system for UK–EU policy shed upon the process of devolution more generally?
- Taken as a whole, would the new arrangements and the responses to such challenges result in devolution constituting a 'critical juncture' in the handling of UK European policy?

The handling of European policy is thus especially revealing as it involves questions that concern multiple tiers of government: largely a new development in the UK.[6] For devolution looked likely to have the effect of bringing the UK more in line with the established pattern of dispersed power in several EU member states, such as Germany, Spain and Belgium (see, for instance, Rometsch and Wessels 1996). In particular, devolution requires a new relationship between Whitehall and the devolved administrations on European policy-making. For, although European policy is reserved to the UK government, its formulation and implementation has to involve the devolved governments. The effect of devolution is to increase the potential for tension between the two levels and to expand the opportunities for different agendas to develop. For these reasons alone, European policy-making offers a potentially revealing area for analysis, especially if we wish to comprehend the broad impact of devolution on the UK polity and beyond.

The distribution of responsibilities on EU matters was set out in the White Papers and the legislation setting up the devolved governments. The UK government leads on negotiations in Europe and on dealings with our partners in Europe. As the Member State government, it has responsibility for relations with EU institutions and with the other Member States. Under the UK legislation, overall responsibility for European policy is reserved to it.[7] Yet matters determined in the EU affect extensive areas of policy handled by the devolved institutions. To effect 'joined up' government, the sub-state institutions need to be drawn into the development of the UK's negotiating position. Also, the devolved administrations are responsible for the implementation of those EC regulations and directives which fall within their remit although, again, the UK government, as the Member State government, remains responsible within the EU for implementation across the UK. This situation means that in effect the operation of, if not the formal responsibility for, European policy is divided between the national and devolved tiers of government in the UK. Under these circumstances the salience of the above questions should be clear.

In researching the above empirical questions we have concentrated on exploring institutional arrangements for European policy-making before and after devolution. This 'before and after' approach is reflected in certain analytical propositions about change which we develop from an historical institutionalist perspective as well as in the organisation of our findings in subsequent chapters. We turn our attention first to the propositions, which are set out in the next section of this chapter. They concern both the ways in which institutions change and the dimensions along which they change. We return to these criteria in our concluding chapter, where we evaluate the magnitude of change that British devolution has brought about in European policy.

1.3 Institutional change

Historical institutionalism holds that institutions usually change at the margins and in keeping with existing formats and ways of operating.[8] Thus institutional change typically tends to involve a high degree of continuity, and, as it also tends to be resisted, it is usually tardy and slow. There are, however, occasions when change can be quite fundamental and a distinctive break is made with existing ways of doing things (Krasner 1988). This happens at those 'critical moments' when there is an objective opportunity for significant change (Bulmer and Burch 1998). If this opportunity is taken up and exploited the result will be a 'critical juncture' at which there is a clear departure from previously established patterns as fundamentally new institutional formats are set (Collier and Collier 1991; Thelen and Steinmo 1992). Development thereafter tends to take place in accordance with these new formats in a path-dependent manner. Notably not all critical moments lead to critical junctures.

Thus change can be evolutionary (i.e. a series of small changes taking place at the margins) or it can be transformative with slow, accretive alterations interspersed by occasional and significant restructuring (Krasner 1988). A third, hybrid variant of change, however, is where it involves a process of incremental transformation, comprising separate and emerging patterns which crystallise and become established as a coherent whole distinctly different from that which previously existed (Bulmer and Burch 1998; Cortell and Peterson 1999).

On the face of it devolution would seem to be a critical moment opening up the prospect for significant and transformative institutional change. Yet whether devolution is in practice a radical shift and a critical juncture in the development of UK governance is a matter for empirical enquiry. In order for that to take place we have to be more precise about the dimensions along which we will examine change.

Historical institutionalism holds that change is not uni-dimensional; rather it takes place to different degrees across the various parts of an institution. Accordingly, it is possible to distinguish the various dimensions of institutions along which change can be plotted. These are summarised in Bulmer and Burch (1998) and are adapted here. They cover change along:

- the *systemic* dimension affecting the constitutional rules and the framework of the state;

- the *organisational* dimension affecting the formal structure of offices and key positions, and including the formal distribution of authority and resources of money and staff;
- the *process-related* (or *procedural*) dimension affecting the processes whereby business is handled, information distributed and policy decisions determined, and including the networks established to fulfil these tasks; and
- the *regulative* dimension affecting rules, guidelines and operating codes and also capacity for strategic guidance.

In addition to these dimensions, change in the *cultural* aspects of institutions – the norms and values affecting activities across all of these dimensions – must also be taken into account.

Change may be significant within one dimension and not within another. It may take time to penetrate across all of them. In the case of devolution the situation is complicated by the fact that the assemblies and political executives are new and yet they are embedded in a bureaucratic structure which has been little altered; in particular the fundamental principle of a unified UK civil service that has been preserved intact. So innovation in one area may be constrained by continuity in another and is bound to lead to tensions. Civil servants, for instance, are presented with two potential masters: one in Whitehall and the other in the devolved administration. Thus, when talking about institutional change in relation to devolution, it is essential to distinguish it not only along the institutional dimensions mentioned above, but also across the various components of the polity. Broadly speaking we can distinguish six of these as outlined in Table 1.1. In this study, our concern is with change in state institutions and consequently we concentrate our inquiries on the representative, political executive and bureaucratic components. That is not to deny that changes in electoral patterns and behaviour, and amongst parties and pressure groups affect and are affected by the other components of the polity. Indeed we touch on

Table 1.1   The components of the polity

- Electoral
- Political parties
- Pressure groups
- Representative – which covers the parliamentary arena
- Political executive – which covers the ministerial element
- Bureaucratic

these matters in our outline and return to them in our conclusion. They are not, however, the central concern of our analysis.

Our task in what follows, therefore, is to look at the changes being brought about by devolution across both the various institutional dimensions and the relevant components of the polity. In the next two substantive parts of this chapter we turn our attention to two specific questions:

• How did Labour develop and operationalise its devolution policy?
• What specific provisions relating to European policy are to be found in the White Papers and the legislation?

1.4   The process for developing and operationalising Labour policy on devolution

Policy on devolved government emerged initially from within the policy processes of the Labour Party. The 1974–79 Labour government procured legislation for devolution to Scotland and Wales, but these proposals were rejected in subsequent referendums (Drucker and Brown 1980). In opposition Labour re-formulated its devolution position, allowing a lot of leeway in this process to the Scottish and Welsh Labour parties. Hence, the pathways leading towards Labour's 1997 policy on devolution are quite different in the case of Scotland, with its Constitutional Convention and strong support for a Parliament, and Wales where the idea of devolution was long resisted within important sections of the Labour Party. These different routes towards Labour's 1997 manifesto commitment to establish, subject to referendums in each country, a Scottish Parliament and a Welsh Assembly (Labour Party 1997: 33) are well documented elsewhere (Morgan and Munghan 2000; Paterson 1998; Mitchell 1996). They account in part for the very different nature of the constitutional settlements in the two countries.

Within Whitehall, preparations for devolution began in December 1996 when the Cabinet Secretary, Sir Robin Butler, authorised the customary arrangements for contacts between senior civil servants and the Opposition leadership and their aides in preparation for the possibility of a Labour victory in the 1997 election (due before June 1997). He discussed with colleagues the administrative arrangements needed to handle Labour's wide-ranging constitutional reform programme, should Labour be returned to office. It was evident that the Cabinet Office would have to have a co-ordinating role if only to organise the relevant materials for the ministerial and official committees that would need to be established to deal with the constitutional programme. It was decided that such a task could not be handled within the existing Economic and Domestic Secretariat and would require the creation of a new secretariat, probably with a more pro-active remit akin to the more interventionist approach characteristic of the European Secretariat.[9] One possible option was to follow the practice of the 1970s, when a Devolution Unit was established in the Cabinet Office and was in charge of the whole process. This unit had led on the devolution bills, was headed by a permanent secretary and had a large staff pulling the policy together. The alternative was to give the lead on each bill to the Scottish and Welsh Offices with co-ordination responsibility being placed in the Cabinet Office. The view in Whitehall was that the 1970s approach of placing the policy lead in the Cabinet Office had not been especially successful; it had failed to drive policy in a timely manner and the Scottish and Welsh offices did not have a big enough stake in the exercise. Final decisions about the exact machinery could not be made until, and if, Labour entered office. However, contingency plans were made, including, during the election campaign period, clandestine interviewing of likely candidates, for the staffing and remit of whatever facility was to be established at the centre. This was sensible planning as Labour's programme was extensive and needed to be put into place immediately on gaining office. Very little, in fact hardly any, expertise on most of the matters involved existed in Whitehall, since the Conservative Major government had had no constitutional policy agenda.

Less was done prior to the election period on the detailed content of Labour's plans. In part, this was because little detail was available, but also because it would not be constitutionally proper to make detailed policy plans.[10] Once the election campaign began, however, a shadow body known as the Inter Departmental Group on constitutional reform (IDG) was assembled. This brought together a small number of senior officials from the departments most likely to be affected by devolution. The group was co-ordinated from the Cabinet Office and was serviced from the relevant departments and reported to a group of permanent secretaries. These officials looked at Labour's plans for constitutional reform, pulled together whatever information was available on these, including the reports of outside bodies such as the Constitution Unit at University College London. They also worked out a timetable for carrying through the reform programme with devolution as the priority for immediate action, and produced skeleton drafts of the devolution White Papers and an options paper on how the policy should be handled in government. A sub-group of the IDG, led by a senior (ex-MAFF) official from the Cabinet Office European Secretariat (COES) and with participation from the territorials and a small number of other UK departments, examined the implications for the handling of European policy by mapping out the existing arrangements and how these might be revised in the light of devolution. The work of this sub-group was to feed into the European chapters of the White Papers. All this activity was helped by the fact that the election campaign period was an exceptionally long one of six weeks duration. As is standard practice, contingency plans were also prepared for the return of a Conservative government.

The options paper was presented to Prime Minister Blair on the 2 May 1997, the day after Labour's election to government. The option of creating a pro-active constitution secretariat in the Cabinet Office to co-ordinate the constitutional reform programme across Whitehall, with the relevant departments taking the lead on individual items, was agreed to by Tony Blair and Lord Irvine. The latter, the newly appointed Lord Chancellor, had drafted the relevant sections of the manifesto and was designated to oversee the enactment of Labour's constitutional reform programme in office. The first meeting of the Constitution Secretariat, complete with staff, came just three days later on the Bank Holiday Monday. These arrangements meant that the lead on devolution was placed in the hands of the Scottish and Welsh Secretaries of State, Donald Dewar and Ron Davies respectively, and their departments and did not rest, as in the 1970s, with a unit in the Cabinet Office. This was one of the most critical decisions affecting the development of the policy. It caused some consternation for giving the lead to the 'territorials' was, to some in Whitehall, tantamount to letting the animals loose.[11]

Thereafter, the White Papers and the legislation were developed in the ministerial Cabinet Committee designated DSWR (Devolution to Scotland, Wales and the Regions)[12] chaired by Lord Irvine and its shadowing official committee(s). The operation was co-ordinated across Whitehall by the Constitution Secretariat with the lead in the hands of the Scottish and Welsh Offices, whose officials usually wrote the drafts for discussion. The Cabinet Office Constitution Secretariat (COCS), in consultation with the European Secretariat, was in charge of ensuring that the UK government's interests in retaining its co-ordinated approach to European policy-making would be protected in reserved matters. As one key participant said: 'It was our job to make sure that they [the territorials] didn't get away with murder, as some might have predicted'.[13] Following the publication of the White Papers in July 1997, the proposals were endorsed in referendums held in both countries in September 1997. The Acts establishing the National Assembly for Wales and the Scottish Parliament and Executive were passed by the Westminster Parliament in July and November 1998 respectively.

1.5   Devolution and European policy: powers and responsibilities

Responsibilities for European policy were broadly set out in the White Papers and the relevant parts of the legislation. These are outlined in Tables 1.2–1.4. The proposals centre on five aspects of the handling of European matters covering formulation of UK policy and negotiating

Table 1.2   Formulation and negotiation of European policy

1. Formulation of the UK line

Wales

- Assembly to 'be involved as closely as possible' in those areas that concern it (WO 1997: 21–2, 3.46).
  - ○ The Secretary of State continues to represent the Welsh interest on European matters within the UK government.
  - ○ The Assembly must make its own judgements on EU matters that concern it and communicate these to Whitehall (22, 3.47).

Scotland

- Scottish Executive to 'be involved as closely as possible in UK decision making on Europe' (SO 1997: x).
  - ○ Scottish Executive ministers and officials to be fully involved in the UK Government's formulation of the UK position on all issues which touch on devolved matters (16, 5.4).
  - ○ The Secretary of State for Scotland represents Scottish interests in reserved areas (14, 4.12).

2. Negotiations with EU partners

UK

- Lead UK minister remains responsible for settling (after full consultation across UK government) and co-ordinating UK negotiating line and the conduct of negotiations.

Wales

- Secretary of State may (by invitation) participate in relevant meetings of the Council of Ministers and even represent the UK on relevant items (22, 3.59).
- The Assembly will need to keep the negotiating delegation 'advised of its views. The Secretary of State and the Assembly will need to liaise closely to establish the necessary arrangements' (22, 3.50).

Scotland

- 'Ministers of the Scottish Executive can [by invitation] participate in relevant meetings of the Council of Ministers (and other negotiations with EU partners). As determined by UK lead minister, they could, in appropriate cases, speak for the United Kingdom' (x; 17, 5.6).
- Role of Scottish ministers and officials in negotiations is to support and advance the single UK negotiating line which they have helped to develop (17, 5.6).

Table 1.3   Scrutiny and implementation of European policy

---

1. Scrutiny of proposed EU legislation

Wales

- The Assembly will have an 'opportunity' to scrutinise relevant proposals from the EU and thus ensure any implications for Wales are considered (WO 1997: 22, 3.48).

Scotland

- The Scottish Parliament will be able to scrutinise EU legislative proposals. UK government will take into account the views of the Scottish Parliament, as may the UK Parliament in its scrutiny process. The Scottish Parliament's views need to be available early enough to enable this to happen (SO 1997: 17, 5.7).

2. Implementation of EU policy

Wales

- A Community obligation of the UK is also a Community obligation of the Assembly.
- Ministers of the Crown can require by order that the Assembly fulfils such obligations should it fail to do so.

Scotland

- Scottish Executive must implement relevant EU legislation.
- UK Parliament maintains the ability to legislate to give effect to EU obligations in Scotland (x).
- Arrangements to be made with the UK government to ensure:
  - that differences of approach are compatible with consistency of effect;
  - that, if any financial penalties are imposed on the UK for any failure of implementation, or arise from infraction proceedings, 'responsibility for meeting them would have to be borne by the Scottish executive if it were responsible for the failure.' (17, 5.8).

---

responsibilities (Table 1.2); scrutiny of European legislation and implementation of European policy (Table 1.3); and representation arrangements in Brussels (Table 1.4).

Table 1.2 makes clear the willingness to involve the Scottish Executive in both the formulation of UK European policy and negotiations. In the case of Wales, in both these activities, the primary role is given to the Secretary of State. Officially the Secretary of State for Wales has always been able to participate in negotiations, though has seldom done so in practice. Potentially, then, the post might become more important in European policy-making. However, in both cases the UK 'functional' department in Whitehall has the policy lead in developing European policy. The rule is that Scottish Executive ministers may lead negotiations, but only if they are agreeable to the overall UK line. Moreover, it is the lead Whitehall minister who can determine whether his/her

Table 1.4   Representation in Brussels

Wales

- UKRep continues to represent the Secretary of State and 'other Welsh interests' (WO 1997: 22, 3.52).
- 'It will be open for the Assembly to decide the form of its own presence in Brussels' (22, 3.52).
- Members of the Assembly to represent Wales on the Committee of the Regions (22, 3.53).
- Assembly can forge closer links with other regions in Europe (14, 2.25).

Scotland

- A Scottish representative office in Brussels to be established to 'complement' the role of UKRep (SO 1997: x).
  - ○ UKRep remains responsible for representing the views of the United Kingdom to the European Institutions.
  - ○ New Scottish representative office to 'provide an effective channel of communication with the Scottish Executive' – distinct from that fulfilled by Scotland Europa (18, 5.10).
- Scottish Executive staff will continue to be seconded to UKRep and to the institutions of the European Community (18, 5.11).
- The Scottish Executive will, subject to the approval of the Scottish Parliament, nominate the Scottish representatives on the Committee of the Regions and the Economic and Social Committee (18, 5.9).

Scottish counterpart can take an active part. So far as Welsh input into UK policy formulation is concerned, the onus is placed upon the Assembly to ensure it makes its views known, whereas in the case of Scotland the involvement suggested for the Parliament is more extensive and comprehensive.

Table 1.3 indicates that thinking on scrutiny and implementation had been developed much more extensively in the Scottish case than the Welsh. From the very start the Scottish Parliament is expected to comment on forthcoming EU legislation, whereas for Wales there is an opportunity for scrutiny, though whether and how that opportunity will be taken up is left vague and uncertain.[14] Equally, in the Scottish case implementation is more advanced in terms of detail than is the Welsh one. Notably, as in determining and negotiating the UK line, it is the UK government that has final responsibility and can thus override the actions of the SP and the NAW in these matters. Implementation is one of the few points specifically relating to European policy mentioned in the Government of Wales and the Scotland Acts.[15] This provides an indication of the importance attached to ensuring that EU requirements are adhered to under devolved government and to establishing that the costs of any failure actually fall on the level of government responsible for it. The rationale for this position was, first, that devolution should not undermine the UK's good record in transposing European legislation (see Armstrong and Bulmer 1996). Second, the view from London was that devolved authorities should explicitly be made responsible for the financial consequences of inadequate legal transposition of European legal requirements: this was a stipulation on the part of the Treasury.

As Table 1.4 illustrates, on the matter of representation in Brussels, the Scottish settlement in extra-state relations is also far more developed than is the Welsh one. This does not preclude the same arrangements being developed for Wales, but what it does indicate is that at the time the legislation had passed Parliament the details of these matters for Wales had not yet been determined.

1.6 Summary

Overall, the framework of proposals on the handling of European policy established in the White Papers and the legislation reveals significant differences between the Welsh and Scottish models. These documents are more detailed in the case of Scotland, revealing a pattern that has characterised the whole of the preparatory phase of the devolution process: the tendency for the settlement in Wales to be drawn along on Scotland's coat tails. Overall, these documents provide a very skeletal framework for devolved government, a point which is especially telling so far as the legislation is concerned. Many questions are left unanswered, such as, how will the Secretary of State for Wales and the Assembly handle their joint involvement in UK European policy-making? Or what, if any, is to be the role of Secretary of State for Scotland in UK European policy-making? In sum, the documents provided a broad outline of some of the key features of the settlement, but they required further and detailed clarification before the devolved governments could ever begin to operate.

1.7 Structure of the report

Our report documents this process of clarification and institution building. In line with the nature of our approach, we look at the situation before and after the establishment of devolved institutions in each instance. This 'before and after' format is followed from Chapter 3 onwards. What then are the functions of each of the succeeding chapters of the report?

- In Chapter 2 we outline, as essential background, the way in which UK European policy was formulated prior to devolution. This provides a basis against which to measure change in the various facets of European policy-making in the subsequent chapters.

- In Chapter 3 we examine arrangements at executive level. How did the UK and the devolved authorities prepare for, and undertake the transition to, devolution?

- In Chapter 4 we look at the role of the assemblies. How did they envisage their respective roles in EU–UK policy-making ahead of, and in the early months of, devolution?

- Chapter 5 provides an examination of institutional and policy adaptation in agricultural policy-making. How did the UK Ministry of Agriculture Fisheries and Food (MAFF) and its counterparts in Cardiff and Edinburgh adapt to the new challenges of devolution in a policy area which is overwhelmingly conducted within a European framework? Brief consideration is also given to the handling of environmental policy after devolution, concentrating on Scotland only. Both cases are designed to illustrate an emergent system of multi-level governance in the new devolved Britain.

- In Chapter 6 we explore the ways in which the devolved governments have developed arrangements for direct engagement with the EU in Brussels.

- In the concluding section of the report we pull together our findings and consider what the case of European policy-making reveals about the nature of the devolution settlement. Crucially, we argue that devolution marks a critical juncture in the handling of European policy in the UK and the reasons leading to this judgement are explored in full in the Conclusion. At the very end of our report we outline some practical proposals for the further reform of European policy-making in a devolving UK.

2
Adapting to Europe: the Pre-Devolution Story

2.1 Introduction

The devolution of power to Scotland, Wales and Northern Ireland makes explicit that UK governance has become more multi-levelled in recent times. Prior to devolution the most obvious manifestation of this multi-levelled situation was the interaction between the UK government and the EU. A clearly anticipated impact of devolution was the formal introduction of 'third-level' governance into pre-existing patterns of handling European policy within the UK.[16] Whilst European policy was to be reserved to the UK government, much of its substance was to be devolved. Outlining the preparations for, and introduction of, this development is the purpose of the chapters which follow this one.

In order to understand what issues arise as a consequence of devolution, we need to consider beforehand how the polity adapted to European integration and the challenge of European policy-making in the period prior to devolution. This requires, first, a brief consideration of the sources of institutional change that lay behind institutional adaptation in a multi-levelled context. Second, we examine the empirical impact of EU membership upon Whitehall and Westminster in the period up to 1999. In conducting the second of these tasks we will follow the framework set out in Chapter 1. A particular focus of attention is how the Welsh and Scottish dimensions were incorporated into UK European policy prior to devolution.

These twin tasks help us to highlight the challenges which devolution poses for the interaction between the new pattern of government in the UK and the EU. These challenges will be considered in the third part of the chapter. Specifically, how will the existing UK system cope with the new division of policy responsibilities between devolved executives and assemblies, on the one hand, and central government, on the other? Further, how will the devolved executives and assemblies themselves adapt to Europe in the new constitutional order?

2.2   Adapting to what? The sources of institutional change

Changing patterns of governance affect UK political forces (Parties, interest groups and public opinion), the polity (Parliament, the executive and the legal system), and many areas of public policy. Our interests here relate centrally to the polity: principally institutional change in the executive branch of government but also including parliamentary assemblies.[17] But what are the sources of change in the polity? From one perspective they derive from changing politics and new governments, most obviously the arrival in May 1997 of a Labour government with a radical constitutional programme (Burch and Holliday 2000). More subtly, the polity responds to new policy challenges, as illustrated by the emergence of the regulatory state in Europe from the 1980s (Majone 1996). However, alongside these sources of change, there is a 'vertical' re-ordering of state responsibilities under way in Europe. We identify three dynamics of institutional change:

- change emanating from the EU, and often loosely termed as 'Europeanisation';[18]
- domestic change at the level of the Member State; and
- 'third-level' change beneath the Member State, deriving from territorial politics.[19]

We need to be aware of these three sources of institutional change because devolution is not happening in isolation. For instance, devolution might go hand-in-hand with greater self-reliance within the devolved polities, thereby acting as a driver or enabler of Europeanisation.[20] Equally, the UK government might continue to be seen as the key conduit to influence in the EU. But at the same time as these questions are being considered, UK governance is itself undergoing wider constitutional change, including modernisation of the House of Commons, reform of the House of Lords, electoral reform, freedom of information legislation and incorporation of the European Convention on Human Rights (ECHR). Moreover, treaty reform continues at the EU level, notably with the coming into force of the Amsterdam Treaty in May 1999 and agreement of the Treaty of Nice in December 2000.

Europeanisation has become an increasingly utilised term in European politics, but it is conceptually rather under-developed. Drawing upon

a valuable recent paper on Europeanisation we offer the following definition, which is an adaptation of that made by its author, Claudio
Radaelli (2000):[21]

> A set of processes through which the EU political, social and eco-
> nomic dynamics interact with the logic of domestic discourse, identi-
> ties, political structures and public policies.

We draw attention to two important points arising from this definition.

- Multi-level governance entails the interaction of competing logics,
  located at the EU, Member State and, where extant, third levels. It
  is dangerous to attribute institutional change to any one level in
  isolation.
- The challenges arising from the interaction of logics are most acute at
  the points of interconnection between the levels of governance.

What does this amount to in practice? It means that, first, the various
branches of the UK polity – and most particularly central government –
must identify an appropriate institutional response to the political and
other dynamics of the EU. They must find suitable ways of processing
EU business. This is likely to occur by means of incorporating it into the
pre-existing domestic logic of governance through some switching
mechanism. However, they must also adapt their procedures so as to be
able to make an effective contribution to those EU dynamics. Elsewhere
these two components in understanding the polity's institutional
response to Europeanisation have been referred to respectively as 'reception' and 'projection' (Bulmer and Burch 2000).

Reception and projection are crucial adaptive responses by actors in
the polity since the need to engage in European policy-making is a consequence of Europeanisation. They are responses to be made at the
Member State level as well as at the level of the devolved authorities.
A further point to make is that we must not fall into a mistake often made
by those writing on Europeanisation. Look for Europeanisation, and you
will surely find it! However, not all the adaptation may be attributable to
an EU-effect. This caveat has application to our (less conceptual) concerns in this volume. Not all the institutional changes that we identify
are attributable to devolution. Constitutional change at UK level, and
continuing reforms at EU level mean that we cannot hold those two
variables constant. But this situation is rather new. Institutional change
from devolution is new. Constitutional change at UK level is new on the

current scale. Thus, in outlining the institutional changes up to 1999 associated with European policy-making in the UK, we are concerned with a rather different situation from the present. The 'third level' was not a source of change, and the UK government was subject to evolutionary change. It was European integration that posed the main challenge.

2.3 Institutional change and European policy-making prior to devolution

What are the origins of the system for the UK system of handling European policy? They can be traced back to 1961 when the Prime Minister, Harold Macmillan, decided to make an application for membership of the then European & Economic Community. As part of this decision a ministerial committee was set up to shape policy for negotiations with Brussels and comprised the ministers from the main departments affected. Beneath the ministerial committee were two tiers of official committee, chaired from the Treasury, to tackle the substance of negotiating issues. In addition, a committee of Whitehall legal advisers was set up, chaired from the Treasury Solicitor's Department (Bulmer and Burch 1998: 608–9; Tratt 1996).

With one major and some minor adjustments this pattern of machinery was adopted when the Heath government secured British accession with effect from 1973. The task thenceforth was no longer to negotiate accession but to participate in the full range of ongoing negotiations. The minor adjustments reflected endogenous changes to government's organisation, such that the departments involved from 1973 superseded some of those in 1961–63, such as the Colonial Office. In addition, the Cabinet Office had taken over the responsibility within Whitehall for co-ordinating economic and other policy areas, thus replacing the Treasury's role in the early 1960s. The major adjustment was the establishment of a weekly meeting to discuss the tactics of European policy over the short- to medium-term (see below).

The machinery for handling European policy operates at several different levels: from the prime minister down to the many officials across all departments of British central government. The prime minister is involved in key European policy decisions as well as in European summit meetings (the European Council, established in 1974) and bilateral summits. Ministers are extremely active in the various formations of the Council of Ministers, such that ministers from the Foreign and Commonwealth Office (FCO), the Treasury and the Ministry of Agriculture, Fisheries and Food (MAFF) meet approximately monthly in the EU. The civil service is active in the preparation of policy. It is also involved through supporting the appropriate national minister or through participation in the EU's Committee of Permanent Representatives (COREPER) and its related committees and working groups. Civil servants are involved from across all ministries: from the FCO to the Department of Media, Culture and Sport. In addition to home-based officials there are also those seconded to the UK Permanent Representation in Brussels (UKRep), formally part of the FCO but staffed by home civil servants as well as diplomats. Finally, civil servants and ministers have an involvement in transposing Community law into national law where this is necessary.

Up to 1999 these characteristics remained unchanged at that level of generality. But where was the input from beneath the Member State level into this policy? In the situation prior to devolution the Scottish, Welsh and Northern Irish Offices were all involved in EU policy-making and implementation as part of the UK government. None of these Offices had a policy lead; the appropriate UK department took that responsibility. Consequently, it was somewhat unusual for a minister from one of the Offices to attend an EU Council meeting. But in that event there was no practical reason why that minister could not represent the UK government's policy, since s/he was part of that government. Of course, prior to devolution ministers reflected the party elected into governmental office on a UK-wide majority rather than the balance of political opinion in Scotland or Wales. By contrast with their ministerial superiors, civil servants from the three Offices were quite regular participants in EU working-level meetings. At both ministerial and official levels the Scots were the most involved in this way. Amongst the reasons for this were the Scottish Office's prioritisation of European business in 1991 (see below); its greater range of interests in European policy (because of its greater range of domestic responsibilities); and its greater resources.

How does the adaptation of Whitehall and Westminster over the period up to 1999 fit in with the different dimensions of change identified in the previous chapter?

The systemic dimension

There has been a significant EU impact on the systemic character of UK governance. The principal changes have been on the UK legal system arising from the doctrine of the supremacy of EU law; the impact upon parliamentary sovereignty; and a creeping constitutionalisation of the UK via Brussels. Each of these developments occurred with entry into the EU but did not manifest themselves in practical terms until later (see Steiner 1992 for a review). Of these developments, the parliamentary dimension is relevant to our study. How did parliament adjust to the new situation, in particular through trying to maximise control and influence over the EU policy process? For the House of Commons the adaptation was quite slow, and was through various procedural changes introduced gradually over the period since accession (see below). The impact upon the executive branch by contrast created little by way of systemic change until the interaction of Europeanisation and devolution under the Blair government. We concentrate in the first instance on adaptation in the executive branch.

The organisational dimension

Already in 1961–63, when the first effort to join the EEC was made, a clear core group of affected ministries had emerged (Bulmer and Burch 1998: 608–9). Their present-day counterparts are the FCO, the Department of Trade and Industry (DTI), MAFF and the Treasury. The FCO is not the lead department on all European policy, but it does have some areas of particular influence, including its lead on EU institutional matters, the Common Foreign and Security Policy (CFSP), and responsibility for chairing the Cabinet Committee on European policy (see Box 2.1). The key co-ordinating agency is the Cabinet Office European Secretariat (COES). Apart from the COES a further central co-ordinating agency, the Cabinet Office Legal Advisers (COLA – based in the Treasury Solicitor's Department) emerged with key responsibilities in respect of legal advice on European policy and litigation involving the UK government before the European Court of Justice. Strong organisational co-ordination is important to the UK's good record at transposing European legislation into national law. Also central, particularly to the negotiating stage, is UKRep. It comprises some 50 officials, drawn from both the home civil service and the diplomatic service. It provides a wealth of formal and informal communications channels between British government and the EU institutions.

Although these departments and bodies have remained the key players in the European policy-making network, one clear development since accession has been the expanding impact of European business to nearly every department, including the Ministry of Defence, and several Executive Agencies. A number of EU developments have spawned subsidiary policy-making networks, such as that triggered by the Treaty on European Union (TEU), and centred on the Home Office, related to justice and home affairs (JHA) policy.

The general pattern of adaptation has been for each department to set up a European co-ordinating division or unit. This entity is responsible

Box 2.1   Membership of the Ministerial Sub-Committee on European Issues ((E)DOP), July 2000

Secretary of State for Foreign and Commonwealth Affairs
(Chair)

Deputy Prime Minister and Secretary of State for the Environment,
Transport and the Regions
Chancellor of the Exchequer
Secretary of State for the Home Department
Secretary of State for Education and Employment
President of the Council and Leader of the House of Commons
Minister for the Cabinet Office
Secretary of State for Scotland
Secretary of State for Defence
Parliamentary Secretary, Treasury and Chief Whip
Secretary of State for Northern Ireland
Secretary of State for International Development
Minister of Agriculture, Fisheries and Food
Secretary of State for Trade and Industry
Secretary of State for Wales
Attorney General
Minister of State, Foreign and Commonwealth Office
Minister for Energy and Competitiveness in Europe
Lord Privy Seal, Leader of the House of Lords and Minister for Women

The Minister of State, Cabinet Office receives papers.
Other Ministers are invited to attend as the nature of the business
requires.
The United Kingdom's Permanent Representative to the European Union
is also in attendance.

Terms of Reference:
To consider questions relating to the United Kingdom's membership of
the European Union and to report as necessary to the Ministerial
Committee on Defence and Overseas Policy (DOP).

Note: The Secretaries of State from the UK government remain as members of this sub-committee both prior to, and following, devolution.

Source: http://www.open.gov.uk/

for disseminating EU-related business to the appropriate functional specialists within the department. At the same time it has the task of ensuring departmental responsibilities are adhered to for keeping Parliament informed of the ramifications of EU legislative proposals through Explanatory Memoranda (EMs). These units are also responsible for monitoring EU institutional developments or treaty reform discussions.

The COES's co-ordinating role is important in that it is neutral of any departmental interest. With the increasing importance of the European Council as a policy-making arena, the Head of the Secretariat has become a key policy adviser to the prime minister. Although staffed with only nine senior staff, the Secretariat has considerable authority in its co-ordinating work, since it is in some senses the prime minister's department. The involvement of the so-called territorial ministries also came about incrementally. The larger Scottish Office was always more geared up to the requirements of engaging with Brussels, although until the early 1990s this awareness was largely confined to the agricultural and fisheries functions. With the growing impact of Europeanisation across the Office, including as a result of the increasing impact of the structural funds, a management review was conducted in 1991 (SO 1991). Co-ordination across the Office came from the European Central Support Unit, located in the Scottish Office Development Department. In Cardiff, where staff resources and policy responsibilities were both more limited, and the need for separate legal transposition was absent, adaptation did not experience such a jolt as that induced in 1991 by the Secretary of State for Scotland, Ian Lang. In Wales coordination was undertaken by the European Affairs Division (EAD(WO)) in the Economic Development Group, although agriculture had its own separate arrangements. In England the growth of the structural funds was one factor behind the creation of the Government Offices in the Regions.

The process-related (or procedural) dimension

The principal procedural requirement which adhesion to the EU brought about in 1973 was the need for the British governmental machinery to work according to the timetable and rhythms of the EU rather than those of Whitehall and Westminster. The co-ordinating procedures for European policy within Whitehall are based around a traditional cabinet committee structure, whose origins can be traced back to 1961–63 (Bulmer and Burch 2000). The structure has three tiers of formal committees (see Table 2.1): the Cabinet Sub-Committee on European Issues (E)DOP; very senior officials EQ(O*), formerly EQ(S); and EQ(O). EQ(O)L is a specialist sub-committee comprising the lawyers' network radiating out through Whitehall from COLA. In addition, the Friday meeting (see Table 2.1) was developed after accession as a forum for the main affected Departments in Whitehall to review the major short- to medium-term issues of European policy. Beyond these more or less formal meetings there existed all manner of opportunities for *ad hoc* meetings, sometimes chaired by the COES, as well as numerous informal contacts.

For the Scottish and Welsh Office participation in the formal meetings was assured, should personnel and time be available, and if business perceived to be of relevance were on the agenda. However, the fact that

Table 2.1 Handling European policy, 1999

Cabinet

DOP (Defence and Overseas Policy)

(E)DOP (Ministerial Sub-Committee on European Issues, chaired by the Foreign Secretary) *Ministerial consideration of European policy, e.g. Inter-governmental Conferences, reform of structural funds, budget and Common Agricultural Policy (CAP). For composition, see Box 2.1.*

EQ(O)* (senior officials' co-ordinating committee – known until 1998 as EQS) *Relatively infrequent oversight meetings – also smaller ad hoc meetings and occasional special groups, e.g. to oversee IGC negotiations. Chaired by Head, Cabinet Office European Secretariat.*

Friday 'Wall/Bender' meetings (Permanent Representative and affected departments) *Examines tactics on short-/medium-term issues arising in the EU. Held in Cabinet Office. Takes name from the then incumbent Ambassador to the EU (Sir Stephen Wall) and Head of the Cabinet Office European Secretariat (Brian Bender).*

EQ(O) (official committee) *Detailed co-ordination of policy at official level. Chaired by Cabinet Office European Secretariat.*

EQ(O)L (lawyers) *Coordination of legal advice on policy and of responses to Commission infraction proceedings, ECJ litigation etc. Chaired by Cabinet Office Legal Adviser from the Treasury Solicitor's Department.*

many of the meetings were organised in London did lead to occasions where Scottish or Welsh Office civil servants might fail to be invited to *ad hoc* meetings, due to oversight or neglect. Under the Major government London became more sensitive to these concerns and one senior official in the Cabinet Office's Economic and Domestic Secretariat was charged with keeping an eye on complaints from Edinburgh, Cardiff or Belfast relating to poor consultation, whether on European or domestic policy matters. One policy area which was particularly 'territorially'-sensitive was agriculture.[22] During the negotiations for EU membership in the early 1970s, MAFF set up a Departmental Committee on Europe (DCE). This committee came to offer officials from the territorial agricultural departments the opportunity to insert their often substantively different agricultural interests into European policy-making at the working level (see Chapter 5).

The growth of traffic of UK-based officials, ministers and prime minister to attend EU meetings was incremental from 1973. The territorial ministries were part of this picture, although once again the Scots led the others. The Scottish Office was also particularly active following its

1991 review to ensure that its officials secured temporary postings in the EU institutions, in UKRep and so on. Scottish Office ministers, notably with responsibility for fisheries, were occasional participants in the Council; their counterparts from Wales and Northern Ireland much less so.

The regulative dimension

The general pattern at the regulative level has been the proliferation of rules, such as COES Guidance Notes, departmental handbooks, evolving departmental practice and so on (see, for instance, Humphreys 1996 for an account from the perspective of the then Department of the Environment). The COES Guidance Notes were designed to ensure conformity across Departments on the handling of standard items of business, such as infraction proceedings initiated by the Commission against the UK government. Another regulative feature consisted of Treasury rules, which were devised in the early 1980s at a time of concern over UK net contributions to the Community budget. They were designed to ensure that receipts from EU spending programmes did not distort the domestic public expenditure (PES) settlement (see Bulmer and Burch 1998: 618–19). The impact of these arrangements upon the Scottish and Welsh Offices was mitigated by virtue of the fact that they were not lead-departments on any EU spending programme. Hence the block grant according to the so-called Barnett formula (Thain and Wright 1995: 307–27) acted as a kind of buffer between their departmental budgets and receipts from Brussels.

A further point concerns the strategic capacity of the European policy-making system. Here the general lack of capacity at the centre of Whitehall combined with the contested politics of European policy to provide little scope for forward thinking on European policy. Unsurprisingly this state of mind was replicated in the territorial departments, although the Scottish Office's management review in 1991 certainly entailed strategic thinking.

The cultural dimension

An important part of participation in European policy-making is the acculturation of ministers and officials to the different character, rhythms and norms of the EU. The general features of the EU policy process may be seen as fluid, open, network-based, rule-guided, multilingual, sectorised, and characterised by significant inter-institutional bargaining (for more discussion, see Mazey and Richardson 1996; Wright 1996, 150–3). These features do not correspond to the skills which UK officials traditionally acquire as part of their induction into, and acculturation to, the centralised system of Whitehall. Nor do they correspond to the adversarial norms of Westminster. At ministerial level personality matters. Politicians able to deploy multiple language skills, such as the former Labour Minister for Trade and Competitiveness in Europe, Lord Simon, could network with counterparts in the EU very effectively. But even those with less prolific linguistic skills, but who relished meeting their European counterparts, could thrive at networking, such as the former Conservative ministers Kenneth Clarke or John Gummer. Euro-sceptic ministers, such as Norman Lamont, or those who simply have not been personally predisposed to the Brussels routine, such as Gordon Brown, have excluded certain negotiating opportunities from their repertoire.

At official level, training and learning through experience offered the opportunity for acquiring the skills to be effective in the EU political system. Training can provide a basic set of skills for understanding how to be effective in the EU. Language training offers additional networking skills. However, learning on the job, through a posting in Brussels, offers the optimal way of developing the best tactical awareness of negotiating in the EU. In practice, departmental personnel policies and management reform may not always facilitate this ideal. Officials spending their careers dealing with European business while located in London may develop a formidable knowledge of the EU but tend to do so on Whitehall's terms. The traditional values of Whitehall stress information-sharing and an expectation that a collective policy should be agreed ('singing from the same hymn sheet'), if necessary through bringing in the COES as broker. Of course, going beyond this in adapting to the norms and values of the EU is contested terrain. An alternative term for acculturation is 'going native', something which has been regarded critically by less Europhile politicians and, indeed, governments. Officials in the Scottish and Welsh Offices also had the opportunity to engage in this way, with the former emphasising detachments to Brussels, whether in the European institutions or in UKRep, following its 1991 management review.[23]

2.3.1 Institutional change 1960–99

Having measured the various dimensions of adaptation on the part of the executive branch of UK government to the EU, it is worth underlining that the overwhelming pattern of change has been incremental in nature. The main upheaval came with the first attempt at accession in the early 1960s, when, at the organisational and procedural levels in particular, the task of 'organising for Europe' was given a clear focus. If that provided a critical juncture of sorts, accession in 1973 did not. It provided an opportunity to review arrangements – a critical moment – but the existing ones were simply adjusted to the new task of negotiating from within the European Community. Thereafter, change has been accretive and incremental. As regards the origins of change, they have been overwhelmingly from the EU level. New institutions, such as the European Council, and new supranational policy responsibilities have been the major source of change. Whilst the policy-making machinery of UK government has not been static, it has been very stable by contrast. Change was largely the result of Europeanisation. The result is the system outlined above, and which was facing a further critical moment with the introduction of devolution in 1999. Before moving on to the challenges which devolution poses, it is worth highlighting the strengths and weaknesses of the UK system before making some brief observations about the parliamentary arrangements.

Strengths and weaknesses

We can summarise the strengths and weaknesses of the system as a set of bullet points (for fuller discussion, see Bulmer and Burch 2000). First, the strengths:

- its effectiveness in distributing information around government;
- its well co-ordinated and well briefed approach, with all negotiators in Brussels 'singing from the same hymn sheet';
- its highly prepared nature, which is good at the 'reception' response to Europeanisation;
- its good record on implementation, facilitated by the role of COLA, which has kept the UK as one of the best performers in avoiding infringement proceedings launched by the European Commission for failure to transpose or implement EC legislation;
- its strong tactical awareness, facilitated through the COES, UKRep and the Friday meetings; and
- the skill of an inner cadre of officials in using the Brussels network to get views across.

Secondly, the weaknesses:

- the tendency of some not well versed in the EU policy style to be cautious about networking and engaging at the key, early stages of policy discussions;
- a bias, doubtless encouraged by the lack of language skills, to rely on bilateral contacts with northern European countries in building alliances;

- a tendency to be over-prepared and thus inflexible, for early co-ordination may weaken the scope to cut deals in end-game nego- tiations and leave Britain in a more isolated position;
- a tendency to conform to the Whitehall norms of policy-making at the cost of flexible and effective bargaining in the quite different policy-making environment of the EU itself;
- fluctuating levels of 'political will' on European policy due to its con- tested, party-political status; and
- weakness in terms of the long-term strategic planning of European policy.

In summary, the strengths lay in the reception response to Euro-peanisation. The weaknesses lay in the 'projection' response, exacer-bated of course by the party-political divisions over integration for much of the period since 1973.

From the above account of the evolution of the UK machinery up to 1999 for dealing with the EU we can derive a set of issues which devolu-tion challenges. Similarly, devolution challenges the system's strengths and weaknesses. Before exploring these further we need to give a brief account of Parliament's adaptation, since both the Scottish Parliament and National Assembly for Wales envisage playing a role in connection with European policy. But how would these roles interact with the exist-ing role performed by Westminster?

2.3.2   Parliament and the EU[24]

Europeanisation has had a considerable impact upon Parliament, just as it has had upon the executive branch. At the symbolic level accession represented more of a critical juncture for Parliament. On the one hand, the doctrine of parliamentary sovereignty was overturned with the advent of the supremacy of EC law over domestic legislation. On the other, the privileged access which government has to EU decision-making via the Council of Ministers had the effect of tilting the balance of executive-legislative power (further) in favour of the former. The con-junction of these two circumstances created an unprecedented challenge to Parliament's place in the institutional framework of the UK.

Following the 1974 report of the Mowbray-King Committee, the Lords found a niche in conducting detailed scrutiny reports on issues of major significance. The reports of the Select Committee on the European Communities (and its six sub-committees) command respect – in the UK and across the EU – because of the expertise of the evidence and the avoidance of adversarial politics.

The House of Commons, by contrast, following the 1974 report of the Foster Committee, opted for a different approach whereby the Select Committee on European Legislation sifted through EU documents – now renamed the European Scrutiny Committee to reflect this function – with a view to identifying those on which a debate should be held. This system was changed during the 1989–90 session because lack of parliamentary time often consigned such debates to unsocial hours, resulting in poor attendance. Instead, two special standing committees[25] were established for the debate of different domains of EC legislation. However, such standing committees rarely captured public attention and party discipline generally ensured a fairly smooth passage. To make matters worse it was not until that time that MPs *were allowed* by their terms of reference to look at anything broader than proposed legislation, e.g. planned European treaty reform measures. Continuing weaknesses of the scrutiny system were the pressure on timing, problems discussing proposals before they were formalised as European proposals, and the exclusion of the increasingly important work on CFSP and JHA. Only in November 1998 were these two areas of EU business brought within the scope of the scrutiny committee as part of Labour's modernisation programme for the Commons. At the same time they were brought into the remit of the other main control mechanism of the Commons, the 'scrutiny reserve' power. This is an agreement with the government, dating from 1980, that no minister should agree to legislation in the Council of Ministers if the 'scrutiny committee' had not previously been consulted. But perhaps the most high-profile manifestation of parliamentary engagement with the EU has come with episodic controversies of European policy, especially at the time of ratifying the TEU. Whilst these occasions have played to the lower House's ability to act as a forum for debate on key issues, they have done so because of the parties' divisions over the European issue as enhanced by the adversarial culture of the Commons.

Overall Parliament's impact upon the European legislative process has so far been limited. In part, this reflects the way the Commons has prioritised the 'reception' of EU business as its response to Europeanisation rather than trying to explore innovative means of securing a voice earlier in the Brussels policy process ('projection'). Of course, this pattern of adaptation is understandable, since the embedded institutional and cultural history of the Commons is difficult to transform in response to the new stimuli stemming from EU membership. We should note that some improvements were being made in parallel to the devolution process as a result of the Labour government's commitment to modernisation of the House (see Chapter 4 and Carter, 2001).

2.4 The challenges posed by devolution

Thus was the *status quo ante*. It was to be anticipated that devolution would pose a number of challenges to the UK–EU policy processes as set out above and an important first step of our research was to isolate and identify specific challenges for contending with EU business. Since many of the challenges, and the planned solutions, will be discussed in the following chapters we can give a summative account here following the organisation of the previous part of the chapter.

Systemic adaptation

- European policy is reserved to the UK but much of its substance, such as agriculture, is devolved to the authorities in Edinburgh, Cardiff and Belfast. How would a balance between the different responsibilities of the two levels of government be accomplished?
- This constitutional issue is potentially politicised by executives with different political stripes in the four capitals. Would the political diversity after the first devolved elections be of such magnitude as to fuel political disputes between central and devolved executives over European policy?
- The asymmetric nature of devolution is a further complicating factor. Policy responsibilities differ; the aspirations (including law-making needs in Edinburgh) of the assemblies differ; and the relations between assemblies and executives differ between each of the cases. Will this make the framework for handling European policy unstable?
- How would this asymmetric pattern of parliamentary/assembly arrangements impact on the democratic input into European policy-making?
- An 'English problem' appears emergent, with ministries in London having to combine English and UK functions in a more territorially-aware context.
- Finally, the interaction of devolution with other types of constitutional change being introduced by the Blair government provides further potential instability. Of relevance are: reform of the House of Lords, modernisation of the House of Commons, devolution of power to the English regions and the Greater London Authority (GLA), and,

last but by no means least, the ongoing reform of the EU, culminating in a new treaty at the Nice European Council in December 2000.

Organisational adaptation

- What organisational adjustments would devolution require of the UK government to manage the setting up, and functioning, of European policy arrangements?
- How would the Scottish Executive and the Welsh Assembly organise themselves for dealing with the EU? Would simple continuity of the pre-devolution arrangements suffice?
- What specific mechanisms would be set up in the Scottish Parliament and Welsh Assembly to ensure democratic accountability at these levels of governance? Would their involvement be occasional issue-based scrutiny along the lines of the Lords? Would they seek to create a forum for debate along the lines of the Commons or of some other kind?
- What representational arrangements would be needed for Scotland and Wales in Brussels, and how would their relationship with UKRep be defined?
- Would continuity of a unified British civil service be compatible with a devolved UK?

Process-related (or procedural) adaptation

- What access, if any, would ministers and officials from Scotland and Wales have to the long-standing policy-making committees, such as the Cabinet Committee and EQ(O), given that these would be subordinate to the UK Cabinet, which would become entirely separate from the political leaderships in Cardiff and Edinburgh?
- What vertical co-ordination arrangements would be set up between Whitehall Departments and their devolved counterparts, e.g. in succession to MAFF's Departmental Committee on Europe, to facilitate European policy-making in specific policy areas?
- Would crisis-management arrangements be needed, given the potential for major political disagreement over European policy under the new constitutional settlement?
- Would the direct engagement of officials in Edinburgh and Cardiff with the European institutions continue unchanged?
- Would co-ordinating procedures be needed within each devolved executive?
- What procedures would be established to ensure suitable flows of information such that the Scottish Parliament and Welsh Assembly could carry out their democratic accountability functions? How

would the Scottish Parliament approach the fact that it would be responsible for transposing some EU decisions into Scots law? Would it try to conduct prior scrutiny?

Regulative adaptation

- How would existing codes of practice for handling European policy be affected by devolution? What new arrangements would be needed? How would information-sharing be affected?
- What would be the impact of devolution upon the existing financial arrangements (the Barnett formula), and how would this bear on funds received in Scotland and Wales from the EU, especially the structural funds?
- Would a strengthening of strategic capacity for European policy be needed in the executive and parliamentary institutions in Edinburgh and in the integrated model of the NAW in Cardiff?

Cultural adaptation

- Would civil servants in Cardiff and Edinburgh remain as well connected with their counterparts in London, or would they become somewhat detached from the flow of information around Whitehall? Given the importance of information-sharing to the success of Whitehall's handling of EU business, this is a critical question.
- What priority would the Scottish and Welsh administrations give to training and placements in Brussels?
- Would the Welsh and Scottish administrations be able to sustain European career tracks, which appear important for seizing the policy opportunities offered by the EU?
- What would happen when there is a real disagreement between London and Edinburgh or Cardiff? Would the traditional pragmatism of the UK constitution be dispensed with, e.g. by resort to legal mechanisms, and in what spirit would any formal consultative machinery operate?
- Finally, would the accountability mechanisms of the Scottish Parliament and Welsh Assembly contribute to a change in the 'politics' of the European issue by departing from the adversarial approach characteristic of Westminster?

Impact on strengths and weaknesses

From the above series of questions it is clear that changes are possible in all five institutional dimensions. That is indicative of the fundamental nature of the challenge posed by devolution for European policy-making. Not surprisingly, the outcome of these challenges has important implications for the traditional strengths and weaknesses of the UK system. Will the UK as a member government remain as well-informed, coherent, and tactically prepared for negotiating in Brussels? Will it retain its reputation as a hard negotiator but dutiful implementer? On the other hand, might the devolution process prompt clearer thinking about European integration, whilst bringing about a new, multi-levelled approach to UK governance that is much more in keeping with the predominant pattern of politics in other EU states, and in the EU itself? Will the UK government become more pro-active in EU matters, increasing strategic capacity so as to promote a 'projection' response to Europeanisation, whether as a result of devolution or of the Labour Party's commitment to a more constructive diplomacy in the EU? Will agreed policy lines come about later in the EU policy cycle, with potential benefits to negotiating flexibility, especially as EU decision-making moves increasingly towards qualified majority voting? Whichever of these happens, there is likely to be some recalibration of the UK's strengths and weaknesses.

For Scotland and Wales, too, there is a question about how they should strengthen the 'reception' and 'projection' responses to Europeanisation. Should they adapt more to Europe? Or, given the UK government's reservation to itself of European policy, should they prioritise adapting to Whitehall? Potentially, there are a three competing logics at work:

- that of the EU;
- that of the UK because of its continued centrality on European policy (and Whitehall will logic prefer 'once-size-fits-all' solutions since they will reduce administrative adjustment costs); and
- the asymmetrical logics of devolution whereby the unitary body in Wales suggests a different response compared to the arrangements in Scotland.

How all these challenges were addressed over the period up to the Spring of 2000 is the task, in their respective domains, of the chapters which follow. In doing this we shall be conscious that devolution is not the only source of change in the arrangements for European policy-making. Devolution represents but one 'logic' of three. Thus, we must bear in mind Blair's other constitutional reforms as well as his wish to create a new more constructive European policy at member state level, and of the reform processes under way at EU level.

In the Conclusion to this volume we will return, in the light of evidence, to whether devolution has represented a critical juncture in the handling of UK European policy.

3
European Business and the Executives

3.1 Introduction

A key expectation arising from devolution was that it would impact significantly on the UK's EU policy administration structures – both at the centre (Whitehall) and within the former territorial administrations (Edinburgh and Cardiff). That devolution was bound to have important consequences for the political Executive and bureaucratic components of the polity at all levels arose in part from the commitment by the UK government to involve the devolved administrations in what is, after all, a reserved matter. In addition, this expectation reflected the fact that, in Scotland, approximately 80 per cent of the competencies assigned to the devolved administration would be affected by European legislation. Although it might be argued that the retention of the Scottish and Welsh Offices suggested that they could input the territorial perspective on UK European policy, the fact that both were considerably down-sized in terms of resources (and respectively re-designated Scotland Office and Wales Office), as well as considerations of 'legitimate' governance, made this approach both impractical and in some senses inappropriate. Rather, in such a situation, the common sense notion of 'good government' which emerged accepted that the devolved administration in Edinburgh, and by extension in Cardiff, *should* have a part to play in the UK–EU policy process. In this chapter, we examine how the three administrations adapted their existing EU policy arrangements – or acquired new capacity in that area – to suit the new constitutional situation and to respond to the challenges that devolution introduced.

The reserved status of UK European policy meant that, in principle, the template for deciding policy would remain unchanged in its essential features. In practice, the Whitehall European policy process – its formulation and development – typically proceeds along one of two intersecting (or overlapping) administrative 'pathways' (Bulmer and Burch 1998). The first (and most frequently used) involves the relevant Whitehall department assuming the 'lead' on the issue under consideration and providing policy advice to the relevant minister(s) at the appropriate stages as the policy process unfolds. Generally the 'lead' will be taken by that department which has domestic responsibility for that EU portfolio and, *inter alia*, it will co-ordinate input from other government departments having an interest in the policy area. In specific cases, however, a second pathway will be preferred whereby responsibility for co-ordinating the government position on an EU matter will be assigned to a dedicated EU unit within the central Whitehall administration. Frequently it will be the Cabinet Office European Secretariat (COES), but it may also be a specialist unit within either the Foreign and Commonwealth Office (FCO) or the Treasury. This pathway will be preferred where the EU issue under consideration requires an input from a number of departments, and where a high element of inter-departmental co-ordination is necessary – for instance where the issue impacts on broad national interests.[26] These two policy pathways need not be mutually exclusive. There may be a number of points at which they overlap or intersect, and the preferred pathway may change as the policy process unfolds. The choice of pathway is largely a matter of routine, decided by officials in light of the nature of the issue. However, if the issue becomes politicised the Cabinet machinery and the COES would most likely be involved.

Prior to devolution, input from the territorial ministries in the UK's EU policy process depended on the issue under review, although territorial ministries were never 'lead' departments. In the majority of routine EU matters, the territorial perspective was represented to the Whitehall lead department via counterpart officials in the territorial ministries. Where the alternative, central government, pathway operated, the territorial ministries tended to input via the Cabinet Office EQ network (see Chapter 2, Table 2.1).[27] Under either scenario, however, it was the responsibility of territorial Secretaries of State to represent the territorial dimension of EU policy issues within UK government. Accordingly, both the Scottish and Welsh Secretaries of State were (and remain) members of the Cabinet (Ministerial) Sub-Committee on European Issues ((E)DOP – see Chapter 2, Box 2.1).

Although accepted from the outset that the devolved administrations would have a role to play in reserved matters (especially EU policy), neither in the devolution White Papers nor in the subsequent legislation were any specific modalities proposed to facilitate this. Instead, it was left to officials from UK government and the to-be devolved administrations jointly to develop mechanisms that would meet the commitments given in the White Papers but which did not compromise the constitutional position with respect to reserved matters. By late in 1997 the idea had rooted that a series of 'concordats' should be prepared setting out provisions for policy co-ordination between UK government and the devolved administrations. The concordats would deal with reserved matters where the devolved administrations had legitimate interests, and for devolved matters where UK government had a legitimate interest.

UK–EU policy was a reserved matter of particular importance to the devolved administrations. As noted above, almost all the devolved policies were also subject to EU policy decisions – i.e. the problem of concurrent powers. Not only did this mean that the autonomy of the devolved administrations was circumscribed by dint of EU legislation, it also meant that the position taken by the UK government with respect to EU policy generally was of direct relevance to the devolved administrations. At the very least this implied that the domestic policy objectives of the devolved administrations and the European policy objectives of UK government should be congruent. Moreover, in some EU policies – for instance actions financed under EU structural funds – any decision reached by the UK government would have a direct and significant material impact on the devolved territories. These considerations pointed to the need to have inter-administration co-ordination arrangements with respect to UK European policy in which the devolved administrations were adequately involved. Also pertinent in this regard was the continuing liability of the UK government in the event of non-implementation of, or non-compliance with, EC law on the part of the devolved administration. While the UK government could – and did – make the devolved administration liable to pay any punitive damages that might arise in the event of a breach of EC law, it was the UK government that would be held to account at the EU level.

The priority that the Labour government accorded to devolution within its overall package of constitutional reform was such that officials had to begin thinking about the structure of inter-administration policy co-operation and co-ordination early on in the process. From the perspective of the devolved administrations, three organisational issues had to be addressed;

- *Capacity building*: the organisation and management of the Scottish and Welsh Office European business was to be (re-)configured (i) to create an administrative structure capable of generating an independent Scottish/Welsh input to this UK government's EU policy process, (ii) to execute the legislative responsibilities that would fall to the devolved administrations with respect to the implementation of EC law.

• *Inter-administration relations*: modalities were to be developed to enable the administrations in Edinburgh and Cardiff to interact with their counterparts in Whitehall on EU-related matters with a view to co-ordinating a representative UK view. This might involve co-ordination between the responsible departments or between central units within the different administrations. The key issues were (i) maintaining information flows between the different administrations to ensure a continuation of established European policy-making practices, and (ii) enabling the devolved executives to discharge (EU-related policy) actions required of them by the devolved Parliament/ Assembly.

• *Inter-governmental mediation*: decisional and accountability structures whereby ministers from the devolved governments were able to represent to UK government the territorial position on European policy matters. Provision for both bilateral (department–department) and multi-lateral (centre–centre) co-ordination was to be made.

3.2   Establishing the new arrangements: July 1998–October 1999

It was during the period between July 1998 and October 1999 that the organisational and institutional foundations were laid in readiness for this fundamentally new phase of UK governance. However, as we have seen in Chapter 1, preparations for devolution had begun immediately upon the new Labour government assuming office, heralding an intense phase of institutional adaptation within the central apparatus of UK government in Whitehall and the territorial administrations in Edinburgh and Cardiff. As was noted in Chapter 1, devolution was dealt with by the Devolution to Scotland, Wales and the Regions (DSWR) Cabinet Committee, chaired by Lord Irvine, the Lord Chancellor.[28] The work of that committee focused on the preparation and publication of the devolution White Papers and the requisite parliamentary legislation. The territorial departments had the lead role 'on their own soil' in the preparation of the White Papers. This transferred a degree of policy ownership of devolution to the territorial offices – thereby increasing their 'stake' in the process[29] – and also avoided over-burdening central government in a phase of considerable constitutional activity. Accordingly, the early drafts were written by the territorial offices themselves, including those chapters providing for territorial participation in the UK European policy process. This was to become a controversial issue as the legislation passed through the House of Commons, since the to-be devolved administrations sought an entitlement to attend and speak at relevant meetings of the Council of Ministers. The outcome was to leave the authority over the UK delegation squarely in the hands of the relevant UK minister but with the provision that a minister from a devolved government might speak, if invited so to do by the UK lead minister.

Institutional preparation and adaptation for devolution gathered momentum with the entry into force of the Government of Wales Act in July 1998; the Scotland Act receiving Royal Assent in November 1998. Although the new arrangements largely were in place by the time devolution took effect on 1 July 1999, this process could not be fully signed-off until the inter-administration concordats setting out agreed inter-administration practices had been published. This process commenced on 6 October 1999 with the publication of the Memorandum of Understanding (MoU) signed by the UK government and each of the devolved administrations, and was followed by the publication, one by one, of inter-departmental concordats.[30] On 7 October 1999, the MoU was debated in both the Scottish Parliament (SP) the National Assembly for Wales (NAW): in the former the document was endorsed by a vote of 75 to 32; in the latter it was 'noted' with no vote being taken.

In many respects the concordats are the centrepiece of the new (post-devolution) governance of the UK, and considerable time and effort was devoted to drafting and agreeing their content in the run-up to devolution. Concordats detail the arrangements whereby UK and devolved administrations will manage policy co-operation and co-ordination post-devolution with a view to maintaining 'good' governance over the UK as a whole. They address two specific problems that arise with devolution – concurrent powers and policy contagion (Scott 2001). Concurrent powers describes the situation where the UK government and the devolved administration effectively share competence with respect to a particular policy area and, as a result, must find a common position if jurisdictional (and political) conflicts are to be avoided. The problem stems from linkage (or spillovers) between reserved and devolved policies. As noted, this situation arises with respect to UK European policy and a host of devolved competencies. Policy contagion describes a situation in which policy decisions taken by one administration have an effect on the policy options facing another administration – for instance, where one administration finds itself under political pressure to conform to policies adopted by another administration. Although inter-administration policy divergence is an inevitable consequence of devolution, it was considered desirable that each administration was given adequate forewarning of policy developments of others in areas where contagion was likely to occur. This was commonly framed in terms of a 'no surprises' approach.[31]

Various options were considered for setting out the inter-administrative arrangements that would be established post-devolution, including voluntary or statutory 'codes of practice'. Concordats were adopted because they implied that a necessary degree of flexibility was desirable, but one which did not sacrifice the underlying objectives of inter-administration co-operation and co-ordination as required for 'joined-up' UK governance.[32] Concordats set out provisions[33] that will direct both the UK government and the devolved administrations as they embark upon a new constitutional phase characterised by joint policy-making, inter-administration exchange of information, and inter-administration dispute settlement. As such, the concordats underpin the new constitutional situation in which there are two tiers of UK governance, and are designed to facilitate policy co-operation and co-ordination between them with respect to reserved and devolved policies.

Ultimately two kinds of concordat emerged. The first was presented as the MoU and was a group of five quadrilateral concordats signed by each of UK government and the (three) devolved administrations. The MoU elaborates the overarching framework of post-devolution inter-administration policy co-operation and co-ordination (to which all other concordats must conform), and covers (i) inter-administration dispute settlement arrangements; (ii) devolved administration involvement in UK European policy (see Appendix I); (iii) financial assistance to industry;[34] (iv) devolved administration involvement in UK international relations; and (v) the exchange of statistics. Second was a series of bilateral concordats signed between specific departments of a devolved administration and the UK government to prescribe arrangements for inter-administration co-operation and co-ordination in specific policy areas, e.g. agricultural policy, health, cultural issues, home affairs, and so on. Neither the quadrilateral nor the bilateral concordats are legally binding agreements. Instead, they are 'codes of conduct' between the UK and devolved administrations, although it is expected that the provisions of the concordats will be closely followed – both in letter and in spirit – by the signatories. From the perspective of this study it is the EU concordat which is the most important, although a number of the bilateral concordats also make reference to EU policy issues – most notably the one on agriculture (see Chapter 5).

As we discuss later in this chapter, it is evident that those responsible for drafting the EU concordat (both within Whitehall and the territorial administrations) began from the premise that the prevailing administrative arrangements for handling EU business in the UK operated extremely well. In that sense the challenge facing officials was to ensure that any changes to the UK's European policy procedures did not weaken a tried and proven policy process.

3.2.1 Change at the centre

From the outset, discussions concerning the management of UK European business post-devolution involved close liaison between Whitehall and the territorial administrations in Cardiff and Edinburgh.[35] Government policy was that the UK negotiating position within the EU decisional structures must continue to reflect the 'legitimate interests' of all parts of the UK and this required that it had the support of the devolved administrations. We use the phrase 'legitimate interests' to suggest a distinction between EU policy issues in which the devolved administrations (and their predecessor Offices) have a direct interest, and for which their input is needed to ensure that the UK policy position adopted is the optimal one, as against EU policy issues which raised explicitly political considerations of strategic *national* importance and in which the Scottish and Welsh Offices customarily had considerably less direct involvement. There was no intention that devolution should (or would) enhance the role of the devolved administrations in this latter aspect of UK European policy. But retaining their involvement in day-to-day EU policy matters was not without problems. In particular, it was felt important to the success of UK negotiations that confidentiality was maintained during the domestic deliberative phase of the policy process – that is, ahead of negotiations with other EU Member States. There was some concern that including the devolved administrations would make this more difficult as is the case in some other Member States, notably Germany. Any breach in confidentiality would be likely to weaken the UK's negotiating effectiveness. Consequently, including the devolved administrations in the UK's European policy process raised sensitive political issues and, unsurprisingly, the EU dimension to devolution was regarded as problematic by some Whitehall officials.

In the run-up to devolution, general responsibility for overseeing arrangements between the devolved administrations and Whitehall was assigned to the Cabinet Office Constitution Secretariat (COCS).

In conjunction with the territorial administrations, COCS was responsible for initiating discussion about how to modify the UK's European policy process after devolution. Much later in the deliberations, at the beginning of 1999, ownership of this European policy co-ordination 'segment of the devolution cake' passed to COES, although ultimate responsibility for all inter-administration relations post-devolution (as were set out subsequently in the MoU) remained with COCS.[36] In practice, however, the COES assumed responsibility for preparing the EU concordat and for drafting the EU-related clauses in the overarching MoU.

Although the initial administrative impact of the decision to proceed with devolution was confined to the Cabinet Office, it quickly spread to all other parts of the Whitehall machinery. This was indicative of the all-encompassing nature of devolution. The FCO is a key UK government department involved in the formulation of UK European policy. Within the FCO, EU policy is divided between four departments: EUDI which deals with broad EC issues, especially institutional structures; EUDE which deals with external policy matters including the common commercial policy; EUDB which covers bilateral relations with other Member States; and a division servicing government policy towards EU Common Foreign and Security Policy (CFSP). On 1 February 1999 a new Devolution Administration Department (DAD) was created within the FCO. The DAD comprised two elements: a Devolution Unit and an Ireland Section, the latter in recognition of the special status now accorded to Anglo-Irish diplomacy. The creation of the DAD was an acknowledgement that devolution would impact on a number of aspects of the FCO business – generally in the realms of international (and so European) relations, and particularly with regard to Anglo-Irish relations. The DAD brought together the FCO's various devolution functions that had emerged since the 1997 election, and assumed responsibility for preparing the international relations concordat.

Elsewhere, all Whitehall departments had, by the spring of 1999, established desks or units to handle policy co-ordination with the devolved administrations. In the course of 1998 the principal activity assigned to these units was the preparation of concordats. Some departments went further than others in committing resources in anticipation of devolution (e.g. to the preparation of concordats), notably the then Ministry for Agriculture, Fisheries and Food (MAFF), DETR, the Treasury and DTI – each of which had a large involvement in EU policy or, as with the Treasury, related issues (e.g. EU-related public spending control).[37] MAFF and the DTI were particularly affected by the EU-policy dimension of devolution, and the drafting of the concordats covering these policy areas was complex and, on occasion, contested. This reflects the importance the devolved administrations assigned to EU agricultural, fisheries, and structural fund policies – policies that impacted directly on their economies and where the former territorial offices had been closely involved in the UK policy process.[38] In other departments (e.g. DETR), EU-related policy discussions had tended not to involve the territorial offices to such an acute degree. In these cases, devolution presented a slightly different problem – namely, providing for the devolved administrations systematically to input to the Whitehall process, possibly for the first time.[39] For instance, as liability for implementing EU environmental policies would be part of the devolution package, inevitably the devolved administrations would need to be included in the UK policy process in this EU policy area.

Devolution had wide-ranging implications for the machinery of UK government in Whitehall, and preparations for devolution necessitated the creation of new administrative units involving the deployment of considerable internal resources. In the arena of UK European policy arrangements it was clear that accommodating devolution raised complex administrative (and sensitive political) questions. However, there was no suggestion that devolution required any fundamental change in the underlying mechanics of the UK European policy process. Current UK European policy procedures were deemed to be both internally efficient and externally effective. Accordingly, the EU policy process would continue to be managed from the centre – operating through the two 'pathways' described above – and the challenge for Whitehall was to establish new administrative arrangements that could be grafted onto current procedures without compromising the smooth and efficient functioning of these procedures. Crucially, from the perspective of UK governance, there was no expectation that devolution would effect a shift in the internal balance of political authority with respect to UK European policy.

3.2.2   Change within the devolved administrations

Within the territorial administrations, the European policy dimension to devolution was assigned to officials who already had an EU policy responsibility, or who had direct experience of the EU policy process.[40] The lead role in deliberations between the territorial administrations and the Cabinet Office tended to be taken by Scottish Office officials rather than their Welsh counterparts. This reflected two aspects of the evolving situation. First, the European policy capability within the Scottish Office was larger (in terms of personnel) than its Welsh counterpart and therefore had more resources to devote to this issue.

Second, the asymmetry of the UK devolution settlement inevitably meant that the Scottish Office had a greater 'stake' in the arrangements subsequently agreed than did the Welsh Office.

In Scotland, responsibility for the European segment of devolution was assigned to the European Support Unit (ESU).[41] In July 1998, once devolution went 'live', the ESU was revamped to become the European Affairs Division (EAD(SO)), whose remit covered the range of EU-related issues raised by devolution in addition to discharging on-going EU-related functions inherited from the ESU. The EAD(SO) was charged with (i) leading on discussions concerning the consequences of devolution for the Scottish Office internal European policy-making structure, (ii) codifying in concordats the arrangements to enable the Scottish position to be factored into UK European policy deliberations, and (iii) advising on the development of a European policy-deliberative capacity for the new Scottish Parliament.[42] To facilitate its new range of tasks, the EAD(SO) was divided into two 'branches'. One branch focused exclusively on addressing EU issues arising directly from devolution, including parliamentary oversight, while the second branch continued to handle 'routine' EU policy matters although it also contributed to the preparation of the EU concordat. Outside of the EAD(SO), and where relevant, various Scottish Office departments had to make provision internally for the EU-policy aspect of their own duties, subject to the terms of their bilateral concordats with Whitehall.[43]

The Welsh Office established a Devolution Unit in Spring 1997 – ahead of the general election – to prepare the groundwork in the event of a devolution referendum. Subsequently the Devolution Unit assumed responsibility for the central co-ordination of the concordats under negotiation with the Cabinet Office, including the EU concordat. As in Scotland, each policy division/group within the Welsh Office negotiated the details of the relevant bilateral concordat with Whitehall counterparts. Unlike the Scottish Office, no specific structural changes were made within the European section of the Welsh Office in anticipation of devolution. Responsibility for European policy lay with the European Affairs Division (EAD(WO)), one of three divisions in the Economic Development Group. The EAD(WO)'s European Affairs Policy Branch (EAPB) focused specifically on the probable needs of the National Assembly for Wales (NAW), including scrutiny arrangements for EU legislative proposals and the working arrangements of a European Affairs Committee of the Assembly. The Welsh Office played little active part in drafting the terms of the EU concordat, adopting instead an essentially 'responsive' mode. At the same time, there was some contact with officials in Scotland and Northern

Ireland on the EU concordat, this being a matter of common concern to each of the devolving territories.

The pattern of the discussions within and between the central and territorial administrations during this preparatory phase can best be described as contingent. There was no prescriptive 'master plan' to guide the design of post-devolution arrangements – only an implicit understanding that nothing should be done that would compromise the effectiveness of the prevailing UK European policy arrangements.[44] However, it was clear that devolution required the territorial administrations to develop or augment existing internal EU policy resources in the form of:

- implementing systems for handling EU business after devolution;
- constructing policy co-ordination arrangements on EU matters between Whitehall, Edinburgh and Cardiff;
- meeting the EU-policy needs of the (Scottish) Parliament and the (Welsh) Assembly;
- collaborating in the design of inter-administration dispute settlement machinery for EU policy; and
- enhancing the territorial administrations' representation in Brussels.

Capacity building: the handling of European policy in the devolved administrations

It was implicit that the UK's European policy arrangements post-devolution would continue broadly as before, with the devolved administrations inputting to the process much as the territorial offices had done previously. Nonetheless, new administrative arrangements were required for two reasons.

First, because the devolved administrations were not part of UK government, the management and co-ordination of European policy in Edinburgh and Cardiff had to be arranged to compensate for their exclusion from the machinery of UK government, and the implications this had for the representation of territorial interests in European policy discussions. No change was anticipated in UK arrangements for handling European policy. Issues subject to a department 'lead' would continue to be dealt with as previously, with Whitehall officials working in bilateral or multiple bilateral mode with counterparts in the devolved administrations.[45] Essentially the territorial administrations would rely on existing structures for contributing to policy discussions. A different procedure would be necessary where the EU issue raised matters of strategic national importance, and where co-ordination of a UK response fell to a central unit within government (e.g. Cabinet Office, FCO, Treasury).[46]

Prior to devolution, and only when relevant, officials from the territorial offices had access to – and would input territorial interests through – central administration networks (e.g. Cabinet Office).[47] At the same time, territorial Secretaries of State could input to UK European policy directly through their membership of the Cabinet.[48] With devolution, a new administrative capacity had to be created in the devolved administrations to distil and agree the (Scottish or Welsh) territorial line on European policy issues of strategic importance. Moreover, resources had to be made available to enable the devolved administrations to service their end of the Joint Ministerial Committee (JMC) machinery through which inter-administration policy disputes – including those on European policy – would be resolved.[49]

Second, devolution imposed new EU-related obligations on the devolved administrations for which provision had to be made – particularly in Scotland where it would fall to the Scottish Executive to implement EC law.[50] While the precise nature of the new EU-related tasks to be undertaken in Edinburgh and Cardiff differed (reflecting the difference in the devolution settlements, and the 'needs' of the new assemblies), both administrations anticipated a growth in the range of EU functions required of them.

Early in 1998 the Scottish Office created an Executive Secretariat to provide 'common' services to all departments following devolution. EAD(SO) thus ceased to be and some of its functions were now brought within the Executive Secretariat. Amongst other tasks, the Executive Secretariat (External) was to co-ordinate the Scottish Executive response to EU policy issues which impacted on a number of departments, and which would liaise with the COES. In the Welsh Office, the existing EAD(WO) would discharge this function, although it was expected that this might be appropriated at some future date by the European Committee of the Welsh Assembly: 'The European Committee will focus on strategic issues which affect the relationship between Wales and the European Union' (Eur-02-99: p. 6).

Appraising the changes introduced within the Scottish and Welsh administrations in the run-up to devolution reveals the extent to which the wish for continuity rather than change shaped developments. Although by necessity devolution altered certain aspects of the process of UK European policy-making, the response both in the territorial administrations and in Whitehall was to embark on organizational changes only where this was shown to be necessary, and with minimal disruption to the *status quo ante*. The situation in Wales deserves special mention with respect to the EU-related administrative changes implemented between 1997 and 1999. Two factors are relevant. First, the corporate nature of the Welsh Assembly meant that the administration would service the entire Assembly, and not an Executive of that assembly – as was the case in Scotland. Accordingly, any changes in the Welsh approach to EU policy-making would be led by the Assembly, or the European Committee within that Assembly. Although the Welsh Office did enhance its EU-related staffing during the period running-up to devolution, in anticipation of a greater workload post-devolution, the scope for institutional innovation was restricted by virtue of the type of bureaucracy which the Welsh Office would become following devolution. Second, this period coincided with extensive preparations in anticipation of the west of Wales being recognised as eligible for regional assistance under Objective 1 of the EU structural fund regulations. Indeed, the greater part of the EU-related administrative changes implemented within the Welsh Office at the time were driven by that expectation – and eventuality – rather than by devolution *per se*.

Inter-administration relations

This refers to modalities to enable the separate administrations in London, Edinburgh and Cardiff to co-ordinate EU policy-related advice, whether on a departmental basis or centrally. As noted above, devolution brought with it a need to establish new procedures and arrangements for maintaining policy co-operation and co-ordination between UK government and the devolved administrations. These procedures and arrangements are set out in the concordats signed between the UK government and each of the devolved administrations in Scotland and Wales.[51] The objectives of the concordats were two-fold: (a) to maintain a broad measure of co-operation and co-ordination between central and territorial administrations with respect to the development of devolved policies, and (b) to achieve a UK-wide consensus on policies reserved to UK government but which nonetheless impact substantially on the devolved administrations.[52]

Concordats tackle two specific problems arising with devolution: (i) managing policies characterised by joint competence (i.e. concurrent powers), and (ii) managing policies where the actions of one (devolved or central) administration will impact on the policy environment of the other (central or devolved) administration. The first describes the problem of policy 'spillover', the second one of policy 'contagion'. As noted in the devolution White Paper, *Scotland's Parliament*:

> The Scottish Executive will need to keep in close touch with Departments of the UK Government. Good communication systems

will be vital. Departments in both administrations will develop mutual understandings covering the appropriate exchange of information, advance notification and joint working. The principles will be as follows:

- the vast majority of matters should be capable of being handled routinely among officials of the Departments in question;
- if further discussion is needed on any issue, the Cabinet Office and its Scottish Executive counterpart will mediate, again at official level;
- on some issues there will need to be discussions between the Scottish Executive and Ministers in the UK Government.[53]

Concordats elaborate these principles of inter-administration co-operation and define the framework within which joint policy-making will evolve. It was implicit from the outset, and stressed on many occasions subsequently, that concordats would *not* create legal obligations or restrictions on any signatory.[54] Instead they were voluntarily agreed codes of conduct to guide the work of officials, and could be re-negotiated in the light of experience.[55] Accordingly, concordats were construed as neutral political and constitutional documents, whose purpose is to effect a seamless transition of the UK policy process from a system involving one administrative entity to a multi-player system involving a number of participants.[56] The concordats are based on four guidelines:

- full communication and consultation between the administrations on matters of joint interest, with each administration giving due consideration to the views of the other;
- co-operation between administrations in all stages of the development of policies for which each had competence;
- a full exchange of information between the administrations on all relevant policy-related matters – the principle of 'no surprises';
- each administration would respect the confidentiality of information passed to it by the other, subject to safeguards where necessary.

As befitted their functional nature, the preparation of concordats was left in the hands of middle-to-senior ranking officials during the run-up to devolution and normally would be signed by senior officials in Whitehall and their counterparts in the territorial administrations. Ministers would become involved only where the subject matter was politically sensitive, or where officials were unable to agree the precise terms of a particular concordat. The intention was that the concordats would be published once ready, and the expectation was that this would be prior to the inaugural elections to the devolved assemblies scheduled for May 1999. In the event, the first concordats were not published until October 1999. A number of reasons were given for the delay, the most convincing of which was that the concordats were not ready on time. However, the implication was that the relevant time frame incorporated a political 'window' which closed ahead of the date of the Scottish and Welsh elections to avoid the concordats becoming an election issue.[57]

The officials involved in drafting the concordats have indicated that in large part they were making up the 'rules' as they went along. There was no master plan; no pre-existing model; no political agenda. The only guiding principle was that, wherever possible, prevailing inter-departmental practices should be codified in a concordat thereby becoming recommended inter-administration 'good practice' after devolution, with – as noted earlier – new arrangements being devised only where necessary.

The concordats were published in two tranches. In October 1999 the MoU was published, including within it five quadrilateral concordats. The MoU is an overarching agreement that sets out the general principles of, and mutual responsibilities for, policy co-ordination and co-operation between the UK government and each of the devolved administrations. It covers issues such as inter-administration correspondence and information flows, arrangements for consultation and co-operation, confidentiality of information, involvement in reserved matters, and dispute settlement procedures. Appended to this are five specific quadrilateral concordats which stipulate the mechanics of co-operation and co-ordination in the following areas: dispute settlement (the structure of the JMC); EU policy issues; financial assistance to industry; international relations; and statistics.

The second tranche of concordats was published piecemeal once agreed upon between individual Whitehall ministries and the devolved administrations. These prescribed inter-administration 'good practice' procedures for individual policy areas affected by devolution – essentially all other devolved or reserved policies – e.g. agriculture and fisheries; social security; home affairs; environment, transport and the regions; defence and so on. Many of these concordats have sections dealing with EU-related business.[58] In all such cases, these provisions have to conform to the principles elaborated in the overarching MoU as well as the EU concordat.

The intention initially had been to prepare a single concordat on EU policy applicable to all devolved administrations, however the structure adopted ultimately was to divide the concordat into three sections: one applicable to Scotland, one to Wales, and a common annex which applied to both.[59] While responsibility for drafting the EU concordat rested with the Cabinet Office, inputs came from a number of different sources including, of course, the territorial administrations – particularly Scotland, reflecting the high profile a Scottish administration would assign to its role in shaping UK European policy. Not only did this reflect the asymmetry of the devolution settlement,[60] it also pointed to expectations in Scotland that the devolved administration should have real clout over UK European policy.[61]

Responsibility in the Scottish Office for contributing to the EU concordat lay with officials within the Executive Secretariat (External). In the Welsh Office it was the EAD(WO) who led on the EU concordat, although officials in the Cabinet Secretariat of the Welsh Office had responsibility for the overseeing the Welsh end of the concordats as a whole.

In the main, and perhaps surprisingly given the novelty and complexity of the undertaking, it appears that few procedural problems were encountered in preparing the EU concordat,[62] confirming the view that the prevailing arrangements for handling European business were generally satisfactory. Nonetheless, devolution did raise some tensions on issues of principle. In the first place EU policy is a reserved matter and there was a view within Whitehall that it should remain solely a matter for national government with no involvement by the devolved administrations. This reflected concern that devolved administration involvement could undermine the strengths of the traditional UK approach to intra-EU bargaining – chief amongst which was the long-standing convention that all parts of UK government adhered to an agreed line in EU policy negotiations.[63] There was a risk that this would be jeopardised by giving devolved administrations a role in formulating UK European policy – particularly as these administrations could not be bound by the principle of collective responsibility. Further, their involvement would make it more difficult to maintain confidentiality when formulating a common UK position. This was not only about 'trust'. Under the Welsh settlement all members of the Assembly had, in principle, access to minutes of inter-administration deliberations and it might prove difficult to maintain confidentiality under these circumstances – regardless of the terms of the concordats.

The concerns of the devolved administrations, naturally, were somewhat different. For them there was pressure to establish arrangements that would be (and could be shown to be) effective in ensuring that territorial interests were incorporated in UK European policy. In part this was indicative of the significant overlap between UK European business on the one hand, and devolved competencies on the other hand. Close inter-administration co-operation was essential in order to ensure that legislation introduced by the devolved government did not conflict with the UK's European obligations or objectives, or that the UK's stance on putative EU legislation reflected properly the views of the devolved administrations.[64] Indeed, one of the more controversial debates concerning the EU concordat was whether ministers of the devolved administrations should have a right to attend meetings of the Council of Ministers where these were discussing matters in which they had a direct interest.[65] This was successfully resisted by Whitehall on the basis that it would undermine the reserved status of UK European policy and could undermine the strengths of the UK bargaining in that Council. Instead, and as set out in the EU concordat, it was for the lead UK minister to decide on the composition of the UK delegation attending Council meetings, and to respond to a request from a minister from a devolved administration to be a member of that delegation.[66] However, where a minister from a devolved administration was invited to participate in a Council meeting, that minister would be required to represent the agreed UK position.

From a review of the provisions of the EU concordat it is tempting to conclude that devolution had little effect on the day-to-day mechanics of the UK's European policy process. European policy continues to be managed by UK government through the well-established Whitehall procedures, with the provisions of the concordat simply enabling the *status quo ante* to prevail. However, this may be to present the new arrangement in a somewhat naive light. The reality was that the devolved administrations no longer were an integral part of the machinery of UK government and, consequently, no longer were involved routinely in the UK European policy process. This loss of 'insider' status *possibly* could impact on the influence that territorial administrations exerted on EU policy simply because their officials might no longer participate (or enjoy their former status) in key Whitehall meetings, nor might they receive, as a matter of routine, documents which may be deemed to be sensitive from a political or negotiating perspective. Although it is too early to determine whether this has happened, our research did reveal quite widespread concerns of this nature within the territorial administrations. Moreover, there was some indication within Whitehall that these administrations now *were* effectively 'out of the Whitehall loop' which carried inevitable consequences with respect to the policy information they could expect to receive (see also Chapter 5).

Consequently, and notwithstanding the formal provisions of the EU concordat – designed to buttress the *status quo ante* – there was a risk that the devolved administrations would find, as a matter of practice, that their post-devolution 'voice' in the UK European policy was becoming less compelling.

Inter-governmental mediation

This refers to decisional and accountability structures whereby ministers from the devolved governments together with their counterparts in UK government resolve disputes over the former's conduct with respect to devolved competencies, or the latter's conduct with respect to reserved competencies. The need for a procedure for resolving inter-administration disputes arose from the policy overlap between devolved and reserved competencies created by devolution, and as a result of the commitment made by UK government to permit the devolved administrations to input to reserved matters. While it was expected that most disputes would be resolved by officials within the relevant departments, exceptionally it might be necessary to involve the relevant ministers from the devolved and UK administrations. Dispute settlement machinery raised complex questions of procedure and constitutionality. While any arrangement could not violate the constitutional position, which stated that authority ultimately lay with the UK government and Parliament, political realism dictated that disputes between the devolved administrations and Whitehall – hitherto resolved by the relevant inter-departmental or Cabinet committee – should be handled by an impartial and fair procedure. Neither the devolution White Papers nor subsequent legislation addressed this issue, and it received its first airing in a House of Lords debate when Baroness Ramsay, a government whip, announced the UK government's intention to establish the JMC of which the UK government and the devolved administrations would be members. Baroness Ramsay explained that:

> There will be one joint ministerial committee. The idea is that the devolved administrations will be represented on it, plus representatives of the UK Government. There will be representation of each administration. That representation will vary according to the specific issues under consideration. Fisheries Ministers would be involved on fisheries matters, for example.[67]

Although announcing that a JMC would be established, at that point little thought had been given to its structure and *modus operandi*.

A number of issues had to be decided, namely: (i) at what ministerial level would the JMC operate; (ii) who would chair meetings of the JMC; (iii) should it meet in bilateral mode, or must it always involve ministers from each of the devolved governments; (iv) would the JMC only convene to address inter-governmental disputes over reserved matters; (v) what status would be given to its consultations within Cabinet discussions; (vi) would the devolved governments be expected to observe 'collective responsibility' for UK policy which had been subject to the JMC procedures; and (vii) what role was envisaged for territorial Secretaries of State in the context of the JMC?

For their part, officials expected that the composition of JMC meetings would depend on the subject under consideration along similar lines to the EU's Council of Ministers, with its variations formations. Further, when convening to discuss an aspect of UK European policy, JMC participation most probably would be drawn from the departments between whom the disagreement had occurred. Moreover, other than in 'ceremonial' mode, the JMC would convene only when it had an issue which had to be resolved.

Although its role was consultative, it was clear that the JMC would have a crucial role to play in facilitating smooth governance once devolution took effect. Responsibility for developing prospective JMC arrangements was given to the COCS. Once established, responsibility for servicing the JMC would fall to the departments responsible for the policy issue under discussion. Should the JMC meet to discuss UK European policy, the Whitehall lead would be taken by the COES. In the devolved administrations this role would be discharged by the relevant central secretariat – in Scotland this being the Executive Secretariat (External) and in Wales the EAD(WO). Finally, in Whitehall the Constitution Secretariat would retain an overall responsibility for the JMC and it would have counterpart officials undertaking similar duties in the devolved administrations.

Details of the JMC machinery were published in October 1999 as one of the five Supplementary Agreements (concordats) to the MoU. With respect to UK European policy, it stated that the JMC '… will operate as one of the principal mechanisms for consultation on UK positions on EU issues which affect devolved matters'.[68] In practice, however, the expectation was that the JMC procedures would be invoked only where officials from UK government and the devolved administrations were unable to agree a common position to be placed before the relevant ministers, and where alternative channels of mediation (e.g. via territorial Secretaries of State) had failed. The JMC was, therefore, a measure of last resort. Moreover, as the concordat made clear, the JMC was to be a consultative body rather than an executive body.[69] Its conclusions would be advisory and have no constitutional standing.

3.3   Arrangements post-devolution

The publication of the MoU on 1 October 1999 and, later, the bilateral concordats between the territorial administrations and individual UK government departments effectively signalled the end of the inter-administration transition phase in the devolution process. By then, of course, the Scottish Parliament and the Welsh Assembly had been operating for six months, while the devolved administrations in Cardiff and Edinburgh had already begun to operate the procedures subsequently set out in the concordats. The publication of the concordats triggered a political controversy in Scotland and Wales. Many (opposition) Members of the Scottish Parliament (MSPs) and some Welsh Assembly Members (AMs), argued that the concordats should be subject to ratification by both territorial assemblies before entering into force (Scott 2001).[70] In the event, the MoU was debated and endorsed by both assemblies on 7 October, although neither body had the authority to amend or nullify the provisions set out within that document.[71] Following the publication of the MoU and the supplementary concordats, the devolved administrations and the UK government embarked on the task of making a success of the new arrangements and, in Cardiff and Edinburgh, of meeting the EU-policy related needs of the newly elected representatives in the Scottish Parliament and the Welsh Assembly.[72]

In the following section we examine the evolving structure of the EU-related element of inter-administration arrangements. We do this by examining post-devolution developments in each of the territorial administrations – Whitehall, the Scottish Executive, and the Welsh Assembly.

3.3.1   Whitehall

Whitehall: the Cabinet Office

By the time devolution took effect, all departments and ministries within UK government had established specialist devolution desks or units. It fell to these officials to implement the provisions agreed upon in the concordats, i.e. to make the system work. At the core of government – the Cabinet – the Ministerial Committee on Devolution Policy (DP – which replaced DSWR) continued to function under the

Lord Chancellor (serviced by the COCS), while within the structures of the EU policy process, authority continued to reside with (E)DOP, chaired by the Foreign Secretary. The three territorial Secretaries of State were members of both these Committees. Ministers from the devolved administrations were not. Within the cadre of officials, the co-ordination of European business in the Cabinet Office remained through the official committee EQ(O) (and EQ(O)L for legal issues – see Chapter 2, Table 2.1). The Friday meetings between the UK Permanent Representative, the head of the COES and relevant ministries continued. Officials from the devolved administrations no longer had direct access to formal meetings of this Cabinet Office EQ network (although *ad hoc* arrangements have evolved to ensure they were not wholly excluded from that network), but were invited to participate in the Friday meetings, other relevant *ad hoc* meetings, set up by COES, and inter-departmental meetings. Distribution of material was maintained using the JMC(O)EU net in lieu of the EQ(O) net. Although the EU concordat was designed to ensure that officials from the devolved administrations were kept fully informed of UK European policy discussions (at least in so far as these touched on devolved competencies) the language of the concordats and the arrangements being made left considerable scope for Whitehall officials to decide when – and to what degree – to include the devolved administration in government discussions.[73] Invoking the JMC machinery to arbitrate such matters, while possible, carried with it the attendant risks either of over-reacting to what might be nothing more than teething difficulties in a new set of procedures or publicising a more profound dilemma inherent in the devolution process. Instead, further guidance was given to Whitehall officials in the form of Devolution Guidance Notes (DGNs).

In January 2000 the Cabinet Office published a number of DGNs setting out guidelines for government officials in their dealings with the devolved administrations. The DGNs were described as a 'third' level of guidance (the MoU and the bilateral concordats being the 'first' and 'second' levels respectively), and these fleshed out the UK government's understanding of its obligations under the concordats. Exceptionally, DGN1 – Common Working Arrangements – was agreed between the UK government and the devolved administrations within the framework of the new JMC(O), and applies to both parties.[74] The first paragraph of DGN1 explains its role:

The UK Government on the one hand and the Scottish Ministers, the Cabinet of the National Assembly for Wales [and the Northern

Ireland Executive Committee] ('the administrations') on the other have agreed a Memorandum of Understanding (MoU) setting out the principles that will underlie relations between them. Pursuant to the MoU, this guidance sets down common working arrangements aimed at promoting the efficient administration of Government business within the UK in relation to both devolved and non-devolved matters.

UK European policy matters are covered in DGN6, 'Circulation of Inter-Ministerial and Inter-Departmental Correspondence'. DGN6 covers two classes of inter-ministerial or inter-departmental correspondences – Cabinet Committee correspondences, which by their nature may contain politically sensitive information, and inter-departmental correspondences which tend not to contain such information. With reference to Cabinet Committee discussions on, *inter alia*, EU policy, point 1.4 of DGN6 states;

> In particular the Government intends that ministers and officials of the devolved administrations should be fully involved in discussions within the UK Government about formulation of the UK's policy position on all EU issues which touch on matters falling within the responsibility of the devolved administrations. In order to meet the commitment of being fully involved while the UK policy is in the process of being agreed, the general rule should be that the devolved administrations are aware of issues which impact on their responsibilities, whether or not these are the subject of inter-ministerial correspondence, in time for them to contribute views before the UK Government has reached its own policy conclusions. There are however a number of means by which this can be achieved, and Departments will wish to consider, in each case, which method best achieves the commitments given in the MoU and EU concordat, *without exposing significant disagreements within the UK Government.*[75]

DGN6 stipulates that ministers from the devolved administrations will not be copied correspondence addressed to members of a Cabinet committee, i.e. they are *not* to be included in the Cabinet committee network.[76] Instead, it will be for the 'originating Department or Minister' to copy the devolved administrations if it is judged, '...that to do so will not entail unnecessary risk, for example by exposing significant disagreements between UK Ministers'. Further, it is for the originator to decide what restrictions, if any, are to be placed on the usage the devolved administration makes of the correspondence. On the other hand, where the correspondence is circulated other than on a Cabinet Committee net, DGN1 (point 3.1) provides that it 'may be copied directly to the devolved administrations'. DGN6 elaborates the JMC arrangements, and notes that 'all JMC correspondence should be sent to the devolved administrations as of right'. Finally, DGN6 (point 4.1) stipulates that 'the JMC(O), the official-level committee which shadows the work of the JMC, may set up official sub-committees' – one of which, the JMC(O)EU, focuses on the development of UK European policy issues (see Figure 3.1).

Excluding the devolved administrations from the Cabinet committee network, while permitting them to be copied papers addressed to members of that network, reflects the pivotal role that the Cabinet committee system plays in UK government. Not only is it here that a consensus position will be brokered between ministers on a controversial policy issue, and therefore is the forum where intra-government disagreements are voiced, it is also the vehicle for securing collective Cabinet responsibility for the policy position subsequently adopted. It would simply be inconceivable for politicians who are not bound by the edict of collective responsibility to be able – without restriction – to access papers appertaining to the work of Cabinet committees.

It is worth noting that DGN6 permits a restrictive interpretation of how much information would be passed on in the event of exposing disagreements: something which might become relevant if there were serious disagreement between a UK government and a devolved administration, say a Scottish Executive led by the Scottish National Party (SNP). In any event, the UK government already has to be mindful of the fact that the Scottish Executive is a coalition of Labour and Liberal Democrat ministers.

Whitehall: FCO

There are two strands to the post-devolution arrangements in the FCO. The first – at official level – is the role played by DAD. DAD was designed to help address any problems the devolved authorities might have with accessing Brussels, relevant Whitehall officials or diplomats, and to ensure that Scotland and Wales would remain 'in the loop' as far as securing placements in UKRep, the European institutions and so on. By the summer of 2000 it had become clear that a special department in the FCO was an excessive commitment of resources and it was abolished shortly thereafter.

The second is a political strand and relates to the Ministerial Committee for European Coordination (MINECOR). MINECOR is a UK

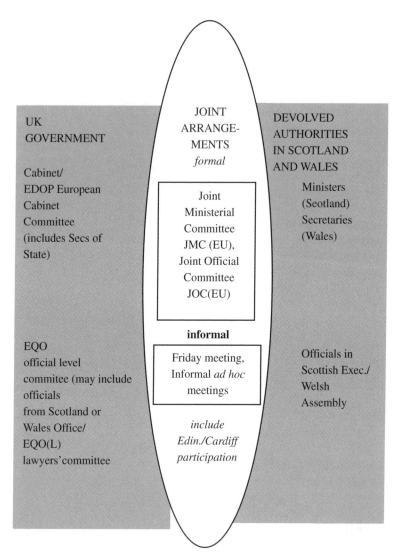

UK GOVERNMENT	JOINT ARRANGE-MENTS *formal*	DEVOLVED AUTHORITIES IN SCOTLAND AND WALES
Cabinet/ EDOP European Cabinet Committee (includes Secs of State)	Joint Ministerial Committee JMC (EU), Joint Official Committee JOC(EU)	Ministers (Seotland) Secretaries (Wales)
	informal	
EQO official level commitee (may include officials from Scotland or Wales Office/ EQO(L) lawyers' committee	Friday meeting, Informal *ad hoc* meetings *include Edin./Cardiff participation*	Officials in Scottish Exec./ Welsh Assembly

Figure 3.1   The co-ordination of EU policy post-devolution

ministerial group on Europe and not a UK government Cabinet committee. It is chaired by the UK minister for Europe in the FCO (then
Keith Vaz, MP[77]). MINECOR was established by the new Labour government with a view to mobilising a more constructive European policy

within government. MINECOR was devised in order to facilitate inter-departmental co-ordination with respect to UK policy towards Europe. It is important to stress that MINECOR has no competence for issues appertaining to the UK European policy process and the devolved administrations – this being mediated under the quite separate arrangements set out in the EU concordat – although ministers from the devolved administrations are able to participate in meetings of MINECOR as are the territorial Secretaries of State. Consequently, while MINECOR is an element in the overall UK co-ordination effort with respect to European policy and includes ministers from the Scottish Executive and the Welsh Assembly in its deliberations, it is neither a product of devolution nor is it a vehicle for resolving EU policy-linked problems arising from devolution.

Whitehall: territorial Secretaries of State[78]

The offices of the territorial Secretaries of State (SoS) were retained after devolution, albeit with a changed remit and a considerably reduced staff.[79] As members of the UK government, and of various Cabinet committees, the SoS are subject to the guidelines set out in the concordats and the relevant DGNs – the latter elaborating the provisions for the circulation of inter-departmental and inter-ministerial correspondences to the devolved administrations. As noted earlier, the roles of the SoS are to fortify devolution in Scotland and Wales by mediating between UK government and the devolved administrations where necessary, and to buttress the political and social legitimacy of UK government in the post-devolution environment.

The devolution legislation assigned different responsibilities to the Scottish and Welsh Secretaries of State. Under the Scottish settlement, the principal role of the Secretary of State (SoS) is to represent Scottish interests on reserved matters. In the area of EU policy, however, executing this assignment rule is not straightforward because EU policies touch upon so many devolved competencies. This raises the question of whether it is the role of the Scottish SoS to argue within government for a UK European policy that is compatible with Scotland's interests, as represented by the Scottish Executive; or to persuade the Scottish Executive to adjust devolved policies such that they accord better with UK European policy.[80] It is likely to be politically tendentious in Scotland if the position advanced by the Executive on a devolved competence is rebutted by the SoS on the basis that it does not accord with the UK's European policy-related interests. Yet, as the SoS is a member of the UK government, this possibility cannot be discounted. While the machinery of the JMC has been created to resolve this type of problem, the JMC is seen as a measure of the last resort, i.e. after mediation by the SoS has been unsuccessful.

In the period of our study, admittedly very early days in the process, no problems of this type were reported, and the JMC(EU) machinery was not invoked.[81] Rather, and despite initial statements that the Scotland Office would remain the voice for Scotland within UK government on reserved matters,[82] on EU issues at least it appeared that the then SoS, Dr John Reid, MP, took his cue largely from the Scottish Executive, this being facilitated by regular meetings between himself and the First Minister and supported by officials from both the Scottish Executive and the Scotland Office.[83] It is worth noting that a distinctive feature of the Scottish settlement is that the lines of communication with respect to Scotland's voice in UK European policy are those between the Scottish Executive and the Scotland Office. They do not involve the Scottish Parliament, it being assumed that the position the Executive adopts is, or will be, endorsed by that Parliament.[84]

Under the Welsh settlement the responsibility of the Welsh SoS to 'speak for Wales' goes further, and s/he is responsible for representing Welsh interests on all legislative matters being considered by UK government, be they transferred or reserved. Moreover, the relevant lines of communication run between the Wales Office and the Assembly generally, mediated by the Assembly Cabinet. Although the SoS for Wales is not regarded as the mouthpiece of Assembly in UK government, this arrangement does acknowledge that s/he will ensure that UK government decisions are taken with '... full regard to any matters where Wales has particular interests or concerns.'[85] In addition, the SoS for Wales must steer primary legislation through Westminster where it affects Wales, a role not relevant to the SoS for Scotland as far as devolved matters are concerned (Osmond 1999: 33). The upshot is that the Welsh SoS must retain a close relationship with the Assembly to ensure that s/he is in a position to represent Welsh interests within UK government[86] – by necessity, closer than the relationship of the Scottish SoS to the Scottish Parliament.[87] By the same token, the Welsh Assembly must maintain a close relationship with the SoS to ensure that s/he is aware of Welsh interests and is fully briefed to represent these interests. In that sense the potential dysfunction that arises between devolved and reserved matters under the Scottish arrangement with respect to UK European policy simply does not arise with the same force in the Welsh case. Unlike the situation in Scotland, the position of the Welsh SoS as representing Welsh interests on all UK policy serves to reduce the scope for 'turf wars' between the SoS and the Assembly First Secretary.[88]

In formal terms, the offices of territorial SoS have key roles to play in the UK European policy process under both variants of devolution. First, responsibility lies with these offices for representing to government the territorial dimension of European policy. Both the Scottish and Welsh SoS are members of (E)DOP and, of course, of the Cabinet itself. Second, in view of the fact that officials from the devolved administrations *formally* are excluded from the EQ network (although *ad hoc* arrangements have been devised to permit them informal access to that network), their formal link to the Cabinet Office – and pertinent information – is via officials in the Scotland and Wales Offices of UK government. Third, the expectation is that the territorial SoS will mediate disputes between the devolved administrations and UK government with respect to policy in reserved matters, and UK European policy is a potential area of dispute.[89]

3.3.2 The Scottish Executive

The main part of the Scottish segment of EU policy business continues to be handled by individual departments now located within the Executive, utilising procedures and arrangements which are, in many instances, little different from those which operated prior to devolution. As we discuss elsewhere, the day-to-day functions of officials within many divisions of the Executive appear to have changed only slightly, if at all, under the new constitutional architecture – albeit inter-administration arrangements now are mediated by concordats. There are, however, exceptions: for specific policy portfolios (e.g. the environment) devolution has necessitated an increase in devolved policy-making capacity in order that the Scottish dimension to UK European policy is adequately reflected in Whitehall.

Outside of individual departmental structures, the main focus of the Scottish Executive's EU-policy relations with Whitehall is the Executive Secretariat (External), which deals with all aspects of external affairs.[90] It is the Executive Secretariat (External) that administers the Scottish segment of the EU concordat, and it is with the Executive Secretariat that responsibility lies for mediating any difficulties between the Scottish Executive and Whitehall with respect to the operation of the EU concordat, i.e. where the prescribed procedures for involving the Scottish Executive in the UK European policy process fail to operate satisfactorily. In the immediate post-devolution phase, problems did appear with officials in the Scottish Executive insisting they were not being sufficiently involved in the UK government's EU-related decision-making process, e.g. being informed of a policy position that had already been decided instead of being consulted on a policy proposal.[91] Problems of this nature are most likely to arise in the context of EU policy issues that have been 'raised' to Cabinet committee level, for instance where there is disagreement within UK government as to the proper policy stance. As the DGNs make clear, UK government is unwilling to have Cabinet committee papers circulated to the devolved administrations other than in an edited form. This restricts the flow of information coming to the devolved administrations and so limits the information they have about the policy choices under consideration and, consequently, their capacity to shape policy. In extreme cases, e.g. where the government's European policy position is the outcome of an inter-departmental compromise brokered at Cabinet level, the devolved administrations may have no independent input to UK policy.[92] Other instances of less than adequate consultation with the Scottish Executive have arisen with respect to EU-related policy advice given to UK government by particular Whitehall departments,[93] although these may simply reflect teething troubles of an administrative or interpretational nature, rather than a structural weakness in the terms of the concordats themselves.[94] The main Whitehall point of contact for the Executive Secretariat (External) is the Cabinet Office. It is its officials who will then pass on to particular departments the complaints or notification of procedural difficulties that arise from the Scottish Executive and that cannot be resolved directly by inter-departmental discussions.

An important innovation within the Scottish Executive has been the creation of an essentially informal network of officials whose work involves them in EU policy issues. This has been described as a European Coordination Group (ECG) and includes the various European experts from different departments within the Scottish Executive, including officials working in Scotland House in Brussels. Although principally a network linked electronically, this group does meet from time to time.

The Executive Secretariat has a number of additional functions appertaining to EU policy:

- It is charged with servicing the Scottish Executive end of JMC (including the JMC(EU)) and collects the papers from the relevant department(s) within the Scottish Executive and ensures that these are circulated to JMC(EU) participants. In the main, Scottish Executive ministers will be briefed by the 'lead' department within the Executive, although on overarching topics (e.g. EU treaty reform) the Executive Secretariat may co-ordinate the briefing. Officials from the Executive Secretariat participate in the Joint Official Committee (JOC), which supports the JMC structure.[95] The JOC will meet when required, although regular stock-taking meetings are likely at least during the initial post-devolution phase.

• The Executive Secretariat has some EU-related responsibilities to the Scottish Parliament arising from the latter's responsibilities for scrutiny of EU documents and implementing EC legislation: (i) where the European Committee has scrutinised an EU legislative proposal, the clerk of that Committee sends its views to the Executive Secretariat for onward transmission to the relevant department(s) within the Executive;[96] (ii) preparation of a Scottish European Brief (SEB) and Scottish Cover Note (SCN) when so requested by the European Committee of the Scottish Parliament. This Scottish information augments the UK Explanatory Memorandum (EM) which the Scottish Parliament receives from Whitehall, and puts a Scottish perspective on the proposal or topic under consideration (see Chapter 4).

• It oversees the activities of Scotland House, the Scottish Executive's office in Brussels. Scottish Executive officials in Scotland House are part of the Executive Secretariat, and 'report back' to the Secretariat on a weekly basis.[97]

The Scottish Executive is responsible for presenting draft legislation to the Scottish Parliament, including legislation required to give effect to EC law (mainly Directives) in Scotland. However, a decision has to be taken at the outset whether or not to implement EC law via a Scottish legislative instrument, or simply to implement the legislation via UK legislation. While the Scottish Parliament may prefer to utilise Scottish legislation, the Executive may prefer to utilise UK legislation – for instance, if there is a real threat of infraction if done by Scottish legislation (e.g. to avoid any delay in the legislation being enacted), or where inconsistencies would result. For the period of our study at least, the Scottish Executive largely decided which road to go down on this matter, based on the advice offered by its officials.

Finally, the relevant minister from the Scottish Executive may be invited by the UK lead minister to participate in a UK delegation to the Council of the European Union, as provided for in the EU concordat (point B4.13). Participation is by invitation, and is conditional on the Scottish minister adhering to the settled UK negotiating line. Should that minister intervene, s/he does so as a member of the UK delegation and not as a minister from the Scottish Executive.[98] Should the

Executive wish to participate in a specific Council meeting, this will be signalled to officials in Whitehall either by the relevant department or division within Scottish Executive, or by the Executive Secretariat. However, ultimately it is the UK minister who decides the composition of the negotiating team.[99]

3.3.3   The National Assembly for Wales

The corporate nature of the Welsh Assembly creates particular problems of terminology, for instance distinguishing between its political side, i.e. the AMs, on the one hand, and the officials who service the Assembly, on the other. Moreover, within this latter group, it is also necessary to draw a distinction between those officials involved directly in servicing the Assembly (e.g. committee clerks), and those who are providing policy advice, interfacing with their Whitehall counterparts, and managing the day-to-day business inherited from the Welsh Office. In this section we will make a three-way distinction involving (a) AMs; (b) Assembly personnel (those working directly to AMs, e.g. Clerks to Committees); and (c) officials of the NAW (civil servants in roles previously associated with Welsh Office business).

The problems are not only terminological. The corporate nature of the Assembly creates an 'open' governance situation in which all AMs, regardless of political affiliation, have access to the officials of the Assembly and the information which they have.[100] This raises problematic questions concerning the access of political opponents of the UK government to information on reserved matters by virtue of their position as AMs. Although the concordats and the DGNs seemingly cover this problem – by stipulating that any recipient of UK government correspondence must observe the confidentiality conditions placed on the correspondence by its originator – the amalgamated nature of the Assembly and its officials implies that 'Chinese walls' must be created within the Assembly organisation if this obligation of confidentiality is to be honoured. And indeed, this has been the upshot of the unique arrangement of devolution as applied to Wales.[101] It is worth noting in this context that the MoU was signed by the *Cabinet* of NAW: a functional status elevated to the status of a structural one.

Responsibility for the Welsh dimension to UK European policy remains principally with the EAD, now of NAW – that section of officials of NAW previously part of the Welsh Office structure. In large measure the day-to-day activities of EAD(NAW) have continued as normal, with a large part of their post-devolution activities linked to preparations for implementing structural fund policies in line with the decision to confer Objective 1 status on the west of Wales. Indeed, the staffing level of the EAD(NAW) has increased in line with these new responsibilities. At the same time, and reflecting the corporate structure of the Assembly, AMs have placed new demands (e.g. commissioning research and policy papers) on officials of NAW in all areas, including EU-related matters, and this has greatly increased their work-load. This factor more generally and the novelty of the Welsh institutional arrangements meant that many of the bilateral concordats between Cardiff and London were slow in being agreed.

The EAD(NAW) assumed formal 'ownership' of the EU concordat and will be responsible for dealing with any difficulties that might arise in its operation. Inevitably the EAD(NAW) retains close contact with its Whitehall counterparts – both directly and through the Wales Office and the SoS for Wales. This latter relationship is much closer than its counterpart in Scotland, reflecting the pivotal role that the SoS retains for representing Welsh interests in UK government on all legislative matters.

Because of the unique nature of the devolution model applied to Wales, and notwithstanding the creation of Chinese walls, the EAD(NAW) necessarily has a much closer relationship with the AMs than its counterpart in Scotland has with its MSPs. The EAD(NAW) will, accordingly, provide support to the deliberations of the European Committee of the Welsh Assembly. That Committee has tended thus far to focus on broader issues appertaining to the EU, leaving to individual subject committees the task of adapting specific EU policy issues to the Welsh situation (see Chapter 4).

3.4 Conclusions

In this chapter we have reviewed the changes that have been made to the organisation of UK European policy process as a consequence of devolution. We have documented the ways in which the UK's pre-existing European policy process – widely perceived as being efficient and effective – was adapted to secure the government's commitment to include the devolved administrations in that policy process. As we have discussed, the UK European policy process was based on an elaborate set of procedures which together secured a high element of *intra*-governmental co-ordination of policy advice, loyalty to the agreed negotiating line, and collective ministerial accountability and responsibility for the ultimate outcome. The problem posed by devolution was how best to open this process to non-government players – the devolved administrations – without jeopardising one or more of these elements and weakening the process as a whole. Notwithstanding the constitutional position under which EU policy was a reserved matter, maintaining the *status quo ante* was not a viable option. Not only had the government given a pledge to include the devolved administrations in the European policy process, the overlap between EU policies and devolved competencies was such as to make desirable the inclusion of the devolved administrations at various stages in that process simply from the perspective of good governance.

In Chapter 2 we concluded by noting the challenges that devolution would pose to the government in its handling of EU business. On the basis of the research reported here, how might we typify the response forthcoming under each heading?

Within the *systemic* dimension it is evident that devolution as a *constitutional* event did not in itself formally necessitate a change to the UK government's arrangements for managing European policy. As a reserved matter, that policy remained the exclusive competence of UK government (a situation buttressed by the provision in the devolution legislation for the UK government to strike down any measure proposed by the devolved administrations that was incompatible with UK–EU obligations). Indeed, notwithstanding commitments given in the devolution White Papers, the legislation itself contained no reference to – or proposal for modalities to facilitate – the involvement of the devolved administrations in the UK European policy process. Notwithstanding the constitutional position, however, the procedures of the domestic European policy process were modified to enable the devolved administrations to be involved in that process. This reflected the extent to which they were – by virtue of the competencies devolved – direct stakeholders in EU policy developments (and so in the UK policy towards EU proposals) and best placed to advise on their territorial impact of EU policy. Although it was understood that devolution required the UK European policy process to be adapted, it was implicit that this should not compromise the perceived strengths of that process – chief amongst which was a willingness by all participants to adhere to the agreed negotiating line, an obligation that would *ipso facto* extend to the devolved administrations.

The (systemic) adaptation of the UK European policy process took place in the administrative – or bureaucratic – sphere and not in the constitutional – or formal – sphere, and involved the creation of structures to facilitate inter-administration co-ordination and co-operation with respect *both* to devolved competencies which had an EU dimension *and* EU policies which had a devolved dimension. The new structures included arrangements for resolving inter-administration disputes – if necessary by referral to the political level by invoking the JMC machinery, although the conclusions of the JMC were not formally binding on either party. There was a general awareness that the success of inter-administration co-operation and co-ordination (and, by implication, the stability of the devolution arrangements) would depend, in part, upon the political complexion of the administrations, i.e. disagreements over policy were expected to be less problematic where the same party held the majority in the devolved administrations as at Westminster. Given the significance of European policy within the devolved administrations, it was likely that this would be a potential source of disagreement – albeit that no instances of this emerged during the period of our study. It is, however, possible to overstate the degree to which this problem might in any event arise. Two considerations are relevant. First, while the UK European policy process at the systemic level has been adapted to fit the institutional realities of devolution, the UK government's political authority over European policy remains intact. Where the devolved administrations have been brought into a policy system hitherto closed to all non-governmental bodies, their involvement is confined to the level of policy or territorial expertise and not – crucially not – to political objectives. There is no intention that the broad thrust of the UK government's European policy will be the subject of negotiation with devolved administrations. Second, if the devolved administrations seek to ensure that 'legitimate' territorial interests are reflected in UK policy, then they have to abide by agreed rules of inter-administration policy co-operation and co-ordination, including being 'bound' to adhere to the agreed negotiating line. Should they breach these rules – for example, to exploit opportunistically a short-term domestic political advantage – they might find themselves being excluded from the policy process as a consequence. Accordingly, it is in the interests of the devolved administrations just as much as it is in the interests of the UK government to make a success of the new procedures.

Adaptation within the *organisational* dimension to European policy-making was a relatively straightforward matter, albeit one that involved a significant degree of capacity-building within the devolved administrations themselves. But the direction of the changes necessary were clearly signposted by the need (a) to retain the strengths of the pre-devolution UK European policy process, and (b) to include the devolved administrations within the UK European policy process. Within the Whitehall bureaucratic machinery devolution progressively acquired importance as the implications it would have over a range of UK policy processes became apparent. But devolution did not trigger a fundamental re-think over the assignment of tasks or responsibilities in the European policy process. In the main, devolution did not prompt any reorganisation of activities in Whitehall departments, although it did require them to follow procedures elaborated in the concordats. At the centre of government, new tasks were implied – especially in maintaining generally good relations between UK government and the devolved administrations, the management of which fell to the Cabinet Office. A more extensive organisational review was required in the devolved administrations, particularly within the Scottish Executive in light of its legislative responsibilities in the European policy field. It seems that the organisational adaptation which took place in the devolved administrations was influenced quite directly by the organisational arrangements in Whitehall with which they had to interact. The principal change in this respect occurred at the centre of the devolved administrations where new functions arose – principally the co-ordination of a territorial policy 'line' with respect to UK European policy options and meeting the requirements of the new assemblies. Even here, however, the devolved administrations generally were able to draw upon in-house expertise, utilising the skills of officials with direct experience of European policy (acquired during periods of secondment in 'Brussels' or participation in specific EU policy training), or officials whose previous tasks had involved giving advice on the territorial dimension of strategic aspects of European policy. For instance, very soon after devolution an informal network of Scottish Executive officials was formed involving those whose responsibilities included EU policy matters (ECG). Additionally, the Scottish Executive had to meet new obligations arising from the legislative role of the Scottish Parliament with respect to the scrutiny of EU documents and the implementation of EC law in Scotland. Although the Executive could opt to use UK legislative measures to give effect to EC law in Scotland, there was an expectation that the Scottish Parliament would generally wish to do so by Scottish legislative measures.

Within the *process-related* (or *procedural*) dimension various new arrangements were designed to meet the obligation in the White Papers to involve the devolved administrations in the UK European policy process. It was *not* intended that the territorial input to UK European policy either should be enhanced or given greater political clout as a consequence of devolution. Instead, the objective was to reconcile current good practices of UK European policy-making with the transfer of competencies and political 'authority' that attended devolution. In practice, this meant retaining the involvement of the devolved administrations in the European policy 'pathways' that lie at the core of that policy process, but from which they now were excluded. This was largely (though not entirely) facilitated by the series of inter-administration 'concordats' – chief amongst which was the EU concordat – and the associated dispute resolution arrangements. There were, however, gaps. In particular, the devolved administrations no longer had ready access to the central machinery of government, such as Cabinet committees (e.g. (E)DOP or the counterpart official network, EQ(O)) within which a consensus policy 'line' was brokered where inter-ministerial divisions had arisen. Excluding the devolved administrations from these discussions implied they would be subject to a policy 'line' which they had not been involved in agreeing: including them in this discussion was unacceptable as that would expose to scrutiny the inner workings of the government at the highest political level. Accordingly, *ad hoc* arrangements have evolved to include officials from the devolved administrations in the Cabinet committee network where there is a direct territorial interest in the subsequent UK policy line. Elsewhere, the terms of the concordats and working practices that have developed subsequently ensure that officials from the territorial departments have fairly ready access to counterparts in Whitehall departments with a view to maintaining the flow of information necessary to ensure that UK European policy continues to reflect the overall interests of all parties. In the main, these arrangements simply utilised established procedures whereby the former Scottish and Welsh Offices had contributed to UK European policy issues. It is difficult to draw any authoritative conclusions about the operation of the inter-administration procedures that accompanied devolution. On the one hand there was no evidence of significant problems having emerged in the European policy area. The JMC(EU) machinery had not been invoked during the period of our research, and in the main the new arrangements seemed to be settling down in a reasonably straightforward manner. On the other hand, we did note a few specific instances during which the lines of communication between Whitehall and the devolved administrations seemed not to have functioned perfectly (see also Chapter 5). In these cases, the problems seemed to involve the lack of adequate notification to, or involvement of, the devolved administrations of important policy matters. However, these were explained as being little more than 'teething problems' that inevitably would arise and which would readily be resolved.

The *regulative* dimension to UK European policy has changed considerably with the publication of the concordats and, to a lesser degree, DGNs. In effect, these documents prescribe the activities of, and obligations upon, both the UK government and the devolved administrations

in shaping, *inter alia*, UK European policy. The EU concordat and specific
subject concordats (e.g. agriculture) elaborate new norms and codes of
conduct which should be followed by each, and include guidance on the
circulation of information and the framework for Whitehall departments
(including 'central' units within government) to keep counterpart officials in the devolved administrations fully informed of, and involved in,
their side of the European policy process. In many instances, the concordats were doing little other than codifying prevailing practices which
were widely understood and unproblematic. This was especially true
where the territorial offices traditionally had participated closely with
Whitehall with respect to European policy – for instance as in agricultural matters. For other issues, devolution raised more significant challenges of including the devolved administrations – challenges either of
procedure (such as the creation of policy co-ordination arrangements
within the devolved administrations) or of substance (involving the territorial administrations perhaps for the first time). Arguably the key
innovation within the regulative dimension was the decision to establish
the JMC dispute resolution machinery. Although this committee had not
met in EU 'mode' during the course of our research, it was intended that
it would broker an agreement between the devolved administrations and
UK government over the latter's European policy in the event of a difference of opinion emerging. In that regard, it is perhaps not an exaggera-
tion to state that the role of the JMC is to stabilise both the devolution
settlement and the UK's preferred approach that all participants adhere
to a single negotiating line with respect to EU policy developments.

Undoubtedly much of the effectiveness of the new arrangements for
UK European policy making will depend on developments within the
cultural dimension to institutional interaction. It is self-evident that these
new arrangements will work properly only with goodwill and determination on the part of officials and politicians from the three administrations. Our research revealed an acute awareness of the importance of this
aspect, and a general determination on the part of those officials directly
involved that devolution would effect the changes in attitudes and practices within the bureaucratic sphere that are required to make the transition to a multi-tiered governance system successful. While the period of
our study was too short for any definitive conclusions to be drawn, it did
confirm to us the significance of this essentially 'human' and normative
element to the process as a whole. Notwithstanding the presentation of
new arrangements and new procedures in the form of concordats and
supplementary working practices, it is the role of the officials to interpret
these obligations and to ensure that the 'spirit' of the new procedures is

observed as much as the specific terms of the concordats. It is this that will help determine the stability and ultimate success of devolution.

Finally, it is worth reflecting on the broader, inter-administration dynamics that devolution may trigger with respect to the UK European policy process. The revised administrative and bureaucratic structures that we have described in this chapter clearly are intended to establish procedures for the effective organisation of UK European policy in the wake of devolution to Scotland and Wales. As noted, a key consideration in this exercise throughout was to ensure that these procedures do not themselves become a source of dynamic instability with a potential to undermine the constitutional settlement. As a review of the concordats reveals, the objective of designing a system which gave the devolved administrations access to the UK European policy process on issues where they had a direct interest (and which, in all its salient features, replicated the *status quo ante*) was achieved. Moreover, these arrangements clearly implied no diminution of the sole authority of UK government on EU issues that raised considerations of 'national interest' or which touched on matters of 'high politics'. Nor did they seem to 'tie the hands' of UK government in their negotiations with other Member States. The overall impression this gives, therefore, is that the UK European policy process after devolution is one that might be portrayed as 'business as usual' in all its essentials, and that continuities and stability prevail. But it may be premature to draw such a strong conclusion. It is worth reflecting that, thus far, the entire devolution exercise has been conducted within a broadly harmonious UK-wide political environment. A quite different reality might materialise should the situation arise in which the political party that governs at the UK level is different from that (or those) in the majority within the territorial assemblies, particularly where any of the governing parties concerned has a narrow majority. For instance, it may be possible for the governing party (or its minority coalition partner) in the territorial assembly to win concessions in the European policy area from a precariously positioned UK government in return for its support in Westminster. Indeed, it is possible to conjure up a range of political scenarios under which the political fortunes of political parties nationally and territorially can be linked. The important point, however, is to note that in a real sense the stability of the devolution settlement – and the European policy process within it – has not yet been subject to the range of challenges that is likely to emerge over time. So while continuity rather than change has characterised the overall process thus far, and has shaped the entire structure of inter-administration arrangements for UK European policy-making, nonetheless devolution represents a critical juncture in the evolution of British governance which, in the future, may generate consequences that were unanticipated by its architects. New institutional opportunity structures, and veto points, have been created for EU policy-making within the executive branch. As yet they remain far from fully tested.

4
European Business and the Assemblies

4.1 Introduction

The new Scottish Parliament and Welsh Assembly were expected to have key and pioneering roles to play in the UK–EU policy process. The central legislative framework for devolution – the White Papers and the Parliamentary Acts – stated this explicitly. The essentially prescriptive and general nature of the legislation meant that the manner in which the two assemblies, and their committees, would interact with the UK–EU system remained undecided at the time of its publication. Importantly, it was left up to the territorial institutions to determine, in accordance with their own consultation procedures, how the Parliament and Assembly would best input to EU business. Furthermore, given that domestic and regional parliamentary influence across the EU varies considerably between Member States, the new assemblies could look to many different models of parliamentary influence to determine 'best practice'. With devolution, therefore, both the Scottish Parliament and the Welsh Assembly had a clear opportunity to create the necessary institutional setting and procedures to conduct effective sub-Member State parliamentary influence over EU affairs.

Two important factors would shape the debate from the beginning. First, at the systemic level, the Parliamentary Acts established two separate models of devolution – the legislative model (Scotland) and the executive model (Wales) (see Preface). The different constitutional nature of the Parliament and the Assembly would circumscribe their respective method of input to the UK–EU policy process. This held less obvious problems for Scotland than for Wales. With a separation of government and parliament in Scotland, the form of parliamentary involvement could more readily be seen as one of influencing and controlling the

Scottish Executive, as well as providing a forum for Scottish debate on European affairs. In Wales, the corporate nature of the Welsh Assembly held no precedent. Thus, how the Welsh Assembly would interpret its 'parliamentary' role in the policy process was far from certain.

Second, at the sub-Member State level, there were high civic expectations that the two assemblies would fashion new and innovative working methods (i.e. be distinct from the Westminster model) and enable the formulation of a more democratic and legitimate European policy in devolved matters (and transferred functions). With devolution, the Scottish Executive would now be subject to *Scottish* parliamentary scrutiny. In Wales, the main focus of the debate was one of ensuring greater accountability of policy implementation, both in institutional and territorial-representative terms. The systemic and cultural dimensions to the new institutions thus established the dynamic of institution-building.

This chapter sets out the challenges faced by the two assemblies in accessing the EU governance system. The chapter describes the process of institution-building in both Scotland and Wales and the creation of parliamentary/assembly machinery to handle EU business. The first section reviews current parliamentary arrangements at UK level for handling Scottish and Welsh input to EU policy – arrangements that continue to operate as far as reserved matters are concerned. The second section documents the preparations for devolution in Scotland and Wales in respect of EU business and highlights key ideas generated during this period. The third section reports on the new institutions and the first set of parliamentary/assembly arrangements for addressing EU affairs. The focus is on capacity-building at territorial level and methods of input to the UK–EU process. Finally, conclusions are drawn with respect to the degree of change post-devolution. Importantly, with respect to the two assemblies, we will illustrate that the degree of continuity is dependent on the parliamentary function under review.

4.2   Parliamentary arrangements for handling EU business: the UK level

Scottish and Welsh affairs in EU business are handled at Westminster as an integral part of the UK system. Although particular procedures and committees exist to represent territorial interests in Parliament (e.g. Scottish/Welsh Question time, the Scottish and Welsh Grand Committees, Select Committees on Scottish and Welsh Affairs), these committees can do very little on Europe and offer a limited form of indirect accountability on EU matters. Rather, Scottish and Welsh interests are represented in the general and specific parliamentary procedures established to consider EU matters. This section reviews those procedures.

UK parliamentary procedure to examine EU policy has evolved considerably since the UK joined the EU in 1973. The last major changes were initiated in 1998 as part of the Labour government's programme of constitutional change – and specifically the modernisation of the House of Commons and the reform of the House of Lords. In general, UK parliamentary practice falls within two broad categories common with other Member States' domestic parliaments.[102] First, the UK Parliament has established committees and procedures to control and influence the UK government at EU level. Second, the UK Parliament is involved in bilateral and collective arrangements with other parliaments which are *independent* of the government.

To exert influence at EU level, parliaments seek to ascertain the government's proposed policy position in the Council of Ministers and to hold it to account for policy decisions reached at EU level. To do this, parliaments across the EU make use of general parliamentary procedures to discuss and scrutinise EU affairs (e.g. ministerial statements, parliamentary written and oral questions, debating of issues, government reports, committees, and so on).[103] Parliaments have also created specialised European committees with specific remits (e.g. to 'sift' EU documents for scrutiny – UK; to conduct *ex post* control of governments – Sweden). In some Member States, specific procedures have also been introduced to handle the scrutiny of EU documents prior to Council of Ministers' meetings (e.g. France, UK, Denmark). Parliaments have also made arrangements for the scrutiny of the implementation of EC law. In addition to these functions, parliaments raise the profile of EU affairs in the public domain through debate in plenary sessions. Finally, they have the all-important function of ratifying treaty reform. Overall, there is a variety of methods in operation across the EU ranging from ones which facilitate close textual analyses of EU documents within strong accountability processes (e.g. UK, Denmark, France) to ones which enable parliaments to raise the profile of EU affairs through informal influence (e.g. Spain, Portugal).

Against this background, UK parliamentary procedures for handling EU business are classified as strong. First, and similar to other Member States, use is made of ordinary procedures to consider EU business.[104] One of the characteristics of Westminster is that Europe has been a massive issue in plenary sessions, especially during the process of treaty ratification (Munro 1999: 209). Arguably, though, the main strength of the Westminster approach is its highly developed scrutiny system. This involves both Houses of Parliament, each with a different method of scrutiny, and has entailed the establishment of specialised committees, specific procedures and a rigorous timescale. The following functions are all part of this scrutiny system:

> sifting of documents; reporting on and clearing of documents; debating the political and legal importance of documents; conducting substantial inquiries; debating on matters of principal and policy of documents; publishing detailed reports; and placing EU issues and information in the public domain. (Carter 2001: 401–2)

The House of Commons' method is one of close textual examination of documents. The main committee is the European Scrutiny Committee (ESC),[105] with 16 members and served by a staff of 16 officials. In response to the demands of time in the EU policy process, the ESC meets on a weekly basis. The ESC's remit is to sift, report on and clear documents from scrutiny. To perform these functions, the ESC has established processes of information and intelligence sharing with Whitehall departments. The ESC scrutinises *circa* 1000 EU documents per year. Each EU document is deposited by the appropriate government department with an accompanying 'Explanatory Memorandum' (EM)[106] and a 'Regulatory Impact Assessment' (RIA). The EM sets out the legal and factual context of the document, and importantly the government's view and where ministerial responsibility lies – the EM *is* the Minister's evidence to the Westminster Parliament (HC Scrutiny Guide 1998: 13–14). The ESC also receives the Council of Ministers' text with highlighted problem areas of negotiation. In addition to receipt of this type of information, the ESC and Whitehall departments exchange intelligence on an informal basis. For example, the ESC produces private intelligence in the form of briefing notes, sometimes used to communicate with the UK ministry concerned.[107] A number of different informal channels exist for intelligence gathering, crucial to the conduct of effective scrutiny of the government's policy position.

Debate on EU documents is conducted in the European Standing Committees, whose role is to deliberate the political and legal importance of documents. Under the modernisation of the House of Commons, the number of Standing Committees was increased from two to three.[108] These have 13 permanent members, but can be attended by all MPs. To date these committees have suffered very low attendance and are considered a weak aspect of the scrutiny system, although this might change as a result of recent reforms.

The method of scrutiny conducted by the House of Lords is, by contrast, one of policy examination. The institutional setting is also committee-based. The main committee is the Select Committee on the European Union (SCEU) established in 1974. It has several sub-committees, specialised in particular policy areas; Economic and Financial Affairs, Trade and External Relations (A); Energy, Industry and Transport (B); Common Foreign and Security Policy (C); Environment, Agriculture, Public Health and Consumer Protection (D); Law and Institutions (E); Social Affairs, Education and Home Affairs (F). The SCEU selects EU documents for scrutiny – about 20–30 each year are subject to detailed examination. The nature and substance of the Lords' reports are quite distinct from ESC reports, being detailed in-depth examinations of substantive and political issues raised by a document or series of documents – e.g. the Charter of Fundamental Rights, E-commerce etc.

Each of the above methods of scrutiny seeks to influence the government's negotiating position (both *ex ante* and *ex post*). Arguably, the predominant feature of the scrutiny system common to both Houses is, however, the Scrutiny Reserve Resolution – commonly referred to as simply the 'scrutiny reserve'. This is the mechanism by which government accountability to Parliament is secured and is the mainstay of the overall system. In the House of Commons, ministers are constrained from giving agreement in either the Council or the European Council to any proposal for EC legislation or to any major decision under the intergovernmental pillars of the Treaty on European Union (TEU) 'which is still subject to scrutiny ... or which is awaiting consideration by the House' (HC Resolution, 17 November 1998: 1250). In the House of Lords, a document will not be considered to have been cleared by the SCEU when it 'is still subject to scrutiny' or when the Select Committee has 'made a report to the House for debate, but ... the debate has not yet taken place' (HL Resolution, 6 December 1999: 1). In both Houses, rules for waiving the resolution exist. One of the important effects heralded by the accountability mechanism is to discipline government provision of timely and accurate information. Under the UK system, Parliament is not simply expressing a view. It is scrutinising the government's position, which is communicated to it, and for which the government is then held responsible under the 'scrutiny reserve' (Carter 2001). This will be seen to be important in the context of devolution.

The UK Parliament also scrutinises the implementation of EC law. National parliamentary control of administrative functions at UK level involves 'technical scrutiny rather than policy oversight' (Armstrong and Bulmer 1996: 276). This type of scrutiny is *ex post* and is concerned with the incorporation of EC law into domestic law. Again, specific procedures exist for consultation between implementing departments at both ministerial and official level, alongside processes for public consultation on proposed implementing legislation (SO 1998a: 8).

The second broad channel for domestic parliamentary influence over EU business entails the establishment of horizontal arrangements for communication flow between Member State parliaments which is *independent* of national governments. To this end, collective arrangements between Member State parliaments have been created and new institutions set up. The most consolidated of these is the Conference of European Affairs Committees (COSAC) which brings together representatives of the national parliaments' European committees and a delegation from the European Parliament (EP) on a twice yearly basis.[109] Other bodies meet less frequently (e.g. the Conference of Presidents and Speakers) or have had a shorter shelf life (e.g. the Parliamentary Assizes which met in 1990). The UK Parliament has participated in these arrangements and is a member of COSAC. The Chairs of the ESC and SCEU, and their Clerks, regularly attend COSAC meetings to represent UK parliamentary interests at the supranational EU level.

In addition to these collective arrangements, national parliaments have established bilateral working relations with the EP and its committees conducive to information flow between parliaments. Again, there are differences in the degree of bilateral contact across the EU. In some Member States, MEPs sit in national parliaments and/or on national parliamentary committees, whereas other Member State parliaments only meet MEPs periodically throughout the year (e.g. Sweden). Some domestic parliamentary committees have direct links between specific EP committees (e.g. Spain). The UK committees have an exchange of papers with the relevant EP committees, but MEPs do not participate in Westminster debates or sit on Westminster European committees. Finally, the UK Parliament has recently set up a National Parliament Office in Brussels (served by one official) to access the supranational level.

In summary, Westminster procedures to handle EU business provide an important contextual reference point for the aspirations of the new assemblies. Two observations can be made. First, UK procedures are themselves not static, but have been (and continue to be) subject to change driven by national modernisation programmes, on the one hand, and by EU reform, on the other (Kerse 2000; Carter 2001). Second, and from the point of view of devolution, we must note that, during our research period, no formal changes were made to the Westminster system for handling EU business as part of the devolution process.[110] Officials in London reported that, during the research period, devolution had had no significant effect on practice at national level. As far as EU matters are concerned, the key impact of devolution on the parliamentary/assembly component of the polity is thus to be found at the devolved level.

4.3 Preparing for devolution: July 1998–June 1999

From a Scottish and Welsh perspective, the Westminster system, as described above, gives rise to a number of concerns with regard to representation. Specifically, questions were raised on the scope for territorially-sensitive parliamentary scrutiny of EU business, particularly in policy areas of direct importance to Scottish and Welsh societies. The UK system, it was argued, was one of scrutiny of an Executive elected on the basis of a UK-wide electorate. For many years, the political make-up of the House of Commons (and the UK government) did not reflect the electoral voting patterns in Scotland and Wales. The House of Lords simply lacked an electoral mandate. In addition, as stated above, Scottish and Welsh committees in Westminster had little specific involvement in EU business. Devolution thus brought with it the potential for far-reaching change in the electoral-representative component of the polity handling EU affairs. This section documents the preparation for assembly involvement in UK–EU matters in Scotland and Wales in terms of first, capacity-building and second, assembly input to the policy process.

4.3.1 Capacity-building at territorial level

> A new … Parliament has an historic opportunity to *innovate*, not merely to create and adopt procedures more effective and more responsive to public opinion than those of Westminster, but to show Westminster and other centres of power that new ways are needed, can work and are better. (Crick and Millar 1997: 2. Emphasis added)

The political reality of Scotland and Wales in 1998 was such that the new institutions had to be designed in a way which would meet high civic expectations. In Scotland, much was made of establishing a parliament *not* organised according to the Westminster model. Historically, the Constitutional Convention had had a key role to play in this regard, demonstrating that a distinct feature of Scottish politics was its consensual approach to decision-making (Crick and Millar 1997: 3). The Convention had moreover been significant in that it brought civic bodies into the decision-making arena – e.g. the churches, the Social Partners, local authorities, women's organisations and anti-racist groups. As such, the norms and principles which would underpin the debate on the institutional structure of the new parliament were ones of transparency, equality, consensus and inclusiveness. The types of committees being created – such as the Equal Opportunities Committee – reflect these aspirations:

> the Scottish Parliament should be accessible, open, responsive and develop procedures which make possible a participative approach to the development, consideration and scrutiny of policy and legislation. (CSG Report 1998: 8)

In Wales, the corporate model posited in the Government of Wales Act would have been sufficient in itself to channel the internal organisation and procedures of the Assembly in a different developmental path from Westminster. Also, in common with Scotland, Wales had high civic aspirations for its new Assembly. Both the remit and the final report of the National Assembly Advisory Group (NAAG) stressed the development of an Assembly based on consensus. NAAG's rationale was to contribute to the establishment of an Assembly which was 'democratic, effective, efficient and inclusive' and which could command the respect of those in and outside Wales (NAAG 1998: 6). There were calls for the different areas of Wales to have a voice. In particular, North Wales was concerned with the prospect of an Assembly dominated by Cardiff.[111] Further, there was a demand for a break from those Westminster traditions based on outmoded practices unsuited to a modern participative democracy, and support for the adoption of new technologies and approaches to support developments in participative democracy. The Assembly would be bilingual and operate family-friendly working practices (NAAG, 1998: 7).

Finally, it was anticipated that the new electoral systems in both Scotland and Wales would give rise to new political patterns and behaviour – ones based on the value of seeking consensus, rather than promoting adversarial debate. In all, the electoral-representative component of the polity was to be shaped by these specific political factors, coupled with a diversity of economy, culture and society.

Scotland

The Consultative Steering Group (CSG) Report (Consultative Steering Group Report on the Scottish Parliament, 1998 (hereafter CSG 1998)) set out the model for the Scottish Parliament in preparation for the standing orders. A key feature of the new Parliament was the enhanced role to be given to committees. In particular, the Scottish committees would have integrated powers of both Westminster Select and Standing Committees, plus some additional powers (SO 1998b: point 31). As such, the CSG proposed that the committees would have powers to scrutinise primary, as well as, secondary legislation. They would also have powers to initiate legislation.[112] There would be a number of subject-based committees which would perform both *ex ante* and *ex post* parliamentary control of the Scottish Executive in specific policy areas. As a unicameral parliament, the Scottish Parliament would thus see an enhanced and potentially innovative role for committees generally in the conduct of parliamentary business. Against this backdrop, it was decided early on that the institutional setting for the conduct of scrutiny of EU documents would be in committee, and that there would be a specialised 'European' committee (SO 1998b: point 1).

Following these decisions, the Scottish Office issued two key consultation documents (SO 1998a: SO 1998b) in which it set out two possible approaches to capacity-building. The first was to remit EU documents to the subject-based committees for scrutiny. This would encourage specialised scrutiny of documents and introduce an element of speed in the scrutiny process (SO 1998a: 16.5). The main disadvantages of this approach were that it would not allow for the handling of cross-cutting issues and that the workload of sifting and discussing the documents might be excessive for the committees. The main proposal that emerged, and was adopted by the final report of the CSG, was instead to create a 'hybrid' European committee 'whose membership should be drawn from members of other relevant committees' (CSG 1998: 61). The advantages of the hybrid committee would be its ability to identify important EU documents which cross-cut the subject committees' responsibilities (SO 1998a: 16.5) and to allow members to amass considerable expertise and 'ensure cross fertilisation of experience' (SO 1998b: point 1). This, it was anticipated, would enable an effective sifting mechanism to be developed.

With regard to the number of members, the CSG report proposed that the committee have between 5 and 15 members and that the Convenor of the committee not be a Convenor of another committee considered relevant to the Scottish European Committee (SEC) (CSG 1998: 38). Any Member of Parliament could attend and speak at Committee meetings, but could not make formal proposals or vote (CSG 1998: 61). Both these proposals originated in the Scottish Office. With regard to the former, this was to ensure 'dispassionate recommendations' were made by the Convenor in the scrutiny process. In the preparatory phase of May 1999, it was expected that Convenor and Deputy Convenor would be from Executive and non-Executive Parties in order to 'de-politicise' the convenorship.[113] With regard to attendance of non-members, this was adapted from the Westminster European Standing Committee rules. On the question of meeting times, officials preparing guidance rules prior to devolution anticipated that the committee would meet every week to ensure timely input to the EU decision-making system.

The institutional setting for the scrutiny of implementation of EC law in Scotland would be the subject committees. It was anticipated that these committees would have a direct involvement in the actual passing of legislation to implement European directives.[114] It was proposed that the subject committees individually – rather than the SEC acting on their behalf – would scrutinise any Executive subordinate legislation issued to fulfil EC objectives (CSG 1998: 62). This was a grey area, however. Certainly, there was an expectation that it would be up to the SEC to conduct any necessary inquiry: it was also not clear how this would relate to the intended function for the Legislation Committee, which would act in a similar way to the Westminster Joint Committee on Statutory Instruments (JCSI).[115] Capacity-building for this aspect of scrutiny was not specifically related to considerations arising out of EU membership. Overseeing the implementation of EC policy would be undertaken as part of an overall duty of the subject committees to regulate their allotted policy area. The general structure was thus expected to be established in such a way as to incorporate the EU dimension, rather than being driven by it. The EU dimension to policy areas was not distinguished from the domestic dimension in this sense.

Finally, the institutional setting for debate would be the European committee itself, as well as plenary sessions.

Wales

In Wales, the legal focus for capacity-building designated in the Government of Wales Act (Section 46(1)) was the standing orders of the Assembly. Under the Act, standing orders were to be made by the Secretary of State for Wales and put in place prior to the Transfer of Functions. In December 1997, the Secretary of State for Wales established the National Assembly Advisory Group (NAAG) to assist in preparing guidelines for the Standing Orders' Commission. Commissioners were appointed in August 1998 and reported at the end of January 1999, after which the Secretary of State made the standing orders.[116] Given that the standing orders could be changed only by a two-thirds majority, NAAG set out to distinguish clearly those matters which should be regulated in this way as opposed to by codes of practice or guidance:

> Standing orders will need to set out the procedures which govern the handling of Assembly proceedings – for example the way in which members of committees are elected, the rules covering questioning of Assembly Secretaries, and how subordinate legislation is passed. (National Assembly Advisory Group Report, 1998: 6 (hereafter NAAG 1998))

The corporate structure for the Assembly foreseen in the Government of Wales Act implied that all the Assembly's powers were to be vested in the Assembly as a whole. They would be exercised by the plenary Assembly unless it should delegate them through its standing orders or by a separate decision. Such delegation could be rescinded by the Assembly. As required by the Government of Wales Act, the Assembly would have to approve the election of the Presiding Officer; the First Secretary; chairs of the subject committees; and committee members (Government of Wales Act 1998: ss. 52–7; NAAG 1998: 24). In addition, NAAG recommended that standing orders require the approval of the full Assembly for certain actions of the Assembly Executive Committee (now commonly referred to as the Cabinet) (NAAG 1998: recommendation 18, 24).

The Government of Wales Act required the Assembly to establish subject committees and regional committees. It provided for only two specific statutory committees: a subordinate legislation scrutiny committee for the quality control of legislation and an audit committee, an equivalent of the UK Public Accounts Committee. In addition, NAAG recommended that standing orders provide for two further types of committee: 'programme' committees to co-ordinate policy development on issues which cut across subject areas and 'task and finish working groups' to monitor and evaluate progress with implementing these cross-cutting programmes (NAAG 1998: 32, 36–7).

There had been no mention of a European committee in the Wales Paper. The idea of a programme committee for European Affairs was developed during the course of 1998–99 in Welsh Office discussions. One influential source shaping these discussions was the report of the European Strategy Group (ESG). This Group had been set-up by the Secretary of State in June 1998, was chaired by Hywel Ceri Jones and reported in December (European Strategy Group Report, 1998 (hereafter ESG 1998)). It fleshed out some of the points raised by NAAG which, in its August 1998 Report, had made a series of recommendations for the handling of EU business. NAAG identified the Assembly's relations with the EU as one of its most important concerns and specifically recommended that a European issues committee be established as a 'standing programme committee' (NAAG 1998: 53–4). It further proposed that each subject committee appoint one of its members to act as European co-ordinator for that committee. This co-ordinator should report to the subject committee each month as appropriate on events in Europe affecting the committee's responsibilities. By contrast, the scrutiny of the implementation of EC law – when transferred – would be undertaken by the subject committees with responsibility for scrutiny of legislation in their area, including European legislation.[117] The Assembly's responsibility for overseeing the administration of the structural funds would thus be delegated to a subject committee in accordance with the First Secretary's allocation of responsibilities to Assembly Secretaries (and not be a function of the European committee) (NAAG 1998: 53–4).

One key area of concern expressed during the consultation exercises held by NAAG was that the Assembly must have effective accountability mechanisms. In particular, NAAG addressed this concern by proposing checks and balances in the scrutiny mechanisms of the Assembly. The report noted: 'In Westminster there is no equivalent check on subordinate legislation before it is made by the relevant Minister' (NAAG 1998: 40). The clear implication was the suggested arrangements would be superior to those at Westminster. Key to this were the role of the subject committees, held to be of 'high importance', in scrutinising, debating and amending subordinate legislation.[118]

Finally, to conduct 'Welsh' debates on EU matters, NAAG recommended that the Assembly in plenary should debate the handling of matters related to the EU at least once a year (NAAG, 1998: 25, 53).

4.3.2 Assembly input to UK–EU decision-making

There are a large number of different ways in which the new assemblies could input to UK–EU decision-making and develop a pro-active EU policy.[119] Here we isolate three main areas for input to the policy process:

- Scrutiny of EU documents: intra-parliamentary/assembly procedures (*ex ante* and *ex post*); executive/legislative relations (Scotland); bilateral relations with national parliament (inter-parliamentary arrangements).
- Scrutiny of the implementation of EC law: intra-parliamentary/ assembly procedures; executive/legislative relations (Scotland); checks and balances (Wales).

- Independent influence in the policy process: independent 'voice'; Scottish and Welsh debates on EU matters; general inquiries; bilateral relations with EU institutions; collective arrangements with other sub-state parliaments/assemblies; relations with civic society.

Scotland: arrangements for the scrutiny of EU documents

The White Paper for Scotland anticipated that a central role for the Scottish Parliament would be one of scrutiny of EU documents.[120] This was also accepted by Scottish MPs at UK level:

> We envisage the Parliament having more time to scrutinise European Union legislation, and that is increasingly important in the life of the country and in terms of this House. (McLeish, HC Scottish Affairs Committee, 2nd Report: Q299, 01-07-98)

Initial discussions on the procedures to be adopted were conducted under the umbrella of the CSG. In the summer of 1998, Scottish Office officials prepared two consultation documents for the purposes of CSG discussions, setting out issues pertinent to the development of an effective Scottish scrutiny system. In February 1999, a number of members of staff of the Parliament were appointed. These officials were given the task of considering draft rules and procedures and guidance for the yet-to-be-elected MSPs, below the level of the Standing Orders. CSG and Scottish Office ideas on procedure were used with a view to drafting guidance notes. At this time, too, the 'Clerk' of the European committee and other officials met with the Clerk of the Westminster ESC to discuss possible future bilateral relations and other issues related to information sharing. This section sets out the key ideas developed during this period.

Two issues were resolved early on in the discussions. The first was that the primary institutional setting for the conduct of Scottish scrutiny would be the SEC. The second was that the SEC would be involved in *two* different types of procedure. First, the SEC would conduct a form of scrutiny which would be independent of the Westminster scrutiny system: it would scrutinise the Scottish Executive's policy position. An intra-parliamentary procedure was thus necessary to enable the Scottish Parliament (via the SEC) to communicate directly with the Scottish Executive and its administration. Second, the SEC would also input directly to the Westminster scrutiny system. An inter-parliamentary procedure was thus necessary to establish lines of communication between the two SECs.[121] Here, the SEC would be communicating its views via the ESC to the UK government.[122]

It was acknowledged within the Scottish Office in the spring of 1999 that a new Scottish intra-parliamentary scrutiny procedure would bring with it an expectation that the Scottish administration would produce written information for the SEC (for example, in a form similar to the UK Explanatory Memoranda – EM). Such information would stress the Scottish perspective. This was a point of departure from past practice, where the Scottish administration would make use of Whitehall departmental documents for their own purposes. Now, with a new parliament to which it was to be held accountable, it was understood that the Scottish administration would have to write their own reports on EU documents: this might create a 'potentially sizeable bundle of work, for people, for colleagues in the department actually working in the subject areas'.[123] It was also accepted that there would be a need to co-ordinate with the SEC, once it had established its own procedures, and agree a timetable for the production of such information necessary for the conduct of scrutiny. The precise details of the types of material which could be produced were left to be resolved once devolution took effect. What was agreed at this stage, however, was that the Executive Secretariat would act as the conduit for information flow, and oversee contact between the committee and the various divisions to 'keep track of it all'.[124]

With regard to the inter-parliamentary scrutiny system, and the question of information flow between parliamentary SECs, detailed discussions were held on the types of information which could be made available to the SEC. The UK government's EM, as a public document, would certainly be available. The ESC (House of Commons) also considered at this stage the possibility of granting access to its in-house briefing notes – intelligence which it considered important in aiding an efficient sifting of documents in Scotland.

The question of whether the Scottish should develop their own 'scrutiny reserve' was discussed in the summer of 1998. An initial Scottish Office document considered this idea, but it subsequently fell off the Scottish Office agenda. As stated above, the 'scrutiny reserve' is the mechanism which underpins an effective scrutiny system, encouraging an Executive body to provide its Parliament with timely and accurate information as to its negotiating position. It introduces an element of accountability into the system which is otherwise missing. It became clear that during this period the Scottish Office was not keen to pursue this aspect of scrutiny.

Two highlighted problem areas were:

- Time. The Westminster scrutiny system operates to a rapid timescale to fit in with EU policy procedures. Would there be time for the

Scottish committee to sift and debate documents? Would the ESC wait for the Scottish SEC to issue its opinion on a specific matter *before* taking a decision?

- Scope of scrutiny. Closely related to the timing issue, was the question of the scope of the scrutiny. The Scottish Office was firmly of the view that the committee should not attempt to replicate the ESC, but rather should concentrate on matters with a clear Scottish interest and on documents issued early in the EU policy cycle (e.g. Green and White Commission Papers). The Committee should not attempt to scrutinise documents in the final stages of legislation. Two different questions were raised. Which policy areas should the Scottish system be focused on? Which kinds of EU documents should the Scottish system be examining?

Scotland: arrangements for the scrutiny of implementation of EC law

The CSG Report proposed that the subject committees would have a direct involvement in the implementation of EC legislation as part of their overall duties. It was left slightly ambiguous, however, to what extent the implementation of a subject area would fall exclusively to the specific subject committee, and/or whether the SEC would have any function in policy implementation. What was agreed, was that the SEC would be expected to have a responsibility to 'take an overview on' the implementation of EC legislation. Precisely what this required in procedural terms was not clear, however.

Scrutiny of the implementation of EC legislation takes on an important dimension in the devolution debate. One of the key objectives of devolution is to enable the Parliament (and the Executive) to implement EC obligations in a manner which would best serve Scottish needs. It was thus anticipated that the approach adopted in Scotland might at times differ from that adopted in Whitehall. Furthermore, EC framework Directives allow for differential implementation to suit local concerns. As such, scrutiny of implementation might not only involve the technical aspect – but might also be concerned with policy decisions. For a number of important (political) considerations come into play when one considers the appropriate level for implementation of a particular Directive. For example, a decision might be taken (by the devolved governments and the UK government) that a particular Directive should be implemented in London for the whole of the UK, rather than in the devolved territories – even if the matter itself is not reserved. In such cases, it can be envisaged that SEC might act, for example, to question – or dispute – such an Executive decision. This is not a matter of *vires* but rather one of shared powers.[125] This aspect to the parliamentary scrutiny of the implementation process could be perceived as a responsibility of the SEC (as distinct from the technical aspect of scrutiny which was seen very much as the responsibility of the subject committees). Although recognised as significant, clear processes to give effect to this function were not forthcoming in the preparatory phase.

Scotland: arrangements for independent influence on EU matters

There was a long-standing expectation in Scotland that the role of the Scottish Parliament would extend beyond one of scrutiny. The CSG agreed in July 1998 that the SEC's business should not be exclusively document based (SO 1998b: point 1) and specifically requested the Scottish Office to develop ideas with regard to the broader role of the committee. In response, the Scottish Office stated in its consultation papers that scrutiny was largely viewed as a *reactive* system. To maximise Scottish influence in EU affairs, the SEC should adopt a *pro-active* role. Expectations rose in political debates in Scotland during this period and, by early 1999, the SEC was being discussed as the new forum for debating 'larger' political EU questions. In this way, the idea of a 'European' committee took on an important symbolic significance (a powerful Scottish voice in 'Europe').

There were three main ways in which the SEC could be pro-active. The first was by holding and initiating debates on EU matters. This role was held to be one of great importance, both by the CSG and the Scottish Office.[126] The committee could also conduct general inquiries into policy matters; for example, the use of the structural funds in Scotland. The Scottish Office adopted a clear line on the selection of topics both for debate and inquiry. In its view, the Parliament should not spend too much time on reserved matters, but rather should focus on discussing an improved Scottish strategy both at national and EU level.

The second way was to seek to establish direct arrangements across the EU. First, the committee should establish bilateral relations with the European Parliament and the European Commission. With regard to arrangements with the EP, the most favoured means was the holding of regular meetings between the SEC and the Scottish MEPs. Second, the committee should develop links within the UK at territorial level – with the Welsh and Northern Irish committees. Third, horizontal links with other sub-Member State parliaments would need to be fostered (SO 1998b: point 15):

Links can undoubtedly be helpful where there is a distinctive Scottish interest which is shared by other regions/states but which does not necessarily figure prominently at UK level (e.g. sustainable rural development). (SO 1998b: point 19)

Parliamentary links of this nature would serve to establish common interest between the Scottish Parliament and other sub-Member State institutions, perhaps independently of the Scottish Executive.

The third way for the SEC to be pro-active was for it to establish links with other groupings within Scotland. This would facilitate parliamentary engagement with the wider European constituency in Scotland.

In many respects such initiatives are in keeping with EU trends as set out in Section 1. Good practice across the EU would suggest that one way to enhance parliamentary power at the sub-Member State level is to work through the non-Member State route and to open channels of information flow which can strengthen the hand of territorial assemblies vis-à-vis both the central and devolved governments. The new type of committee being created in Scotland was particularly facilitative in this regard. As the SEC was to be participatory – i.e. open (albeit) non-voting membership – it could be innovative in its composition. Thus, it was hoped that the SEC could meet at times in a wider grouping of members:

> Such a wider forum could feature MEPs, Committee of the Regions and Economic and Social Committee members and possibly representatives of other bodies in Scotland, such as COSLA, STUC, SCVO and representatives of the business community. Consideration should be given to whether Westminster MPs should also be invited, particularly for issues which cross the devolved/reserved boundary. (SO 1998b: point 40)[127]

Such a participatory approach would be in stark contrast to that conducted at Westminster.

Wales: scrutiny arrangements

Up until the publication of the standing orders in 1999, it was not clear whether the Welsh Assembly would conduct an *ex ante* 'parliamentary' scrutiny of EU documents, even though the White Paper made reference to Welsh input via scrutiny.[128] During 1998–99, there was very confused discussion in the Welsh Office with no clear differentiation made between this type of scrutiny and the scrutiny of subordinate legislation to implement EC law. By June 1999, the Welsh Office had grown aware of the need to address questions relating to scrutiny, as 'the whole question of scrutiny of European documents ... is not an area where we put much in at the moment'.[129] The standing orders left it up to the subject committees to develop processes in the Assembly for the conduct of scrutiny, hence delaying any decision on this matter for an elected committee to decide.

During the preparatory period, time and scope were clearly not considered in any detail, though NAAG did note that '... it must be accepted that the Assembly will not have time to scrutinise all European legislation affecting Wales' (NAAG 1998: 54). Where this was discussed within the Welsh Office, it was foreseen that scrutiny functions would have to operate on a very selective basis and consideration had to be given to the extent to which the Assembly might tie in to the Commons scrutiny of documents. There was concern to avoid duplication of scrutiny between the Commons and the Assembly: with the Assembly concentrating on matters pertaining specifically to Wales.[130] In the early spring of 1999, Welsh officials met with ESC officials to discuss inter-assembly arrangements. However, the meeting took place prior to the publication of the standing orders and, at that time, decisions on the role of the European committee and subject committees in the performance of a scrutiny function had not been finalised. As a result, discussions were underdeveloped and a 'wait and see' policy was adopted by both sides.[131]

Wales: arrangements for independent influence on EU matters

By Easter 1999, deliberations on the scrutiny function of the committees took a back seat to more innovative aspects of their operation deriving from the Assembly's unique corporate structure. It was foreseen that the subject committees would provide the practical mechanism for inclusive politics in that they were not merely scrutiny committees (a reactive role), but were also capable of a pro-active role through their ability to set a framework for policy.[132] Through their multiparty membership, the subject committees would therefore provide a forum for genuine cross-party debate and a means of contributing to policy development. In this way, policy development in the Assembly would not be within the exclusive purview of the Assembly Executive Committee.

Since only members of the Assembly itself would be entitled to sit on the committees, the Assembly was requested to consider how best to ensure the necessary liaison and exchange of ideas and information with the Welsh MEPs (ESG 1998: paras. 9.4; 10.3; 11.1). The ESG report recommended the development of collaboration with other regions within the UK with respect to their European links and machinery, particularly with Scotland and Northern Ireland (ESG 1998 paras. 13.1; 14.1; 14.3). Consideration should also be given to links and partnership arrangements with other countries and regions in Europe to bring economic, social and cultural benefits to Wales.

Moreover, the ESG recommended the establishment of a Welsh Forum on European Affairs to provide an interim conduit for consultation with Welsh interests while the National Assembly established routine consultative arrangements (ESG 1998: paras. 4.17; 4.20–21; 4.23–24). The summary report prepared in advance of the first meeting of the European Affairs Committee on 1 July 1999 reiterated the participative ethos of the NAAG consultations, suggesting that the Welsh Forum should bring together 'representatives of the different partner interests to promote a dynamic Team-Wales approach in Europe' (ESG 1998: para. 4.21). A high priority was accorded to Partnership.[133] In February 1999, Alun Michael, as Secretary of State for Wales, called a meeting of the new 'European Partnership' to review this report pending the election of the Assembly.

4.3.3 Summary

During the preparatory phase, the participatory dimension to the fashioning of the new assemblies and their procedures is in evidence. In Scotland, there was wide consultation made by the Scottish Office on the documents prepared and the CSG Report itself was clearly extremely influential in determining the framework for debate – parliamentary officials preparing arrangements in the early spring of 1999 stated that their key source for consideration of procedures was the CSG Report. In addition, Scottish Office documents prepared at this stage were also drafted on the basis of wide consultation, a process reported at interview as being 'relatively novel in Scottish terms'.[134] It is to be further noted that *all* the key suggestions made by the Scottish Office with respect to the organisational, regulatory and process dimensions of handling EU matters within the Parliament were adopted by the CSG.

In Wales, too, the process was initially one of inclusiveness. In drawing up its report, NAAG consulted widely. In January and February of 1998 it held seven initial meetings with representatives of business, local government, trade unions, the voluntary sector, equality groups and Welsh language groups. Following the publication of its consultation document in April 1998, it held further meetings with interest groups and various agencies and authorities specific to Wales, including the Welsh Development Agency, the Institute of Welsh Affairs, and Welsh MPs and Peers. Sixteen public meetings were held in nine venues to publicise and consult on its findings and written responses were accepted on the document. (NAAG 1998: 6–7, Annex A). The consultation responses firmly endorsed NAAG's prioritisation of themes of democracy, openness, inclusiveness and participation.[135] One theme which emerged from the soundings taken by NAAG was a strong desire for mechanisms for consulting the people of Wales and for them to be able to influence the Assembly, particularly at an early stage of developing new policies.

4.4   Post-devolution: June 1999–February 2000

Post-devolution, a political dimension was added to the process of developing the 'parliamentary' role at the sub-Member State level. Proposals drawn up by officials for the development of a pro-active input into UK European policy were operationalised by politicians, with assemblies taking political decisions on the handling of EU affairs. At times this resulted in a departure from pre-devolution proposals. In Wales, the replacement of Ron Davies (in October 1998) as the prospective First Secretary by Alun Michael was of particular significance. Davies, who had supervised the preparations for the Transfer of Powers, had been personally committed to the ideals of consensual decision-making, consultation and inclusivity. In contrast, Michael's leadership style was increasingly perceived as authoritarian and too concerned with political-administrative control and personal attention to minor details.[136] Alun Michael's domination of leadership positions relating to European matters (Secretary of State, First Secretary, Chair of the European Affairs Committee, Chair of the Wales European Forum), together with his pre-empting of the EAC agenda, was to give him extraordinary control over the initial development of Assembly functions with respect to European matters.

In this section, we document capacity-building and the emergence of initial procedural and working arrangements in both Scotland and Wales and initial attempts to foster a pro-active role in the policy process.

4.4.1   Capacity-building at territorial level

Scotland

The SEC was established on 23 May 1999 and held its first meeting on 23 June 1999. Subject committees were also established under the standing orders, with responsibilities in devolved matters, many of which have an EU policy dimension. In its initial incarnation, the SEC had 13 members, and the Convenor was Hugh Henry (Lab.) and Deputy Convenor Cathy Jamieson (Lab.). At the close of the study period, party political representation was as shown in Table 4.1.

Table 4.1 Party representation on the Scottish European Committee, February 2000

Political party	No. of members
Labour	6
Scottish National Party	3
Conservative	2
Liberal Democrats	1
Independent	1

Table 4.2 Committee cross-representation on the Scottish European Committee, February 2000

Membership of other committees	No. of members
Health and Care in the Community	3
Enterprise and Lifelong Learning	2
Transport and Environment	2
Justice and Home Affairs	1
Local Government	1
Subordinate Legislation	1

In terms of party control, the coalition Executive constituted the majority and the convenorship and deputy-convenorship were in the hands of the governing parties. This is a different outcome from that which was anticipated prior to devolution. A further interesting development concerns the nature of the policy areas represented on the committee through membership of other committees which, at close of study, were as shown in Table 4.2.

Policy areas well represented were health and community care and enterprise and lifelong learning. Notable EU policy areas *not* represented on the committee were agriculture, fisheries and regional policy. Also, environmental policy was under-represented by comparison with health. Interviewees could not explain this composition.[137] This departure from the CSG Report's suggestions is hard to fathom in a context where cross-committee membership is expressly stated as conducive to effective performance in the shared policy area.

The Committee is served by two full-time officials and one who works part-time. These are the Clerk and the Assistant Clerk of the Committee (both full-time appointments) and a part-time legal adviser. The number of officials wholly working on the SEC was below what was expected.[138]

In interview, it was stated that the Committee was under-resourced at least in comparison with Westminster.[139] This was seen as a serious matter to be addressed in the coming months, once the Committee had 'bedded down' and had a clearer view on the degree and nature of its work-load. It was also noted that other committees were better staffed.

The Committee agreed to meet initially on a two weekly basis and early in the week – normally on a Tuesday. This decision was taken in the light of the Westminster procedure, where the ESC meets every week on a Wednesday. At the close of the study period, it was too early to say whether this would enable a consistent timely input to the UK scrutiny cycle.

Wales

The First Secretary, Alun Michael, demonstrated a personal commitment to the handling of European matters in the new Assembly. Initially, he had opposed the establishment of a European committee. His concern had been to avoid 'ghettoising' European issues through restricting their consideration to a designated European committee. He believed that EU policy-development should be an integral part of all the subject committees' work and in particular was determined that European issues should be addressed on a wider canvas than the structural funds alone (Eur-01-99: p. 3.3). He was not easily persuaded of the case for introducing a programme committee, but in the end accepted the general thrust of the NAAG and ESG recommendations. He did, however, decide to take charge of European matters personally on account of the potential significance of the area.[140]

Standing orders required the Assembly to elect an Assembly Secretary (Cabinet member) to chair the European Affairs Committee (EAC). Alun Michael determined in advance of the first EAC meeting that he himself would take overall responsibility for European Affairs and would chair the EAC. The Committee rationale expounded by him as Convenor at the first EAC meeting played down the integrative and cross-committee rationale of the Committee found in Standing Orders, limiting *explicit* cross-committee membership of the EAC by Cabinet members to the First Secretary and Secretary for Economic Development. This new impetus (and departure from NAAG's original suggestions) appeared to be largely in the interests of Cabinet efficiency. Apparently with similar integrative intent to the Scottish model, it was decided that the other members should be chosen 'so far as practicable to reflect the balance of political groups in the Assembly, and having regard to the desirability of each subject committee being represented on the Committee'.[141]

The EAC was founded with 11 members (with Labour members heavily over-represented on the EAC, but not able to secure an absolute majority) (see Table 4.3) and is served by a Clerk and a Deputy Clerk.

The EAC was charged with capacity-building measures for European issues. Alun Michael took a strong lead in the Committee's early development. At the July 1999 meeting, he suggested a forward agenda for the next two meetings of the Committee in 1999.[142] He expressed the hope that his chairmanship would allow the Committee's collective views to influence the Cabinet's thinking on the many matters to which European issues were relevant. Michael's vision of the Committee's broad strategic role was one which supported and complemented (but did not duplicate) the work of the subject committees.[143] Going beyond ESG recommendations (ESG 1998: para 4.10) he pushed for a monthly review of the European agenda for each subject committee by exhorting that each subject committee be 'steeped' in the European dimension of its work (Eur-01-99: p. 1). Michael interpreted the standing orders to imply that the EAC ought to meet less frequently than the subject committees, suggesting a cycle of four to six weeks as appropriate. By the end of the study period, the EAC was meeting every two or three months, much less frequently than the subject committees, and the Scottish European Committee.

4.4.2 Assembly input to UK–EU decision-making

Post-devolution it was becoming increasingly clear that the Scottish and Welsh European committees were going to have quite different roles to play in the UK–EU decision-making processes. The Scottish Committee's remit was to consider and report on:

1. proposals for European Communities legislation;
2. the implementation of European Communities legislation;
3. any European Communities or European Union issue.

Table 4.3 Original composition of the Welsh Assembly European Affairs Committee

Political party	No. of members
Labour	5
Plaid Cymru	3
Conservative	2
Liberal Democrats	1

The objectives of the Welsh EAC were defined more clearly at its second meeting of 14 October 1999 (Eur-02-99: p. 6.6).[144] Here three main objectives were proposed for the Committee:

1. to increase the knowledge and understanding of Committee members of the European Union's institutions, policy-making process, major developments and broad directions;
2. to ensure that Wales is responding effectively to policy developments within the European Union;
3. to develop an institutional framework to serve the requirements and opportunities presented to Wales under devolution.

In Scotland, the first nine months of the Committee's operation saw the prioritisation of procedures to deliver on the first of its remits – the scrutiny of EU documents. The Committee also made headway in establishing itself as the forum for political debate on EU matters in Scotland. By contrast, in Wales, the EAC gave most of its attention to the development of a strategic overview of European matters within the Assembly.[145]

Clearly change at the sub-Member State level in terms of parliamentary input to the UK–EU policy process had already commenced along an asymmetric trajectory. These different approaches to the handling of European matters nonetheless secured political consensus in both assemblies. The extremely challenging remit of the SEC secured all-party consensus from the start. In Wales, interviewees reported an 'enlightened attitude which makes it obvious that they are seeking consensus'[146] – even though the EAC was clearly an executive-led committee. Early meetings were 'almost evangelical in the sense of common purpose and co-operation',[147] with hardly any partisan interventions. It was acknowledged, though, in both Scotland and Wales, that this consensus in part reflected the fact that the material dealt with in the early meetings of the Committees was non-contentious.[148]

Scotland: arrangements for the scrutiny of EU documents

As part of its scrutiny function, the SEC sifts and debates EU documents. Contrary to earlier recommendations (and the rationale for the hybrid committee), the Committee decided that some scrutiny and debate of EU documents should also be conducted by the relevant subject committees. EU documents are passed to subject committees where appropriate, thus adding another committee-tier to the scrutiny system. In all cases, the SEC acts as the main point of liaison.

An early priority was to establish processes for information and communication flow. During the research period, the procedures governing receipt of information by the Committee were established. As a result, the SEC is sent EU legislative documents directly by the Cabinet Office in London,[149] and receives the UK EM several days after that. The rest of the information received from 'government' is from the Scottish Executive. Certain co-ordination arrangements were also put in place. The SEC's liaison officer in the Executive is the Head of External Relations in the Executive Secretariat. This person is the principal point of contact for the Committee. Two different types of information emerged from the Scottish administration: the Scottish Cover Note (SCN) – which is attached to a UK EM, reflecting on its substance and building in a Scottish dimension – and the Scottish European Brief (SEB) – a Scottish version of the UK EM. The SEB was only to be requested in cases of urgency. The SCN thus provides the Scottish Executive's position on the document – and whether or not they agree with the UK ministry concerned (e.g. the DTI). During the research period, the Scottish Executive was not automatically providing this information. Rather, it was provided *on request from* the SEC. The route for requesting information is via the liaison officer in the Executive Secretariat, and also the Scottish division dealing with the document. In cases where the SCN did not provide adequate information, the committee had sent it back requesting further information. At the end of the research period, this was a slow process, taking time to 'bed down'.

In addition, a formal process was put in place to ensure communication of the SEC's views to the Scottish Executive. Once the Committee has performed its scrutiny function (and/or received comments from a subject committee), and reached a decision on a document, this view was communicated to the Scottish Executive minister in the form of a report – a letter along with the text of the committee's conclusions. This is copied to the liaison officer in the Executive Secretariat. To what extent this view was taken into consideration by the Executive or minister was unclear.

During the research period, no Scottish 'scrutiny reserve' had emerged. However, what could be detected was an emergent desire to develop parliamentary control of the executive to strengthen the accountability function (of the Executive to the Parliament) in EU affairs beyond that originally envisaged by Scottish Office documents. Such moves by the SEC were not aimed at challenging the constitutional position whereby the negotiation of EU affairs is reserved to the UK government, accountable to the Westminster parliament. Rather, they represented initiatives by the sub-Member State parliament to establish modalities to hold its Executive to account within the UK (intra-state) domestic process in the formulation of the aggregated UK negotiating position within the Council of Ministers. During the research period, however, procedures developed were ones which enabled the Committee to express a 'view' to the Executive, rather than ones which enabled the Scottish government to be held to account to its parliament in respect of its policy negotiating position with the UK government. The early Scottish scrutiny system thus differed considerably from the Westminster system on this point.

With regard to bilateral inter-parliamentary relations, arrangements were still under review at the end of the research period. The main information sent to the SEC by the Westminster ESC was its in-house agenda, which gives some indication of ESC recommendations on EU documents. Otherwise, no formal channels of information flow were established between the SEC and the ESC. Prior to devolution, the ESC had thought of sending their private briefing notes to the Scottish committee. A number of problems emerged, however, with regard to sharing of intelligence *between* parliaments (Carter 2000). A central concern raised was how to protect the confidential nature of certain types of information in an environment of 'openness' fostered by the devolved assemblies. Although a willingness to share information was evident, officials in London stressed the constraints within which they were operating and differences which had arisen in relation to public availability of documents.[150] As a result, the ESC tried to find other ways to help the SEC which did not involve a straightforward exchange of papers. Consequently, what was established was a very informal working relationship between committee clerks (via telephone, e-mail etc.).[151] Two issues are worth especial mention:

- Time: at the intra-parliamentary level, the timing of when documents are referred to subject committees for scrutiny is crucial. Efficiency demands a strong managerial hand by the SEC. Timely receipt of information from the Executive is also pertinent to enable the Committee to sift effectively. At the inter-parliamentary level, the key concern remains the fact that the ESC cannot allow the Scottish scrutiny to interfere with the UK 'scrutiny reserve'. At a certain point, the ESC has to decide to clear a document and the Scottish system cannot hold this up.
- Scope: the Committee has established two different functions and isolated two different types of document concerning the scope of its scrutiny. The first function is to examine proposals in the early stages of the policy cycle and this involves the scrutiny of Green and

White Papers. The aim is to engage in a policy debate with the Scottish Executive. The second function is to scrutinise EU documents at a very late stage in the policy cycle under the six-week time-frame (contrary to previous SO recommendations). Here, communication will tend to be directly to Westminster or to Scottish MEPs, particularly if a proposal is in the process of a co-decision procedure. As such, the SEC appears to be attempting two different methods of scrutiny – one more akin to the House of Lords, the other to the House of Commons.

Scotland: arrangements for the scrutiny of implementation of EC law

By February 2000, the Committee had yet to finalise its procedural role in the scrutiny of the implementation of EC law. The approach adopted at the end of research period was to leave the subject committees to scrutinise the 'fine detail' (e.g. mechanisms of payments to farmers would be a matter for the then Rural Affairs Committee), and grant the SEC the broader constitutional function of holding the Executive to account. To do this, the Committee intended to establish procedures to elicit from the Executive how it intends to implement a Directive; what is the most appropriate route (i.e. through Westminster or through the Scottish Parliament), whether there are subordinate legislation provisions and if so, what they are. The Committee would subsequently hold the Executive to account on the accuracy and timeliness of implementation. As to the appropriate level of implementation (i.e. UK or Scotland), the Committee had been asking the administration a number of specific questions: how is this decided? who makes the decisions? when are decisions made? what are the criteria? The route for seeking such information at official level is between the officials of the SEC and the Executive Secretariat, which pools information from the various divisions and communicates answers to the Committee. If this information does not answer the question, the next route is between Parliament and Executive – i.e. the Convener of the Committee and the minister in a formal sense. Third, a minister might be asked to appear before the Committee for questioning. On interview, it was reported that the administration were being 'helpful' but were not used to dealing with these types of questions.

Scotland: arrangements for independent influence on EU matters

The members of the SEC saw the committee as the vehicle for expressing Scotland's voice in EU matters.[152] In the execution of this function, the symbolic aspect of the institution became extremely significant in a context where, under Donald Dewar's tenure as First Minister, 'Europe' was not recognised as a separate ministerial responsibility in the Scottish

Executive, and no specific minister was allocated the function of speaking on EU matters.[153] The SEC would take pro-active initiation of debates on EU affairs:

> Where else in Scotland can you have a debate on European issues if it is not the Scottish Parliament and the European committee?[154]

On the topics for debate, the SEC did not wish to be constrained by the Executive's own work programme. Rather the Committee wished to respond to interests and demands emanating from civic society in Scotland. To this end, the Committee initiated a consultation process and asked the Scottish public 'what does the European Union mean to you and what would you like the Scottish Parliament, and the SEC in particular, to do about it?'. A shortlist of subject matters was drafted and a committee 'rapporteur' appointed to take it forward (examples include the EU Charter for Fundamental Rights, fish diseases and infectious salmon). The SEC intends to air issues, which perhaps the Executive does not wish necessarily to discuss, e.g. preparations for EMU, and to debate both reserved and non-reserved matters.[155] By proceeding in this way, influence is brought to bear on the Executive to consider matters that are European linked, but not a priority in the programme of government.

The SEC also took the lead in fostering relations across the EU. The Committee had established good working relations with the office of the EP Representation to Scotland, with the Scottish MEPs, and were meeting MEPs and European parliamentary officials in Brussels to strengthen communication lines. The Committee had also established good relations with the European Commission representation to Scotland, with regular meetings between officials to share information. With regard to horizontal links with other domestic parliaments, here too the Committee had made initial contact with, and received a lot of interest from, committees in other parliaments (e.g. Germany, Spain, Sweden, Norway, Italy, France, Ireland) and were in regular contact with the Welsh and the Northern Irish (between clerks). This form of engagement was to share ideas and best practice in policy implementation. The Committee had also made contact with COSLA (with the offices in Scotland and Brussels) and Scotland Europa. In all, the SEC saw this as a key aim of its programme of action.

Wales: arrangements for the scrutiny of EU documents

One of the agreed remits of the EAC was to ensure that Wales was responding effectively to policy developments within the European Union.

This was to be achieved in part through the Assembly's scrutiny of European legislation and with reference to UK White Papers on developments within the European Union. By February 2000, it remained unclear, however, whether the Welsh Assembly was intending to conduct 'parliamentary' scrutiny of EU documents. Negative comments were made about the 'parliamentary' scrutiny process – the main obstacle to the making of a 'meaningful' Welsh input being the time scales of the policy cycle.[156] The concern was raised that the Welsh remained 'out of the loop' in this aspect of the UK–EU policy process.

UK officials, too, were not certain about future bilateral relations and arrangements for information flow. For example, it was not clear whether the EAC wished to receive EU documents and the UK EMs on a regular basis. In addition, whether individual Assembly subject committees would establish (separate) relations with the ESC, or whether the EAC would set up its own system of communication, was unknown. Concerns were raised at UK level over the complexity of establishing multiple and asymmetric arrangements between the ESC and different subject committees 'huge problems [could be envisaged] if some committees wanted to feed their views into [the ESC] and others didn't'.[157] Concerns with regard to confidential information sharing with public and multiple committees were expressed. Reciprocal concerns over accountability were raised by Members of the Assembly in plenary. In relation to European matters, paragraph B4.33 of the European concordat specifically required the UK government to take account of the views of the Assembly as a whole in deciding the UK line. The Welsh Cabinet's input into the UK process should therefore reflect the Assembly's views. Assembly Members (AMs) questioned how Assembly Secretaries receiving confidential information from UK government might nevertheless fulfil their obligation to be accountable to the wider Assembly for the operation of the concordats. This issue was held to be particularly tricky in the context of a minority administration. Could the Cabinet be relied on to represent the views of the Assembly as a whole when dealing with UK government?[158]

In summary, neither internal assembly arrangements for scrutiny of EU documents nor informal inter-parliamentary arrangements for information flow were established during this period. As a result, the representation of Welsh interests in the scrutiny of EU documents continues to be expressed as part of the Westminster UK system (as described in Section 1).

Wales: arrangements for the scrutiny of implementation of EC law

The subject committees have responsibility for scrutiny of legislation in their area (Standing Order 9): in standing orders there is deliberately no distinction made between the scrutiny of domestic, primary and European legislation.[159] The EAC has no explicit role in scrutiny of EU legislation, even if it is charged to 'have particular regard to the need for liaison with Members of Parliament responsible for scrutiny of European matters of particular relevance to Wales' (15.1(iii)).

At the second meeting of the EAC members were asked to agree a process which would enable the Assembly subject committees to take full account of the implications of European Union policies in their work programmes (EAC Eur-02-99: p. 3). Discussion focused on the advice that should be given to the subject committee chairs in order to help them to prioritise European issues and to time their considera-tion to best effect. It was foreseen that the Chair of the EAC would offer such advice in writing to the chairs of the subject committees and that the EAC would receive a report on the progress of subject committees in due course.[160] Thereafter, Assembly Divisions in the administrative branch would be responsible for informing their relevant Assembly Secretary of subsequent developments: he or she would then report these as appropriate to the relevant Assembly subject committee (Eur-03-99: p. 4.6). As a first response to the recommendation of the ESG (ESG 1998: paras. 4.3; 4.5; 4.38; 4.43; 4.49) for a review of the linkages between each of the devolved policy areas and EU legislation, policy and initiatives, the administrative branch had prepared a list of European Union policy areas, categorised by the policy areas of the Assembly sub-ject committees (EAC Eur-02-99: p. 3 Annex A). It was stressed that the list served as a starting point only, that some EU policy initiatives were relevant to the work of more than one Assembly committee and that the subject committees must be made aware of new European policies, par-ticularly those emanating from new EU competencies as Treaties are amended by Inter-governmental Conferences. MEP Jill Evans's sugges-tion that MEPs might input into the list of European policy areas to be considered relevant to individual subject committees was accepted by the EAC.

Wales: arrangements for independent influence on EU matters

The main activities of the EAC were in this area of the policy process and a number of arrangements were put in place. Specifically, whereas European matters have been attended to by the subject committees, wide-ranging matters have been debated in plenary. The latter includes for example, the 'take note' debate on the Memorandum of Understanding and Concordats conducted on 7 October 1999 and the debate on the European Strategy documents of 19 October 1999.

To carry out the broader pro-active role of the EAC, regular communication with relevant institutions and agencies in Brussels would need to be established.[161] This would entail setting up an Assembly representation in Brussels, joining the Wales European Centre, establishing links with the UK's Permanent Representation to the European Union, and institutionalising the Concordat between the Assembly and central government. But progress on these points was slow to develop.

In response to the ESG's request (ESG 1998: paras. 9.4; 10.3; 11.1) to ensure liaison with Welsh MEPs, the First Secretary proposed that meetings of the EAC should be timetabled as far as possible to permit attendance by Welsh MEPs and members of Committee of the Regions (CoR) and the Economic and Social Committee (ECOSOC). The report had also recommended the development of collaboration with other regions within the UK with respect to their European links and machinery, particularly with Scotland and Northern Ireland (ESG 1998 paras. 13.1; 14.1; 14.3). The First Secretary noted his intention to promote contacts between Assembly Secretaries with their Scottish and Northern Irish counterparts and to attend to the development of Wales's links with the 'Four Motor Regions'. However, in a speech in January 2000, Ron Davies, AM for Caerphilly, claimed that the Assembly had failed to develop significant relationships or links with the UK Parliament and the other devolved Assemblies (Davies 2000: 28).

The EAC's 1 July 1999 agenda included the establishment of the Wales (*sic*) Forum on European Affairs (Eur-01-99:agd; p. 1; p. 3).[162] From the outset, it was intended that this body should begin its operation as soon as possible: i.e. between September and early November 1999 and should meet every six months or so to coincide with changes in the presidency of the EU. The Chair proposed the establishment of the Wales Forum as a means of exchanging information on European matters and of promoting public and media debate. The EAC determined that the Forum's participants should include representatives of public bodies, local government, the business and agricultural communities, the voluntary sector, education bodies, Members of Parliament and other relevant agencies (including the Wales European Centre). It was also agreed that Forum should meet for the first time as a conference, but that its subsequent development should be in the hands of its participants. The ESG report had recommended that the Forum should have an independent chair to be appointed by the Secretary of State. In fact, Alun Michael as Secretary of State proposed himself as First Secretary to this 'independent' position. The justification was that the Chair of the EAC should fulfil this role in order that the Assembly would be fully engaged with the work of the Forum. Likewise, the members of the EAC should also be members of the Forum. The first meeting of the Wales Forum on European Affairs took place on 22 October 1999.

4.5   Conclusions

This chapter has explored issues relevant to the development of the 'parliamentary' role of the devolved institutions in the formulation and implementation of EU policy. We may note that the experience of the Scottish and Welsh institution-builders holds many similarities with the experiences of other third-level or sub-state actors across the EU. Regional parliaments and assemblies face similar challenges in accessing the EU policy process – a governance system which prioritises the role of national governments. The chapter isolates features relevant to the successful mobilisation of the parliamentary or assembly component of the sub-Member State. As we have shown, a main objective for the assemblies was to develop a *pro-active* European policy – defined here as both the establishment of a local forum for debate of European matters and also the attempt to gain access to the EU policy system through the creation of effective modalities for parliamentary involvement. Further, we have seen that the discourse of the sub-Member State with regard to its parliamentary role elevates issues such as the representative and participatory aspects of good governance at the local level. A key challenge is to balance the requirements of participatory (local) governance with the demands of efficiency within a multi-levelled policy system – a common difficulty faced by all EU regions irrespective of the national constitutional settlement within which they reside. In all, we conclude that the new assemblies in Scotland and Wales have been inventive in their approach although, in the first nine months of their existence, there have been practical problems which have meant that delivery has not quite kept pace with expectations.

Certain tensions within the system surfaced during the research period. In Scotland, tensions within executive-legislative relations came to light, whereby the 'new' parliament was attempting to gain access to the 'old' institution of the Scottish administration. In Wales, the main general tensions emerged around the assertion of a corporate form of accountability, with AMs struggling to define the role of the Welsh Assembly. At the close of the period of study, the Welsh Assembly was still attempting to assert an 'integrated' mode of accountability in which the entire Assembly upheld this function, as opposed to the traditional patterns of accountability conducted under a separate executive – a model promoted by Alun Michael's leadership.[163] Dependency on the centre also gave rise to tensions for both assemblies. First, the reserved status of EU policy to the UK government had specific ramifications in Scotland, with the challenge to define a 'Scottish' scrutiny system instrumental within the national system. In Wales, there was a dependency in terms of both the transfer and scope of executive functions in EU affairs.

Given this context, we must ask to what extent the Scottish Parliament and Welsh Assembly met the high expectations placed on them in the development of pioneering 'parliamentary' roles in the UK–EU policy system. To begin to answer this question, we deploy the framework as set out in Chapter 1 to analyse change within the five institutional dimensions. In so doing, we note that the systemic dimension set the parameters of institution-building in the organisational, regulative and process-related dimensions.

Change in the *systemic* dimension created a critical moment in the UK–EU policy system in respect of the electoral-representative component. Two distinct models of devolution defined the new constitutional settlement – a legislative model in Scotland and an executive model in Wales – instigating a new and asymmetric quality to the 'parliamentary' control of the formulation and implementation of EU policy. Further, new institutional settings for the debate of EU matters created the potential to render the system more representative of territorial interests through the opening of space for independent 'voice' at the sub-Member State level. Systemic change also provided for a more accountable EU policy within Scotland and Wales. In Scotland, this would be achieved through executive–legislative relations; in Wales through a new 'integrated' mode of accountability in which the entire Assembly would uphold this function. In addition, new electoral systems would give rise to a new political character. Our research findings suggest, however, that the ramifications of the key changes in this dimension for the handling of UK–EU policy have yet to register in any significant way.

Overall *organisational* change has been considerable. First, the effect of devolution has been to create a whole new set of organisations and positions, with powers attached to them in the form of assemblies for both countries. Second, the two assemblies took similar decisions about the type of organisations that would be involved in the handling of EU business. In both Scotland and Wales, decisions were made to create a 'European' committee as part of the respective parliamentary/assembly committee system; both 'European' committees were based on a hybrid model, with cross-committee membership with related subject committees; both committees had a similar party political balance. Similarly, an interesting organisational anomaly now exists in both assemblies in that both the Scottish and the Welsh European committees were under-resourced. Third, one way in which the two assemblies have organised extra-state links marks a key departure from the Westminster approach. Unlike at Westminster, decisions were taken to institutionalise at the local level relations between parliamentary/assembly members, MEPs and members of local civic bodies (public and private). In Wales, this manifested itself as a Wales Forum on European Affairs. In Scotland, it was proposed that the SEC would meet in a broader setting with MEPs and local organisations. This way of handling European affairs is innovative for the UK and perhaps specific to a sub-Member State 'parliamentary' approach (as distinct from a national one).

The standing orders for the Scottish Parliament and the Welsh Assembly constitute the most evident elements within the *regulative* dimension. Strategic capacity for handling EU affairs in both assemblies was divided between the European committees and subject committees. In both assemblies, subject committees scrutinise the implementation of EC law. There were marked differences, however, in the remit granted to the European committees as between Scotland and Wales (and as compared with the Westminster European committees). In Scotland, the SEC was given an extensive remit – an amalgam of the functions of Westminster European scrutiny and standing committees – and this can in part be explained by the new integrated role for committees generally within the Scottish Parliament and the Parliament's legislative function. In Wales, the European committee's remit was innovative and critically related to the structure of the assembly. Change in this dimension is thus considerable, resulting in the creation of two different types of 'European' committee to handle EU business at the sub-Member State level, along with subject committees with power sharing functions (Scotland) and 'checks and balances' functions (Wales).

The main challenges for both assemblies during the research period were to be found within the *process-related* (or *procedural*) dimension. With regard to intra-assembly procedures, in Scotland the main challenge was in the area of executive-legislative relations and the setting up of formal channels of information flow between the Parliament and the Executive. New types of Scottish information appeared (the SCN and SEB), but the Scottish Executive was not providing information to the SEC on a systematic basis. In Wales, no Welsh version of a UK-EM materialised during this period. With regard to information flow between the European committees and the UK ESC, no formal process agreements were put in place. For Scotland, informal arrangements exist.

In Wales, it was not clear to what extent even informal arrangements could be established for information flow. Alongside intra-state relations, both assemblies made pro-active efforts to begin the process of establishing extra-state and bilateral relations across the EU. In all, the Scottish Parliament aimed to input to all stages of the UK–EU policy process, whereas the Welsh Assembly's European Affairs Committee attempted to take a more strategic, managerial role seeking to ensure that European matters are adequately covered in the Assembly's deliberations.

A key finding for Wales, was that devolution brought *no* change as far as the scrutiny of EU documents is concerned, and this as a direct result of difficulties emerging within the process dimension coupled with the asymmetry of devolution where diversity is driven by the systemic and regulative dimensions (there is a difficulty of interpretation of this essentially 'parliamentary' function given that the Welsh Assembly does not hold primary legislative functions and is not a parliament).[164] In Scotland, change in the parliamentary scrutiny system only occurs to the extent that the Scottish procedures are effective and the committee gains access to accurate and timely government (Scottish) information. In addition, the Scottish scrutiny system had not developed a strong government–parliament accountability mechanism. In both Scotland and Wales, a further key challenge was one of 'time', whereby Scottish and Welsh inputs have to enter the policy-making procedure at a very early stage. This renders effective scrutiny of EU documents at territorial level problematic. At the end of the research period, the electoral-representative component of the newly devolved polity was not yet directly included in the internal UK policy formulation process, with Wales holding a latent scrutiny function. To what extent devolution strengthens parliamentary scrutiny of EU documents depends on the extent to which there is a further future strengthening of the process-related dimension.[165]

Arguably the key aspiration for change in both assemblies was in the *cultural* dimension of institution building, and in particular in the cultural aspects embedded in the organisational, regulative and process dimensions. First, both assemblies were to give effect to principles of participatory governance: these included principles of power sharing; accountability; and access and participation. In both assemblies, these underlying values were prevalent in understandings of allocation of committee members; in co-operational procedures between committees; in the value placed on open information sharing. The cultural dimension to institution-building was also felt in the 'models' driving change. First, both Scottish and Welsh societies were heavily influenced by the importance of 'Europe' in the historical development of their respective cultures. This enabled an all-embracing positive approach to the adoption of a pro-active EU policy. Second, one of the central intentions of both Scottish and Welsh institution-builders was to establish models distinct from the Westminster one. The Scottish Parliament seeks to foster a culture of 'new politics'; the Welsh Assembly one of 'inclusive' politics, which, in each case, aims to replace the entrenched partisan conflicts of the Westminster Parliament with a priority for territorial community interests.

To what extent these aspirations can be fulfilled is hard to assess definitively at this stage. Certain problems emerged in the course of our research period. First in Wales, doubts were expressed over the Assembly's ability to promote the 'partnership' ethos which had been the foundation of the consultative documents in Wales. It was asserted that decision-making in the Assembly was being undertaken within an extremely narrow circle within the Cabinet. Instead of corporate, cross-party decision-making, the reality was a much more centralised model of decision-making with Alun Michael in a key role. The Assembly committees, the partnerships and forums were perceived by some as 'smoke screens, they have the illusion of participation but their influence and impact upon the decisions are nil, absolutely nil'.[166] The ambiguous nature of the Assembly's role in handling EU policy had not been resolved by the end of our research period. Second, attempts by the ESC to share intelligence with the third-level European committees were quickly tempered by concerns of confidentiality. This suggested that in practice, the Whitehall/Westminster culture of 'non-openness' may come into conflict with the culture of transparency which the Scottish Parliament and Welsh Assembly are attempting (with difficulty) to foster. If cultural aspirations between the centre and devolved authorities do come to diverge, the sub-state tier may find itself ostracised by the centre, and the scope for sub-state influence in reserved or shared matters may be constrained. The cultural dimension, intrinsic to all other dimensions, thus set up new symbiotic tensions within the overall UK–EU policy system.

5

The Post-Devolution Governance of Rural and Environmental Affairs: Early Impressions

5.1 Introduction

In the report so far we have examined institutional change in a broad sense, not focusing on specific arrangements for individual policy areas. That coverage is important because there are general features relating to the handling of all areas of policy. In addition, we have thereby covered the machinery for horizontal issues that cut across different UK and devolved departments responsible for European policy. However, a lot of European business is dealt with in a more sectorised manner, whereby the functional departments do not have to consult widely across government. Instead, the Brussels–London–Edinburgh/Cardiff triangle comprises officials in one policy area. In this chapter we focus upon agriculture and, in a shorter study, on environmental policy. Our interest is once again in how far the policy machinery has changed as a consequence of devolution.

Agriculture is an interesting case study, since arrangements for its handling have been long-standing and to a large degree separate from other European business in Cardiff, Edinburgh and London. The Common Agricultural Policy (CAP) is an intensely regulated policy area, such that virtually all agricultural policy has a European dimension. Moreover, agriculture is a policy area where territorial interests within the UK are quite diverse because of different patterns of livestock and arable farming. Hence the scope for divergent interests on policy substance is clearly present.

If agricultural policy was already subject to a kind of territorial machinery, environmental policy is rather different. It is a more recent EU policy area, originating in the 1970s. Whilst the CAP places clear constraints on national agricultural policy, environmental policy brings different types of costs through the burdens of regulatory compliance. The EU's responsibilities in the latter domain were regarded as intrusive by some Conservative ministers such that the Europeanisation of the (then) Department of the Environment (DoE) only really occurred under John Gummer, who was Secretary of State from 1993 to 1997 (Lowe and Ward 1998; Jordan 2000). It is perhaps not such a big surprise, therefore, that the territorial dimension of European policy was late in developing, in view of the delayed adaptation to the EU 'at the centre'. The two policy areas highlight divergent patterns of institutional adaptation: operational continuity in agriculture but significant change in environmental policy.

5.2   Agriculture[167]

The UK government had to put in place arrangements for monitoring the CAP from its creation, i.e. prior to accession to the European Communities. The reason was not restricted to accession negotiations, although that was a factor. Of at least equal significance was the fact that the CAP impacted upon neighbouring non-Member States in a similar way as today's single market rules impact on a state such as Switzerland. Upon accession the impact upon UK agriculture was by no means uniform. England has had a comparatively large emphasis upon arable farming; the beef sector has been especially important in Scotland; sheep farming has been a central concern in Wales, where there is little arable farming. In addition, there are certain niche areas of agriculture, such as seed potatoes in Scotland. Even these scant references demonstrate that there is a distinct territoriality to agricultural interests within the UK. A further point to be noted is that the territorial ministries tended to have closer contacts with 'their' farming communities simply on the grounds of proximity, compared to the Ministry of Agriculture, Fisheries and Food's (MAFF) more remote relationship resulting from Whitehall's location at the centre of a huge conurbation. Finally, at the policy-implementation stage, the opportunity existed for policy to be operationalised through different instruments, including in the Scottish case through different legislation. These various points should make clear that, even before devolution, European policy in the UK was rather more variegated than might be implied by the designation 'unitary state'.

5.2.1   Agriculture: *status quo ante*

Agriculture is the most Europeanised policy area. In 1996 it was reported to represent some 40 per cent of proposals emanating from Brussels, although the figure had earlier been 80–90 per cent. As the same senior MAFF official reported to us 'virtually everyone in the Department deals with Brussels'. Moreover, John Gummer, the Secretary of State (1989–93) was wont to say '80 per cent of my budget is controlled from Brussels'.[168] In light of this level of EU impact MAFF has long been recognised as one of the key departments in European policy-making.

Policy-making at the 'centre'

European policy-making within MAFF was handled in the following way:[169]

- Ministerial involvement was extensive, since the Council of Agricultural Ministers meets very frequently. In 1996, for instance, there were 13 meetings – a total unsurpassed (but equalled by foreign ministers) – and this figure excludes five sessions of the Fisheries Council.[170] Ministers attending the agriculture Council are recommended a negotiating brief arising from a meeting of the Departmental Committee on Europe (see below).
- The Special Committee on Agriculture is a key preparatory body for the Council at EU level. Agriculture occupies an important role in UKRep's establishment. Further, the 'traffic' of officials from MAFF's line divisions to various EU committees at the pre-proposal, decision-making and policy-management stages has been extensive.
- Co-ordination in MAFF was handled by the European Union Division, with an all-in staff of 39. Its three principal functions were: co-ordination of CAP negotiations; responsibility for 'horizontal' CAP issues, such as policy reform, the budget; and it acted as focal point for MAFF on issues where other departments held the 'lead', e.g. enlargement and treaty reform (FCO) or EMU (the Treasury). The Division also co-ordinated to ensure that the necessary Explanatory Memoranda (EM) were laid before Parliament setting out the government's view on agricultural policy proposals. EU Division was accountable via the EU and International Policy Group (set up in December 1997) to the Agricultural Crops and Commodities Directorate, one of two in the department, headed by a Deputy Secretary. The Food Safety and Environment Directorate is headed by another Deputy Secretary, and the EU looms large in this work – notably the whole Bovine Spongiform Encephalopathy (BSE) crisis – even if European co-ordination is in another command structure. Both of the Deputy Secretaries report to the Permanent Secretary (to whom fisheries and some miscellaneous services report direct), and thence to the ministerial team.

- The Departmental Committee on Europe (DCE) was set up in the early 1970s as a MAFF-based co-ordination mechanism on European policy, run by the EU Division. It prepared meetings of the Council or the Special Committee on Agriculture. The practice was for the head of agriculture in UKRep to either attend or be 'beamed in' via video-link. Depending on the Brussels agenda the relevant policy line-divisions would be represented and a negotiating position finalised. A 'DCE Notice System' disseminated guidelines on procedures relating to European policy-making.
- MAFF was a key player at ministerial and official level within Cabinet co-ordination. Senior figures, such as the Deputy Secretaries, were likely to have extensive experience of the EU; both incumbents in 1996 had been in the Cabinet Office European Secretariat (COES) and one had been Head of Agriculture in UKRep. The department thus had extensive experience of the Cabinet Office network on European policy and the Brussels network on agriculture. As part of the latter it was engaged in considerable bilateral lobbying with counterparts in other Member States, conscious of the importance of such action in a policy area where decision-making by qualified majority is normally provided for.
- Policy issues with a consequence for other Whitehall departments – i.e. apart from the territorials – would be handled on an *ad hoc* basis or, more formally, through the COES machinery.

Policy-making in the territorial ministries

Prior to devolution MAFF's counterpart north of the border was the Scottish Office Department of Agriculture, Environment and Fisheries (SOAEFD).[171] European policy was handled in the General Agriculture Division, making up approaching 80 per cent of the workload. The Division's European tasks primarily consisted of co-ordination and information-distribution, CAP-wide issues (e.g. broad questions relating to CAP reform) and EU funding (agricultural structural funds, fisheries support).[172] Specific, product-related matters would be dealt with in line-divisions elsewhere within SOAEFD.

How was Edinburgh brought into EU policy-making under these arrangements? On the 'reception' side, the original arrangement was that all information flowed to Edinburgh from MAFF: either between the two divisions responsible for EU co-ordination or, on a more *ad hoc* basis, between desk officers responsible for a specific domain of agricul-tural policy. This arrangement could be haphazard on occasion, for instance both MAFF's co-ordinating division and its line division might very occasionally assume that the other had informed the territorials, when in reality neither had. Alternatively, the information might be passed on too slowly to permit any meaningful territorial input into the UK policy position. Not surprisingly, this arrangement was not entirely satisfactory for the Scottish Office, and on a number of policy issues questions were raised about the effectiveness of the machinery. One instance occurred under William Waldegrave's period as Secretary of State (1994–95). He initiated a consideration of options for CAP reform, supported by the Treasury, but without active involvement from any of the territorial departments. When they eventually saw the results of this exercise there was extensive ministerial correspondence to point out that the proposals had not taken into account the views from Edinburgh, Cardiff and Belfast. The territorial ministries took the view that the proposals were in any case too radical and stood little chance of success in the Commission and even less in the Council of Ministers. It was instances of this type which led to the establishment in 1995 of a reporting mechanism for 'territorial discord' in the Cabinet Office's Economic and Domestic Secretariat, and resultant annual reports.[173] Questionnaires sought views from the territorials on whether they felt they had been adequately consulted, had complaints with their 'lead Department' and so on. The resultant reports included what action should prevent a recurrence of the types of problems experienced. European and agricultural policy represented areas where the complexity of the policy network and dictates of the Brussels timetable provided plenty of potential for such territorial discord. Suffice it to say that the BSE crisis provided a number of such instances.

Not all agricultural policy issues were confined in London to MAFF. For instance the Treasury or the Department of the Environment might have particular concerns about an agricultural issue. In these cases, and as departments of the UK government, the territorials could legitimately expect to receive (or could request) the relevant papers from Whitehall in order to see the wider debates between ministries in London. On issues cutting across Whitehall, such as CAP reform – which might be linked with budgetary policy, reform of the structural funds and so on, as in the EU's Agenda 2000 package of reforms – SOAEFD and its counterparts in Cardiff and Belfast would receive papers for meetings of the Cabinet Committee on European Questions (EQ(O)), since they were on the EQ distribution list, and could attend meetings of it or the 'Friday meeting' if they had particular concerns (see Chapter 2, Table 2.1). If such matters were sufficiently politicised that they came to be discussed at ministerial level, the three territorial Secretaries of State would receive the papers and would attend the Cabinet Committee or utilise the more informal channels offered by ministerial correspondence.

Direct information from Brussels, such as from UKRep, was somewhat haphazard until 1995. At that point a new procedure was introduced whereby the Head of Agricultural Affairs in UKRep assumed a new information-dissemination role. This post has been seen as 'number 3' in UKRep – i.e. after the Permanent Representative and the Deputy Permanent Representative – because of the importance of the Special Committee on Agriculture as a decision-making body, in some ways equivalent to, yet separate from, the Committee of Permanent Representatives (COREPER) (see Hayes-Renshaw and Wallace 1997; Westlake 1995). From 1995 the Head of Agricultural Affairs was to send all reports and papers to MAFF and the SOAEFD (and counterparts in Belfast and Cardiff) simultaneously.[174] This step not only improved the quality of the information received in Edinburgh and Cardiff but, importantly, also accelerated the speed of the information-sharing process. In consequence, the process was no longer such that MAFF would automatically be ahead of the territorials temporally in considering a UK response, although it would likely have a staff resource advantage.

As regards the 'projection' side of the territorials' response to the EU, there were a number of ways in which an input could be made into the policy process:

- The most frequent input would be from line-division officials in the territorials to their counterparts in MAFF.
- Ministerial correspondence or official-level meetings with MAFF counterparts could be utilised on important issues.
- DCE offered an opportunity for input of a limited kind. The territorials were able to play a part in DCE, although resources limited the extent of such participation. The Scottish Office, for instance, tended to rely on its liaison staff, based at Dover House in London, to attend and monitor DCE meetings. Only on a very important matter would a (more specialised) official from SOAEFD attend. DCE is best seen as a monitoring arrangement. The other territorials did not attend some DCE meetings at all.
- For agricultural issues which had wider significance within the government, the EQ network and EQ(O) offered alternative arenas for formal or informal (*ad hoc*) input into policy-making.
- Officials and ministers could attend meetings at all levels of the Council of Ministers hierarchy: from meetings of EU agriculture ministers down to working groups. Participation of officials also applied

to Commission advisory groups at the pre-proposal stage of policy-making and, at the other end of the policy cycle, to product-based management committees for implementing policy. Of course, resource constraints meant that participation in any of these on the part of the territorials had to be highly selective. The Scottish Office tended to be the most active participant but an official-level representation from each of the territorials would be normal for each Council session. At more specialist levels of the Brussels machinery the SOAEFD might send the only UK official where an issue of specific importance, such as seed potatoes, were under discussion in Brussels. Ministerial participation in the Council would be less frequent, but during the BSE crisis the Conservative junior minister in the Scottish Office, Lord Lindsay, attended virtually all related sessions alongside the UK Secretary of State, Douglas Hogg, in order to uphold Scotland's corner.[175] On one occasion during the crisis the Scottish Secretary of State, Michael Forsyth, unusually attended the agriculture Council. In any event, the UK minister would lead the negotiations on the basis of prior agreement reached with territorial counterparts, normally at official level. By contrast, it is worth noting that the fisheries minister from MAFF might permit his Scottish Office counterpart to lead the UK delegation, and thus negotiations, at the Fisheries Council.

One of the key difficulties experienced by the territorials was that, in issues where their concerns departed from MAFF's, and where their interests were particularly affected, such as on beef, the European Commission and other Member States might be very slow to understand the different nature of, say, Scottish circumstances. The principal way of tackling this issue was to invite officials from the Commission, the Agriculture Commissioner's *cabinet*, or agricultural attachés from the London embassies to visit Scotland to see matters for themselves.

In all its work the SOAEFD's European Division saw its role as 'to ensure that Scotland is not discriminated against'.[176] The *quid pro quo* under the above arrangements was that the SOAEFD and Scottish Office ministers had to keep MAFF (and other territorials) briefed of their actions, e.g., through side-copying correspondence to UKRep, and ensuring that they did not step outside agreed UK policy lines.

Compared with the Scottish Office's longer-standing existence and involvement in agriculture, the Welsh Office's separate life (with a separate Cabinet minister) dates only from 1964. Further, agriculture was not taken over in Cardiff until 1977. Previously there had simply been a regional office of MAFF in Aberystwyth. This background bears on the different aspirations and capacity for agricultural policy-making in Wales as compared to Scotland.

In the pre-devolution period the EU's impact on agricultural policy-making in the Welsh Office was significant. An official with two decades' experience in the Welsh Office observed that the impact of the EU was more critical in the Agriculture Department than in any other area in which he had worked.[177] In a normal year about £250 million of CAP money was directed to Wales; it was estimated that in a normal year half the money spent by the Welsh Office on agriculture was spent on sheep premium payments.[178]

The Agriculture Department would meet proposals from the EU with a Welsh perspective formulated on the basis of expertise from line officials, plus information and advice from in-house sources such as the ADAS (Agricultural Development Advisory Service, run jointly with MAFF), the State Veterinary Service, and economists and statisticians in the Welsh Office. In addition, the Secretary of State (SoS) could call on advisory panels: the Advisory Panel on Agriculture, comprising farming representatives, business interests, academics, environmental specialists and so on, which considered the impact of new and existing policies; the Hill Farming Advisory Committee; and the Food Strategy Advisory Group.

EU policy was handled through its Agriculture Department (WOAD), located within the Agriculture, Industry, Economic Development and Training Directorate. Already from its title, the much more multi-functional nature of this Directorate is clear when compared to the SOAEFD, not to mention MAFF. Whilst this presented advantages where policy proposals cut across sectors, e.g. linking with the environment, it was also indicative of the fact that Welsh Office resources were rather more shallow: focused on breadth rather than depth.[179] In fact, the limited nature of staff resources meant that European policy co-ordination within WOAD was less assured by institutional design than through informal, in-house contacts. Thus, even more than with the SOAEFD, substantive European business was dealt with by specialists in WOAD.

Despite the multi-functional organisation of the Welsh Office, non-agricultural European policy was co-ordinated by a European Affairs Division in the Economic Development Group within the same directorate. WOAD tended to play a smaller role in the Cabinet Office's EQ network than its Scottish Office counterpart. Papers were received but attendance was infrequent. Similarly, on liaison with Parliament, most work was left to MAFF, with commentary being added to draft EMs as necessary. WOAD also utilised direct engagement in the Brussels network less than its counterpart in Edinburgh.

We should also note where the UK Parliament came into the arrangements for handling European policy. Parliamentary questions and scrutiny were of course conducted through the normal channels (see above). Whilst parliamentary questions could be tabled for Scottish Office ministers (or their counterparts), scrutiny arrangements had no real territorial sensitivity. The House of Commons Agriculture Select Committee might deal with CAP-related matters as part of its work, but its remit would not cover specific EU legislative proposals. The Scottish Select Committee could (and did) review agricultural policy north of the border – a possibility open to counterpart bodies – but this would be a very indirect route for making an input into EU policy-making, and most likely ineffective as a result.

Finally, it is worth noting that lobbying of the territorial departments, e.g. of SOAEFD by the National Farmers' Union Scotland or the Scottish Landowners' Federation was a regular part of agricultural politics. In Wales WOAD maintained close and active links with the producer interests, particularly the National Farmers' Union (Welsh Area), the Farmers' Union of Wales (a break-away branch from the National Farmers' Union) and the Country Landowners' Association. Nevertheless, on the principle of 'shooting where the ducks are', most lobbying by interest groups was directed at MAFF, since it was seen as where the crucial European policy decisions were finalised in the UK.

5.2.2 Agriculture: post-devolution arrangements

Operationalising devolution at the centre

Before looking at the negotiation of post-devolution arrangements it is worth mentioning the BSE crisis, which emerged under the Major government. Owing to its seriousness and differential territorial impact, it necessitated careful handling.[180] The crisis had the consequence of intensifying meetings at a senior official (Deputy Secretary) level between MAFF and its territorial counterparts. Ministerial contacts also intensified, largely on an *ad hoc* basis, although there was also a ministerial committee on the crisis chaired by Roger Freeman, minister in the Cabinet Office under the Major government. As already noted, more intensive territorial attendance of meetings in Brussels also ensued. Although completely unrelated to devolution, the territoriality of the BSE crisis led to the more regular holding of meetings, and this was to suggest a framework for policy-making following devolution.

MAFF had been engaged in a limited and informal way with the devolution issue during the period of the 1997 election campaign as part of a wider process outlined in Chapter 1. MAFF officials were prominent members of the Inter-Departmental Group on Constitutional Reform (IDG) and of its sub-group on European policy. As noted already, it was then the Scottish and Welsh Offices which were responsible for drawing up the White Papers within a space of two months after Blair's election. However, the Cabinet Office Constitution Secretariat (COCS), in consultation with the European Secretariat, was in charge of ensuring that the UK government's interests in retaining its co-ordinated approach to policy-making would be protected in reserved matters. What were MAFF's concerns at this initial stage? They can be connected with two discrete phases of European business: policy-making and policy-implementation. In respect of the former the key issues were: the role of the devolved administrations in policy preparation and negotiation; and their representation in the Council. MAFF was concerned that provisions should enable a single UK line to be articulated (by MAFF). In respect of policy-implementation there were two particular concerns: that MAFF should not be held responsible – as a department of the Member-State government – for any improper implementation of policy by the devolved administrations; and with the scope for differential forms of policy-implementation within the UK.[181] The solutions to problems relating to these issues, e.g. when a minister from Scotland or a secretary from Wales could attend the Council, ultimately needed resolution within Cabinet or the Cabinet Committee on Devolution to Scotland, Wales and the Regions (DSWR).

Within MAFF initial responsibility for devolution after Labour's election lay with the EU Division. However, the workload became unmanageable, because so much of MAFF business would be affected, so a separate Devolution Unit was already created in the second half of 1997 elsewhere within the Department. However, as a result of an unrelated re-organisation at the end of 1997 the function was transferred back and became one branch (of 4) – in EU Division. Resources were slender: essentially one senior civil servant was given a devolution brief but others were brought in when their responsibilities were affected. With the White Paper published by this time, the tasks of the branch included: the drafting of concordats; preparation for, and then conducting, general relations with the devolved administrations; and keeping the rest of MAFF informed on how to handle devolution, e.g. through guidance.

Within Whitehall MAFF was one of the first departments to make headway with the consideration of concordat arrangements, i.e. for agriculture. The disadvantage of being ahead in concordatry was that MAFF's preparations – and they were principally with counterparts in SOAEFD – ran ahead of wider considerations in the Cabinet Office. Thus, in Autumn 1998, when the COCS decided that there should be a number of overarching concordats, and that one would be on EU business, some of the MAFF-SOAEFD agenda was clawed back to the Cabinet Office. This development was, in the words of one of those involved, 'slightly messy'.[182] The principal reason for the negotiation of a concordat with Wales falling (ever further) behind was the lack of resources in WOAD. However, there had been difficulties in negotiating the Welsh dimension of the overarching concordats owing to the novel constitutional situation in Cardiff. Concordat negotiations were undertaken through a mix of meetings and correspondence exclusively at official level. Subsidiary concordat arrangements, notably for fisheries, were also being negotiated.

The main goal was to put in place working arrangements to operationalise the principles set out in the White Papers. At interview in April 1999 a MAFF official indicated that no special consultation machinery was being established in the bilateral agriculture concordat with Scotland. Instead, attention was drawn to the practice that had emerged from the BSE crisis, namely of monthly meetings between MAFF and the territorials at Deputy Secretary level and infrequent ones between the UK Secretary of State and his agriculture counterparts.[183] When the bilateral concordat was published later in the year, however, para. 5 specified meetings to facilitate relations:

> [T]he senior agriculture officials in MAFF, and the Head of the Food and Agriculture Group of the Scottish Executive Rural Affairs Department (SERAD), will aim to meet monthly (or as appropriate) to discuss matters of mutual interest and co-ordinate any necessary joint action. The Scottish Minister(s) responsible for agriculture and the Minister of Agriculture, Fisheries and Food will aim to meet bimonthly or as appropriate for the same purposes. Similarly, for fisheries there will be regular meetings between the respective Fisheries Secretaries and between the respective Fisheries Ministers. (MAFF/SE Concordat 1999)

The decision to include these meetings was taken in May 1999. A further related development occurred in July 1999 as a result of a government reshuffle. Joyce Quin, formerly Minister of State for Europe in the FCO, was moved sideways to MAFF. Within MAFF she was given an informal designation of minister for England. This designation meant that when the ministerial meetings came to be held under devolved arrangements, Nick Brown, the Secretary of State, sought more of a brokering 'UK' role, whereas Joyce Quin would wear an English 'hat', thus seeking to minimise any conflict of interest in negotiations with their Scottish and Welsh counterparts. A further point to note is that, diaries permitting, the ministerial meetings would be scheduled to be as close as possible before a meeting of the Council of Agriculture Ministers.

Space does not permit an analysis of all the issues raised by the concordat negotiations. Moreover, we are not privy to them all, especially as the Welsh concordat was not published at the conclusion of our fieldwork. However, one of the last issues to be resolved will serve as illustration, namely the question of communication of information to the Commission. The devolved administrations had made a strong case in Whitehall for communicating information themselves direct to the Commission via UKRep where they were responsible for implementing a directive or implementing legislation. The logic behind this case was that where they implement a directive they would be wholly competent for its provisions. That posed a number of problems. First, so much CAP business is regulatory, so implementation comprises a massive amount of activity. Secondly, there are questions of the distortion of competition and a lot of the CAP has to be implemented on a UK-wide basis. Even if the devolved authorities were implementing legislation themselves, MAFF would have to implement the same thing in England.[184] Thirdly, the Commission would want a single reply rather than four separate replies. Eventually a compromise was reached which specifies that communication of information will go through MAFF to UKRep to the Commission except for in a very small number of cases (see MAFF/SE Concordat 1999, para. 15 in Annex for details). One might regard this agreement as MAFF using the reserved status of European policy to keep a prudent check on policy-implementation by the devolved authorities. Alternatively, a nationalist might regard this arrangement as MAFF keeping the whip hand and limiting the freedom of Cardiff or Edinburgh in devolved matters. In reality, it was a pragmatic compromise between both positions.

The operation of the new arrangements was commenced in July 1999, ahead of their publication. It is worth pointing out that the subsequent period has not been one where there have been significant numbers of high-profile EU agricultural proposals. Notably, the reform process associated with the Agenda 2000 package was agreed ahead of formal devolution. However, as will be seen, a number of regulatory or implementation issues arose in these first months. The machinery set out in the MAFF/SE Concordat has been operationalised, with the deputy secretary meetings being held more frequently than monthly. A lot of effort was invested on all sides to ensure that meetings got off to a good start and set a good precedent. EU business is a permanent agenda item. Ministerial meetings have followed the pattern of the concordat.[185] In addition, at working level the option remains of the devolved authorities using DCE(MAFF) to make an input into policy. In the absence of any major disputes between MAFF and its Scottish and Welsh counterparts, these arrangements and informal bilateral contacts have sufficed to facilitate the functioning of European policy.

But where might disputes be resolved, given that the *formal* Cabinet Office machinery is no longer available? There are two possible routes. One is via the agriculture concordat machinery, up to ministerial level. This route is likely to be preferred where the issue is narrowly agricultural. If a solution could not be reached there, then the dispute could be taken to the Joint Ministerial Committee (JMC). Another route would be to involve the COES, which would be likely to set up an *ad hoc* meeting so that officials from the devolved authorities could participate.[186] On a wider agricultural issue, such as hypothetically the abolition of milk quotas, this would be MAFF's preference. The meeting might be skewed towards Whitehall, since the FCO and the Treasury would also wish to make an input from central government side on such an issue. If a matter were unresolved at this level, then the JMC would again be the final forum. It is worth recalling that the JMC is advisory only, so the UK government *could* ignore its conclusions. By the time our fieldwork ended the JMC had not been convened on agricultural issues. However, a number of contentious issues had arisen between London and both Edinburgh and Cardiff. We will review them briefly after considering how the devolved authorities fitted in with the new arrangements.

It is worth quoting a pre-devolution observation from a senior participant on the prospects for disputes:

> I think the main problem will be ... if – as one would expect – Scottish and indeed Welsh ministers come under pressure to assume an independent line on any particular issue ... that will give rise to tensions. Those tensions already exist, obviously, because they are based on economic reality but of course they are resolved within a framework of collective responsibility to which their ministers are bound. I think following devolution Scottish ministers will be under great pressure to make public a different line ....[187]

In the event these prescient comments proved to be more applicable to the situation in Wales.

Operationalising devolution in Edinburgh and Cardiff

There is a more substantive story to relate regarding adaptation in Scotland, compared to Wales, because negotiations were more advanced, with the bilateral concordat published in November 1999.[188] The agriculture concordat was negotiated centrally from the Agriculture Group within SOAEFD ahead of devolution. The negotiations were not without controversy. For instance, the Scottish National Party (SNP) obtained a leaked SOAEFD document at the early stages of the negotiations which, according to *The Herald* newspaper, reported:

> There has been and doubtless will continue to be some tension in the drafting process. From the Maff perspective the concordat is a chance to emphasise their leading UK role and to keep tabs on action by the Scottish Executive. From our perspective it is a chance to keep open the access to the European policy process and to decisions which have to be made at UK level while limiting Maff interference in Scottish business.[189]

This summed up well the Scottish position. However, the SNP agricultural spokesman, John Swinney, issued the following statement in response to the leak:

> This means the agriculture department of the Scottish Executive in the new Parliament will be *under the thumb* of the London-based Ministry of Agriculture, Fisheries and Food.[190] (Our italics)

Once the transfer of power had taken place in Scotland a number of key organisational decisions were taken. These were, first, the creation of the Scottish Executive Rural Affairs Department as successor to SOAEFD. Otherwise, in agriculture and fisheries, the administrative arrangements were largely as inherited from SOAEFD. Secondly, the establishment of the Executive Secretariat at the heart of the Scottish Executive, with EU policy as one of its tasks, established co-ordination arrangements for horizontal issues, such as preparing for the 2000 Inter-governmental Conference on EU treaty reform. The establishment of the European Co-ordination Group (ECG) – principally as a distribution list rather than as a meeting – further reflected the way in which Edinburgh was following the kind of arrangements which had been long-standing in the Cabinet Office (COES and the EQ network). SERAD clearly has a key role in these horizontal matters. Thirdly, in terms of ministerial portfolios, Ross Finnie was appointed the Minister for Rural Affairs: an interesting development, since he was a Liberal Democrat MSP. John Home Robertson (Labour) was appointed a Deputy to the Minister for Rural Affairs with particular responsibility for fisheries. Environmental policy, although located in SERAD, was the responsibility of the Minister for Transport and the Environment, Sarah Boyack (Labour).[191]

Ross Finnie has attended a number of Council sessions, but not as intensively as in fisheries, where John Home Robertson was reported as having attended them all by June 2000 (taking over the pattern prior to devolution).[192] When these ministers have travelled on individual visits to Brussels it has been important for them to 'clear their lines' with UKRep, so that there is no confusion. When travelling to a Council session, clearing lines has to be done with MAFF. The UKRep relationship is regarded as having worked well, with the Brussels embassy registering clearly that they represent the UK, which may not be synonymous with the UK government. One example mentioned where UKRep had been very helpful to a particular Scottish concern was on the culled ewe scheme (see below). With such contacts and the Brussels routine well established in SERAD from the pre-devolution era, no real use has been made of Scotland House. However, the launch of the new arrangements with a 'Scotland Week' did help with marketing the Scotland brand, including for food exports: a task which could hardly be expected of UKRep.

In Wales the principal change from the pre-devolution era was the creation of the post of Agriculture Secretary, thus introducing a post with exclusive responsibility for the principality's agriculture: something which did not exist previously. As will be seen, the first incumbent, Christine Gwyther, was embroiled in some of the early controversies on European policy-making in devolved Britain.

What is the view of approaching one year of the new arrangements in European agricultural policy-making? At ministerial level Nick Brown was regarded north of the border as playing his role very fairly. 'As long as he is on this side of the channel he is the minister for England; as soon as he crosses the Channel he is the minister for the UK'.[193] The overall view, in the words of the same interviewee, is that arrangements have worked 'better than expected', although that judgement was influenced by the lack of contentious policy-making issues over the period thus far. In July 2000 the quadrilateral meeting at deputy-secretary level convened to consider how the machinery has worked, as part of a review process. From the Scottish perspective the main problem had been on a small number of informational issues, including the serious one relating to contaminated rape seed (see below). There had also been some problems with announcing packages of aid for farmers but that was largely due to the involvement of the Treasury and the Prime Minister. Where the latter become involved the devolved administrations are now at a disadvantage compared to the *status quo ante*:

> We don't see the raft of Whitehall correspondence between Whitehall ministers that we used to do between colleagues in the Cabinet. All that stuff has more or less stopped. People, if they want to involve us ... have to make a conscious effort to involve us and send us a separate letter or consciously go out of their way to copy everything to us which they said they would do for a while at least ... and they tend to be a bit reluctant to do that if it's about anything controversial. And that's understandable: Mr Finnie is a Liberal Democrat.[194]

5.2.3   Testing European policy issues

As mentioned already, the agricultural policy-making issue was relatively clear of controversy in the early months of devolution in operation. This situation was slightly unusual and is unlikely to persist into the longer term. An issue such as reform of the sheepmeat regime is likely to expose the territorial politics of agriculture to a considerable degree. However, brief examination of four issues relating to policy-*implementation* will serve to reveal some aspects of the new arrangements. The following issues will be considered: the contamination of rape seed; the culled ewe scheme; the calf reprocessing scheme; and 'modulation'.

   The contaminated rape seed issue is in fact the least directly Europeanised of the issues. The specific European context is that the controlled release of genetically modified (GM) material into the environment is governed by EC directives. The case arose when Advanta Seeds, the Canadian producers, advised MAFF in mid-April 2000 that they believed some rape seed had become contaminated by genetically modified material. For reasons that are not entirely clear, but presumably relate to MAFF seeking to investigate the facts, this information was not passed on to the Welsh or Scottish administrations for about a month. The Welsh Assembly, for example, was only informed on 15 May. Secretary of State, Nick Brown, made a formal announcement in the House of Commons on 18 May. In Scotland the climate and later planting season meant that prompt advice could probably have prevented the seed being planted in the first place. By the time that the

Scottish Executive was informed, the seed had been sown, and had to be grubbed up or poisoned. Legal action has ensued in various directions, but it is clear that legal action by landowners in Scotland might have been avoided altogether if information had been passed on promptly by MAFF. Attribution of the costs faced by farmers – whether to the seed producers, central government or devolved government – was highly contentious.

The situation in Wales was similar, except compounded by a separate aspect. The latter had developed when the Department of the Environment, Transport and the Regions (DETR) allowed a trial of GM seeds to go ahead at a farm with a Chester postcode, but which was actually located in Wales. This occurrence led to the Welsh Assembly seeking to declare Wales a GM-free zone, but with legal opinion divided as to whether such action was within its powers (see Constitution Unit Wales Report 2000). Nevertheless, the cause gathered momentum and a motion to that effect gained unanimous support on 24 May. Michael German, Leader of the Liberal Democrats, is quoted as saying, 'European law, UK law, Assembly law and devolution law are all at odds on GM crops' (quoted in Constitution Unit Wales Report 2000). However, the First Secretary, Rhodri Morgan indicated that his legal advice was that the motion could not be enforced. The attempt to declare a GM-free zone was simultaneously confronted by Nick Brown's announcement in the Commons that rape seed (including that sown in Wales) had been contaminated. The consequence was that the Welsh Assembly was presented in public as being powerless, thereby adding to existing dissatisfaction at its lack of powers. Christine Gwyther, the then Agriculture Secretary in Wales, was reportedly incensed, and stated on a radio broadcast, 'The Whitehall machine does not recognise devolution … There is a mindset there that needs to be altered' (*Wales at One*, Radio Wales, 18 May quoted in Constitution Unit Wales Report 2000). The GM foods issue was regarded as the hottest political issue in the National Assembly during the second quarter of 2000. Although accusatory fingers were pointed by Welsh politicians in various directions – all in London, though! – our information is that MAFF even failed to inform the DETR in Whitehall.[195]

The culled ewe scheme arose because of a large number of grazing ewes which were virtually unsaleable (or reported in the press as sold for 1p). Calls were made in the Scottish Parliament for a subsidy to dispose of the ewes. These calls gave rise to three issues: first, who should notify the European Commission; secondly, whether such state aid could be offered to sheep farmers in conformity with EU law; and thirdly, whether it could be done only in Scotland (and Wales) and still be in conformity with Community law. MAFF and UKRep sought to facilitate the devolved administrations' attempts to get EU approval for such aid. MAFF, however, did not wish to commit the funds to put in place a similar scheme in England. The Commission's decision was that a special scheme for Scotland was not compatible with EU rules. The Rural Affairs Minister, Ross Finnie, and First Minister, Donald Dewar, then scheduled a meeting with Agriculture Commissioner Fischler to complain at the inflexibility of the rules during a Brussels visit in October 1999, coinciding with Scotland Week (Scottish Executive Press Release SE0846/ 1999).[196] Sheep farmers in Scotland and Wales were thus left with a more generalised aid scheme, agreed on a UK-wide basis.

The calf processing scheme was similar except the issue became more salient in Wales and came to a head only slightly earlier than the ewe scheme. MAFF announced that it no longer wished to assign money to the existing support scheme. The Welsh livestock industry was faced with new born calves and plummeting prices. The Welsh Assembly's Agriculture and Rural Development Subject Committee drew up a £750 000 scheme, funded from the Assembly's budget, and this was unanimously agreed on 15 September (Constitution Unit Wales Report 1999). Unfortunately, there seems to have been insufficient consideration of the legal niceties of the scheme in Cardiff beforehand. The Agriculture Secretary, Christine Gwyther, flew to Brussels expecting to bask in the reflected glory of securing such a scheme. Unfortunately, Welsh Office officials, who had been meeting the Commission before her arrival, had been told it was incompatible with EC law – again because differential schemes could not be operated within a Member State. The political fall-out from that episode was a motion of censure against Gwyther and a motion of no-confidence against Alun Michael, the then First Secretary (Constitution Unit Wales Report 1999). Neither succeeded; both led to (separate) procedural disputes about the Assembly's Standing Orders in such motions; and once again EU rules demonstrated limits to the powers of the devolved authorities. Each time MAFF's decision that it did not wish to spend its budget on these schemes left the devolved administrations in a difficult position, bearing in mind their policy preferences. But MAFF was also in a slightly difficult position. It had to argue the case on behalf of the devolved authorities for schemes that it did not want to carry out itself. MAFF's judgement from the start was that the Commission would say 'no', but it was important that somebody independent of them, i.e. UKRep, was able to express a view as well.[197] In other words, UKRep served to confirm MAFF's account, thereby limiting damage in relations between it and its devolved counterparts.

The final case relates to 'modulation'. This is a system whereby CAP funds are diverted from generalised product-support subsidies. A cut is made in the support and the money diverted into rural development expenditure: a scheme agreed as part of the Agenda 2000 CAP reforms. Here again it was necessary for MAFF and the devolved authorities to agree to the same approach to implementing policy. In this case two sets of negotiations were needed. Within Whitehall there was an *ad hoc* committee from MAFF, the DETR and the Treasury, but without the devolved authorities present. At the same time, MAFF was negotiating with the devolved administrations. As one senior official put it, 'you may ask the question why were those two negotiations not brought together and the answer is that those in the centre did not want to bring them together'.[198] This situation leads MAFF into a difficult balancing act. At the same time it reveals how the Scottish and Welsh authorities may not be privy, on a matter of concern to them, to debates under way within Whitehall. In the event, these negotiations reached a compromise, even though the sensitivity to cuts in agricultural support was potentially more politicised in Wales and Scotland than in England. But they raised problems procedurally. Nick Brown wanted to simply 'make an announcement of a big splash, major new policy ...', being certain that he could deliver a majority in Westminster:

> In Cardiff it ain't like that, because ... it is quite hard for the executive to commit itself ... it is a minority administration and, because it is a corporate body, there is no sort of question of agreeing something quietly amongst yourselves, announcing it to Parliament ... and Parliament taking note or accepting ... The Welsh have to put their proposals in draft to the Assembly. It is only when the Assembly has had a draft, had a discussion and a vote that the Welsh are in a position to say yes or no. Fitting that in with our system is quite difficult ... . You have got to find new ways of working to address those sorts of relationships.[199]

Before drawing any conclusions about the extent of institutional change that devolution has brought about, we simply make one observation on the above cases before turning to environmental policy. In each case there is evidence that the European dimension has imposed major constraints on the ability of the devolved authorities to pursue distinctive policies in the new context. Devolution may not increase the range of policy options on matters where the EU requires member state-wide solutions. Thus, an accumulation of such cases might stoke nationalist sentiment.

5.3   Environmental policy[200]

This case study is rather different in nature. Unlike with the agriculture case study, we will not look at the picture across Britain as a whole but will adopt a Scottish perspective, concentrating on changes to institutional arrangements in Edinburgh and in relations with the DETR in London.

By way of context we point out that the impact of the EU upon national environmental policy was both more recent and more contested by UK governments than with agriculture. The UK was originally seen as a 'laggard' amongst the Member States in terms of its attitudes to environmentalism (Sbragia 1996; Sharp 1998). The transformation in its position occurred in the 1990s (Sharp 1998: 37). As a legacy of this late transformation the UK's record on transposing environmental legislation has been inferior to its general performance.[201] A further point to note relates to the organisation of the UK department. The Department of the Environment (DoE), as it was known until Labour came to power in 1997, was originally a department chiefly responsible for overseeing local government and housing in England. Environmental functions accumulated in the 1980s and 1990s. The impact of the EU regarding these functions was resisted by a number of Conservative Secretaries of State, who were more concerned with domestic agenda issues, such as water privatisation, where EU intrusion would be both constraining and costly. Re-organisation of the DoE, particularly under John Gummer (1993–97), brought the co-ordination of European business into a much more central location within the department from 1995. The resultant Environment Protection Strategy and Europe Division (EPSED) was located in the Environmental Protection Group, one of three policy groups.[202] The DoE undertook this change as part of a wider European professionalism initiative (see Sharp 1998: 51–3).

This sense of focus regarding EU environmental co-ordination was challenged somewhat with the creation of the DETR, which created a much bigger 'super-ministry' under Blair's deputy, John Prescott, with five policy groups. The Department of Transport was merged in, complete with its separate European co-ordination arrangements. At the same time, Prescott's political agenda for *English* devolution gave a new focus within the DETR to the government offices in the regions, which had been set up in the 1990s to deal with urban regeneration and to make a more co-ordinated response at regional level to the opportunities afforded by the EU structural funds. In a sense, then, the DETR was developing a strengthened 'English' mission which was potentially at odds with UK devolution in such a Europeanised policy area as the environment. This situation contrasts with MAFF's well-established sensitivity to the territoriality of agricultural policy in an EU context.

Handling European environmental policy in Scotland: the status quo ante

Environmental policy was handled from within the Scottish Office Development Department until the mid-1990s, when it was merged with agriculture and fisheries (DAFS) to become SOAEFD. The traditional arrangement had been for a division amongst the SO environment officials between those engaged as policy administrators and the 'professionals', principally civil engineers. These divisions had been breaking down because of developments such as the creation of the Scottish Environment Protection Agency. The principal feature for our purposes was that there was no central oversight at all of European matters. Much of the officials' work had a European dimension but there was a lack of co-ordination. Liaison with counterparts in London was not as smooth as in agriculture, whether under Conservative or Labour governments. 'There were some examples of good links where our position was taken on board by DoE but there were other areas where, for whatever reason, we weren't consulted, we didn't know what was happening'.[203] One area of EU legislation where this arose was the Natural Habitats Directive, where the different interests of the Scots – and the wish to operationalise policy differently – were not taken into account in London until a late stage of policy-making.[204] It should also be mentioned that there was very little engagement of SO environment officials with Council working groups, with MEPs or with the Commission.

Reformed arrangements in the Scottish Executive

In April 1999, ahead of the transfer of power, the Environment Group of the SOAEFD conducted a fundamental review of its internal organisation. European policy was consequently deemed to be of central strategic importance to the Group, so it became one of three teams in the central Strategy and Co-ordination Unit. Although still only small – some 10 staff – central location in SERAD increases influence. The re-organisation reflected a number of factors:

- nearly 90 per cent of domestic environmental legislation derives from Brussels;

- under devolution all this legislation falls to the Scottish Executive for implementation and any penalties for failure to implement would fall to the authorities in Edinburgh.

These factors rammed home the need for a centrally-located unit to ensure that:

- the Executive made every effort to participate in the policy-making process; and
- that a proper monitoring system existed to oversee and co-ordinate transposition of EU law to ensure a better rate of compliance rather than relying on reminders from the DETR or piecemeal responses in Edinburgh from across the Environment Group.

In other words, the new circumstances of devolution represented both a *critical moment* and a *critical juncture* for the handling of European environmental policy in Scotland. As one official put it:

> ... we have established that there are all these infractions – and there are quite a few – and we have said 'This is a result, a legacy, an inheritance from previous policies, previous incoherence within, between the different divisions' and we are at the position where we can say 'OK we are in this mess but we have got to get out of it'. It is not good to have these infractions. We want to be compliant and indeed the Scotland Act obliges us to comply with European law, so we have to do everything we can to ensure that we do that.[205]

A separate point worth mentioning is that environmental officials in SERAD – as doubtless elsewhere within the Executive – are having to accommodate themselves to the presence of a minister located in their own building with a closer day-to-day interest in their work than in the pre-devolution era. Scottish Office ministers were in London for four days a week when Parliament was in session.

The Europe Team, as it is known, sees its basic task post-devolution as promoting Scotland's interest in European environmental matters. It seeks to do this through making an impact upon the key EU institutions. First, it tries to get the minister involved in meetings of the Council of Environment Ministers.[206] Our information relates to the period of Donald Dewar's leadership as First Minister, when Sarah Boyack (Labour) was Minister for Transport and the Environment.[207] There has been a marked increase in attendance compared to the situation when

Lord Sewel was Labour Scottish Office minister with environmental responsibilities.[208] Secondly, recognising the importance of the co-decision procedure in EU environmental policy-making following the Amsterdam Treaty's implementation in May 1999, the Team also seeks to brief Scottish MEPs on pending legislation. Thirdly, it seeks to ensure that contacts are maintained with the Commission, for instance through meetings between Sarah Boyack and the Commissioner for the Environment, Margot Wallström,[209] but also through supporting staff secondments or *stages* in Brussels from across the Environment Group.[210] Encouragement is also offered to Scottish officials to attend one or two meetings of Council working groups to see how policy-making works. The head of the Europe Team has also taken a study group of environment policy officials from SERAD to Brussels for training purposes.

The Europe Team does not generally deal with the detail of policy; that is for the relevant 'technical' policy unit, such as air/climate engineering. However, it is responsible for contributing to policy debates on very wide issues, such as EU treaty reform, through the European Co-ordination Group (ECG) run from the Executive Secretariat at the heart of the Scottish Executive. The Europe Team is also responsible for those environmental policy issues that cut across policy units within the Environment Group, notably the periodic EU Environmental Action Programmes. In addition, it has responsibility for liaising with the Holyrood on parliamentary questions, scrutiny and other committee work of a general nature on EU environmental policy. Finally, it is responsible for overseeing transposition of EU law and attending to any infraction proceedings that the Commission may launch on such matters (although they would be directed to Whitehall as the Member State government). To this end it has set up a database to track compliance – whether by means of Scottish primary or secondary legislation – with all EU obligations. Co-ordination with other interested parties from Whitehall and elsewhere on infraction proceedings continues through the EQ(O)L network of lawyers working on EU policy. But there is an important change in that these meetings do not take that formal designation but are re-badged '*ad hocs*', because of the participation of officials from outside the UK government.

A noticeable contrast between environmental and agricultural policies lies in the nature of contacts with the UK counterpart department. Whereas in agriculture there were long-standing territorial arrangements, strengthened at senior official and ministerial level by the BSE crisis, such arrangements scarcely existed on environmental policy. Contacts tended to be much more *ad hoc* and based on personal relationships. Post-devolution the contacts still tend to be bilateral rather than quadrilateral as in agriculture. In large part this is due to the Scottish Executive being the biggest of the devolved administrations.

The specific concordat on bilateral arrangements covers the whole of the DETR's responsibilities and therefore goes beyond the Environment Group in SERAD to include other matters handled in the Scottish Executive's Development Department (DETR/SE Concordat 1999). The tone of this concordat is one of the DETR defending its formal rights and is rather different from that of the agriculture concordat, where there is more of a feel of codification of existing practices. The impression one gains from SERAD's Environment Group is that they place more emphasis on the EU Concordat. However, the DETR bilateral concordat does make clear that there must be full consultation of the Scottish Executive on EU business where, beforehand, that tended to be rather haphazard. It is perhaps not surprising, in view of this change of emphasis, that the Environment Group has considered it important to play a full role in the DETR's devolution seminars to 'educate' DETR officials. It appears that relations on European environmental policy are beginning to develop pragmatically along the lines of the various concordats. Nevertheless, the DETR's devolution unit – which is neither concerned exclusively with environmental policy nor with European policy – has taken a rather more formalistic view of relations with the Scottish Executive. This view lays it open to the charge that the DETR is insufficiently differentiating between its role and culture as an English ministry, on the one hand, and its UK-wide responsibilities in negotiating European environmental policy, on the other.

It is perhaps indicative of the way in which devolution has forced environmental policy-makers to *start* coming to terms with the territoriality of the policy area that the bilateral concordat makes little reference to the nature of meetings between the two tiers of government. Unlike the arrangements specified for agriculture, and based on developed practice, there is no explicit provision in the DETR concordat for regular meetings of ministers or senior officials. In this respect the concordat is unspecific; stating for instance in para. 28 that 'DETR and the Executive may set up joint working groups or committees where appropriate'. The only specific forum referred to is the JMC, but it had not been used by June 2000 on environmental matters. In reality there have been meetings twice a year between officials, with the Head of the Environment Group in SERAD meeting his counterpart in London and others from the DETR. These meetings have been concerned with such issues as who pays for regulatory impact assessments of EU legislation. There are no regular ministerial meetings. One senior insider in SERAD, comparing its relationship with DETR to that with MAFF, said: 'the relationship is considerably more difficult'. Comparing the situation with agriculture the same official remarked:

> one of the things that ... we are seeing in MAFF, what they are trying to do ... is trying to work out the UK versus the English role. You wouldn't expect to see a similar thing happening in DETR because they are coming from the opposite spectrum, as it were, as almost a department that has been more comfortable with its English role as opposed to its UK one.

It is also interesting to note that SERAD's Environment Group makes more use of the Scottish Executive's office in Brussels, Scotland House. One of the four officials employed by the Executive includes environment within his brief, and is charged with following a small number of dossiers in this policy area, including liasing on them with the EP. It will be recalled that on the agriculture side of SERAD little use is made of Scotland House because of lengthy experience of the 'disciplined hierarchy' of UKRep. Here again we find the Environment Group taking advantage of devolution to develop new patterns of work.

5.4   Conclusion: continuity or change?

What can we conclude from these two policy cases? How can we analyse the extent of change using the framework set out in Chapter 1?

Within the *systemic* dimension both policy areas have experienced fundamental change. The political leaderships in Edinburgh and Cardiff are not the same as in London. This is highlighted by the presence of a Liberal Democrat Minister for Rural Affairs in Scotland. The party-political dimension has begun to play a significant role in the new territorial politics of European policy. The unstable constitutional arrangements in Wales combined with the party dimension to have a significant impact, both on trying to find new working arrangements and on particular issues such as the calf processing scheme. It is worth underlining that, with Labour in office nationally and the dominant governing party in both Edinburgh and Cardiff, the present circumstances are relatively benign. A more variegated set of parties in power would be likely to present a more politicised European policy process.

Within the *organisational* dimension agricultural policy-making has experienced minimal change in Scotland. There was virtually a seamless transition between SOAEFD and SERAD in agricultural policy. The main change came from new accountability mechanisms to Holyrood. In Cardiff the organisational changes were not significant at official level. However, the unitary status of the Welsh Assembly has led to a protracted period of getting used to a new constitutional situation compounded by a minority administration. In MAFF, where the territorial nature of European agricultural policy was recognised, the organisational changes have also been negligible. By contrast, in environmental policy SERAD has witnessed a fundamental re-organisation. Here change has been very significant. Devolution prompted a re-think of how European environmental policy is handled.

Change in the *process-related* (or *procedural*) dimension has been quite small. Many of the practices present in the pre-existing 'territorial politics' of agricultural policy have simply been adjusted or re-badged. The mechanisms for dispute-resolution through the JMC have not been tested, although these are still early days. The lack of access for the devolved administrations to papers on the *intra-Whitehall* policy debate is perhaps the major change. On the basis of the case studies, once again it is arguably in the Scottish Executive's approach to EU environmental policy-making that there has been greatest change. Devolution has prompted a reappraisal of the processes utilised in the triangular relationship between Edinburgh London and Brussels. By contrast, in agriculture the processes were already well established and simply needed to be adapted to the new constitutional framework.

Within the *regulative* dimension the drafting of concordats covering European business as well as the MAFF and DETR bilateral concordats have been the main items of activity. For agriculture, '...the [MAFF/SE] concordat largely represents the writing down of an arrangement that existed before devolution and continues after devolution'.[211] The Welsh concordat, by contrast, has had to factor in the novel nature of the Assembly's character. For environmental policy, by contrast, the bilateral concordat rather uneasily acknowledges the need to gear up for a new pattern of territorial politics that is less haphazard than in the past. In this sense there is an attempt to innovate. Moreover, within SERAD the mechanisms for monitoring compliance with European law as well as the development of a new, strategic capacity represent significant innovation triggered by devolution.

Finally, we can only make some preliminary observations with regard to the *cultural* dimension, since change is inevitably slower and conditioned by the continued existence of a unified civil service. It is clear that new adjustments are having to be made in MAFF to try to recognise that it is an English department which acts on behalf of the UK in EU negotiations. The informal designation of Joyce Quin as minister for England is one expression of this situation. This kind of step represents an attempt to separate out roles within a Department which has been conscious of the territorial dimension of agricultural policy for a long time. However, the DETR is having to adjust to a more explicit requirement to take account of the territoriality of European environmental policy. At the same time, the Environment Group of SERAD has taken the occasion of devolution to introduce the kind of European professionalisation process that John Gummer had introduced into the DoE in the mid-1990s. How far these cultural adjustments in the DETR and the Environment Group will go requires longer-term observation.

In summary, therefore, our study of agriculture demonstrates quite a measure of continuity in policy machinery, albeit in a new constitutional context with the potential for greater change in a different political climate. But we must underline once again the large measure of continuity has been facilitated by the predominance of the Labour Party at UK and sub-national levels. The continuity in the way policy-making has operated is contingent on these politically benign circumstances. Without them the machinery *might well* operate rather differently: relations between ministers/secretaries might become more fraught; and information-sharing between officials might become more politically contingent. However, this scenario remains for the future. By contrast with agriculture, our analysis of environmental policy in Scotland reveals that devolution has prompted a significant reorganisation of machinery at official level. Relations with the DETR are undergoing something of a rebalancing. And, again, this is under benign party-political circumstances.

6
Relations between the Devolved Administrations and the European Union

6.1 Introduction

In this chapter we report on the considerations which were influential in designing new representative offices to act for the devolved administrations in Brussels. We depart from the approach taken in previous chapters of attempting to integrate the Scottish and Welsh stories within a common chronological framework, instead focusing on each separate administration in turn. Documenting developments in this way helps to illustrate and account for the different paths of development followed in Scotland and Wales in establishing their representative offices. Both this development and the role to be played by each office within the newly devolved system of governance strongly reflect the constitutional asymmetry of the devolution settlement.

Both the Scottish and the Welsh devolution White Papers anticipated that the devolved administrations would develop independent representative offices in Brussels (see Table 1.4, Chapter 1). Their aim would be to provide an additional source of information and advice to the devolved administrations, although their activities would not compromise in any way the authority of the UK Permanent Representation (UKRep) as speaking for the UK government on European matters. By the same token, the creation of European offices of the devolved administrations would not lead to any change in the practice of assigning officials from the territorial administrations to UKRep.[212] Once devolution had been implemented, the issue of a Brussels-based representation for the devolved administrations was addressed in the Memorandum of Understanding (MoU) and supplementary agreements, part B4: Co-ordination of European Policy

Issues: Common Annex:

B4.26   The status and functions of the UK Permanent Representation in Brussels as the institution representing the United Kingdom within the European Union will continue unchanged.

B4.27   The devolved administrations will be able to take part in the less formal discussions with the institutions of the EU and interests within other Member States. Subject to paragraph B4.26 above, the devolved administrations may choose to establish an office in Brussels, to assist direct relationships with other regional governments and with the institutions of the European Communities, so far as this serves the exercise of their powers and the performance of their functions as laid down in the devolution legislation and so far as it is consistent with the responsibility of the UK Government for relations with the EU. If such an office is established, it will work closely with, and in a manner complementary to, UKRep which remains responsible for representing the view of the United Kingdom to the European Institutions, and will respect the responsibility of the UK Government for non-devolved areas, including overall responsibility for relations with the EU. Both UKRep and any office of the devolved administrations will develop working procedures which reflect the need to balance the interests of all parts of the UK.

6.2   Scotland

6.2.1   Preparations

Establishing a Scottish Executive representative office in Brussels – SE (Brussels) – following devolution was recognised in the White Paper as being a likely – though not an inevitable – outcome (SO 1997: point 5.10). Accordingly, as part of the process of preparing for devolution, the Scottish Office initiated a review of the different types of regional representation already existing in Brussels to guide an incoming Scottish Executive when designing its own representative office. The evaluation was conducted by two Scottish Office officials seconded to UKRep, and their conclusions were reported back to the Scottish Office in Autumn, 1998. The starting position in conducting this review was stated in Annex 3 of the resulting Scottish Office Consultation Paper circulated in September 1988:

UKRep will continue to represent the UK in Brussels, however the Scottish Executive will be invited to decide in due course whether and how it wishes to be represented in Brussels ... Options for a Scottish Executive Representation in Brussels are currently being evaluated.

In considering the shape of SE (Brussels), account had to be taken of two factors. First, as matters stood, SE (Brussels) would co-exist with Scotland Europa Ltd (SEL), created in 1992 and, by now, widely viewed as *the* 'voice' of Scotland in Brussels. On the assumption that SEL would continue, a clear division of tasks between the two organisations needed to be agreed. Second, because UK European policy was a reserved matter, the activities of SE (Brussels) had to dovetail with those of UKRep which retained the sole authority to articulate the UK government's European Union policy line in Brussels.[213] Certainly it was taken as a given that the devolved administrations must do nothing to challenge the role or integrity of UKRep. Not only would this violate the constitutional settlement which reserved EU policy to the UK government, but public divisions in the UK European policy position might weaken the UK's overall negotiating strength within the EU – to the possible disadvantage of all parts of the UK.

Scotland Europa Ltd

Scotland Europa Ltd was established in 1992 as a 'joint venture' between Scottish Enterprise and a range of Scotland-based public and private bodies.[214] Its broad remit is to promote Scottish interests in the EU, and to develop links with regional representations from other countries. Since its inception, SEL has developed a capacity in five areas:[215]

- intelligence-gathering, and information dissemination, for members;
- facilitating EU project funding opportunities;
- promoting Scotland's regional interests;
- informing EU policy development from a Scottish perspective; and
- providing a Scottish focal point in Brussels.

With devolution, some of these functions might properly be assumed by SE (Brussels), although others clearly lay outside the scope of a government department to perform. In the light of this, SEL undertook a review (running parallel to the Scottish Office review) as to how its activities would change once devolution took effect.[216] It was realised that devolution would bring with it a need for a type of governmental (including diplomatic) representation in Brussels which SEL – given its essentially 'quango' nature – could not discharge.

UKRep

Defining a working relationship (including a division of tasks) between SE (Brussels) and UKRep was regarded in some quarters as particularly problematic. On the one hand, it was clear that this relationship must do nothing to compromise the integrity of UKRep as the sole voice of UK government European policy within the EU institutions. Consequently, SE (Brussels) could not become – or be seen as becoming – a detached (from the UK), or a political, voice of 'Scotland in Europe'. On the other hand, SE (Brussels) had to serve the distinctive interests of a devolved administration whose legislative authority included many policies which were substantially affected by EU legislation. SE (Brussels) had to provide some domestic 'value added' over and above that available through UKRep, especially given the high profile of EU matters in the Scottish economic and political landscape.

6.2.2   The role of SE (Brussels)

The evaluative exercise conducted by the Scottish Office focused on four aspects of SE (Brussels): (i) its role and its relationship with UKRep; (ii) its relationship with Scotland Europa; (iii) interaction with the EU institutions; (iv) links with other regional representations in Brussels.[217]

The relationship with UKRep

The Scottish Office paper provided an overview and an analysis of the different types of Brussels-based regional representation from which a future Scottish Executive might draw lessons.[218] Clearly, the sheer diversity of national constitutional provisions regarding the position regions occupied in Member State policy-processes meant that this type of comparative exercise could provide only broad pointers to the role that SE (Brussels) could play following devolution.[219] However, the exercise did demonstrate the extent to which regional representations had become an integral feature of the Brussels policy landscape.

The review indicated that the question of the relationship between regional and national representations had been a source of tension for most member states as the trend towards Brussels-based regional offices had gathered pace during the 1980s. This seems to have reflected a widespread concern on the part of Member States that their bargaining strength might be weakened should sub-national authorities publicly depart from the national position on putative EU policy. At the same time, the increasingly important economic stake that regions had in the EU policy process along with the often strong domestic 'voice' given to regions by Member State constitutional structures, had persuaded most national governments of the need to take on board the views of their regions when formulating a national position on EU policy matters. Accordingly, in most EU Member States, regional interests with respect to EU policies were articulated through *domestic* administrative arrangements, typically involving direct regional representation in the Member State capital.[220] In these cases, the role of Brussels-based regional representations was to provide briefings to their home regional authorities on EU policy developments to assist them to contribute in the formulation of the national position. Because regional authorities generally could input to their national European policy-process, regional representations in Brussels had no reason to depart from the line advanced by the permanent representation. Nor did they, as a rule, engage in direct representation to the EU institutions (including the Commission) although they did generally have close contact with all institutions (particularly the Commission), consistent with their responsibilities to their home authorities.

On the basis of their study, the Scottish Office review concluded that there were two fundamental requirements to ensure that a region has an effective role in the national policy-making process;

- The region should have a presence in the Member State capital, or an effective route into negotiations there, to ensure that its voice is heard in the formulation of the national line.
- The region's Brussels office must be well supported from within the region to ensure that information acquired can readily be passed to the regional administration to be used in negotiations with national authorities.

Crucially, there was no reason either in principle or on the basis of the review conducted, to suppose that SE (Brussels) could not engage constructively and co-operatively with UKRep, without in any way compromising any aspect of its activities.

The relationship with Scotland Europa Ltd

Establishing SE (Brussels) would have consequences for the Scotland Europa organisation. Two specific issues were examined: first, the extent to which SE (Brussels) would assume some activities hitherto undertaken by Scotland Europa Ltd (SEL); second, the impact of SE (Brussels) on the Scotland Europa Centre (SEC) as the 'voice' of Scotland in Brussels.

In part, the activities of SEL are shaped by the needs of its membership. These include: the provision of information to its membership;

assisting with (though not engaging in) lobbying; intelligence gathering with respect to EU funding opportunities; contributing to EU policy debates; and developing relationships with other regional representations. In functional terms, only the 'ambassadorial' role of SEL was likely to be wholly supplanted by SE (Brussels),[221] although parts of other functions ultimately might sit more easily with an office of the Scottish Executive than with SEL. At the same time it was clear from the outset that SEL activities linked to the private sector could not properly be undertaken by an office of the Executive – for example, promoting specific economic and business interests within the EU.[222] Beyond this, SEL would continue to service the needs of the non-governmental aspects of the Scottish public sector. However, the role of providing a Scottish perspective on EU policy developments, along with taking responsibility for broader Scottish representational activities would, with devolution, default to SE (Brussels).

The SEC in Brussels is also landlord to a number of resident organisations from Scotland which pursue their own interests – e.g. the Convention of Scottish Local Authorities (COSLA), local authorities, private consultancies and a legal firm. While no formal link exists between SEL and the tenant organisations using SEC, SEL was conceived partly to provide a common base for various Scottish interests so as to raise the profile and strengthen the influence of each. This locational synergy aspect of the arrangement would be weakened if SE (Brussels) were to be located outside the SEC structure. Accordingly, from early in the review the possibility of co-location between SEL and the SEC office was mooted and, in the event, decided upon.[223]

SE (Brussels) and the EU institutions

SE (Brussels) was expected to be a focus for facilitating contact between the Scottish Executive and the EU institutions. Potential activities fell into one of two broad categories – policy oriented and diplomacy.

The policy-oriented aspect reflected the significant EU policy element to the devolved competencies, and involved principally official-level contacts between the Scottish Executive and the European Commission. Of course, this was not a new situation. The Scottish Office had, over many years, developed close contacts with the Directorates-General with responsibility for policies that directly impinged on Scotland's economic and social interests. These contacts played a key role in shaping the Scottish Office input to the UK's response to EU proposals. With devolution, Scotland's voice in UK European policy inevitably would gravitate to the Scottish Executive and not – or not *principally* – be retained by the Secretary of State for Scotland. This simply reflected the post-devolution situation where many of the competencies assigned to the Executive were characterised by a substantial EU element. The expectation was that much of Scotland's EU policy business would continue to be conducted as before (albeit these would become inter- rather than intra-administration business). SE (Brussels) would provide support to particular departments in the Executive where this was necessary,[224] and support any new Brussels-based functions required by the Executive, e.g. on implementation of EC law, advising on European policy, and responding to Scottish Parliamentary debates and questions.

Beyond this, the Scottish Office review identified a number of ancillary functions that SE (Brussels) could discharge. These included liaison with Scottish MEPs; supporting the work of Scottish members of ECOSOC[225] and the Committee of the Regions (CoR);[226] attending working groups of the Council of Ministers where a matter of acute importance to Scotland's interests is under discussion and where there is no other significant UK interest; facilitating contact with other UK devolved representations; and providing access to various Brussels-based regional networks to the extent that their aims are consistent with Scotland's interests.

Networking with other regional representations

SE (Brussels) would be a focus for Scotland to develop links with other EU regions. Hitherto, SEL had regarded this as within its remit. However, with devolution this role would logically fall to the Scottish Executive.

6.2.3   Establishing Scotland House

In the Autumn of 1998 the results of the Scottish Office work were sent to Scottish Office management, and then on to ministers. The outcome was the creation of Scotland House. On 9 February 1999, Donald Dewar – then Secretary of State for Scotland – announced in a speech to Members of the European Parliament (MEPs) that SE (Brussels) would co-locate with SEL, the COSLA and the other SEL residents in a new centre to be called Scotland House. He stated that:

> The office will assist the Executive in supporting the European responsibilities of the Scottish Parliament. It will provide information to facilitate scrutiny of European legislation; it will assist visits to Brussels by Parliamentary Committees … it will ensure that the Scottish dimension is fed in early as European proposals are being formulated. It will work to build links with other European regions and their Member States.

The Scottish Executive office in Brussels needs to work in an open and co-operative way with the UK's Permanent Representation. UKRep will remain responsible for representing the views of the UK Government to the European Institutions … it will continue to represent all of the UK's interests there, including Scotland.

In conclusion, Dewar stressed that devolution would give a new strength to Scotland in the arena of UK European policy-making. Moreover, he insisted that this would strengthen the position of the UK within Europe.

It is certainly my expectation that Scotland will play an important role, in areas where power is devolved, in developing UK policy positions and then presenting them and discussing them with our European partners.[227]

6.2.4   Post-devolution SE (Brussels)

SE (Brussels) is an integral part of the Executive Secretariat (External) of the Scottish Executive, and it reports directly to the head of the Executive Secretariat. It opened on 1 July 1999, coinciding with the formal opening of the Scottish Parliament in Edinburgh. SE (Brussel)'s operation is evolving in two general areas: policy and representational. With respect to policy issues, two principal responsibilities have been identified: to keep ministers and officials abreast of developments in Brussels, and to offer support and advice to the Scottish Executive.[228] Representational responsibilities, as described on the SE (Brussels) web page, are: to assist in influencing EU decision-making; and to raise Scotland's profile in the EU.[229] SE (Brussels) is headed by a senior official from the Scottish Executive (Mr George Calder) and his staff of five – three of whom are policy advisers with responsibility for particular EU policy areas of particular relevance to Scotland – (i) agriculture, fisheries and industrial matters; (ii) regional and social funding, research and development, and education policies; (iii) environmental, transport and legal matters (including police co-operation).[230]

Although a formal part of the Scottish Executive governance machinery, SE (Brussels) has also been described as '…part of the UKRep family'.[231] And while this may appear to place it in a somewhat ambiguous position – potentially serving two political 'masters' – it conforms precisely to the situation which was envisaged in the MoU[232] thereby avoiding SE (Brussels) being misconstrued as representing a separate (to the UK) 'voice' of the Scottish Executive in Brussels. Accordingly, although reporting directly to the Scottish Executive, and to the Minister within the Executive with responsibility for Europe,[233] SE (Brussels) works alongside UKRep in promoting general UK European policy interests in Brussels. Because the domestic UK European policy process should, as a matter of course, reflect the interests of the devolved administrations, the position advanced by UKRep will be that agreed upon in discussions between, inter alia, UK government and officials and ministers from the devolved administrations.[234] In that way, the activities of SE (Brussels) should never be in conflict with those of UKRep – rather, the objectives of SE (Brussels) and UKRep will remain congruent.

SE (Brussels) therefore operates within the remit of negotiated and agreed UK European policy, while at the same time providing specific advice to the Scottish Executive in areas where devolved competencies interact with EU policy.[235] Not only does this ensure that the Scottish Executive is properly informed when going into EU policy discussions with UK government, it also ensures that officials in Edinburgh are kept informed about developments in relevant policy portfolios.

It is this combination of overlapping powers (between devolved competencies and EU policy) in conjunction with the significant territorial dimension to UK European policy-making, which in sectors such as fisheries and agriculture is considerable, that provides the fundamental rationale for the creation of SE (Brussels). The role of SE (Brussels) will vary from policy to policy. In some policy areas – for instance agriculture and fisheries, and structural funds – the former Scottish Office had, over many years, acquired considerable EU-related expertise and had established close links with counterpart officials both in Whitehall and the European Commission. In these areas the policy process tends to continue as previously, with much of the day-to-day Brussels-related business continuing to be handled bilaterally by officials in the relevant departments.[236] In other policy areas, where there is less home-based experience and/or resources available, SE (Brussels) may expect to play a more significant role in briefing counterparts in Edinburgh, and taking a lead on initiating a debate within the relevant Scottish Executive department, e.g. on environment policy (see Chapter 5).[237] This may be a reflection of prior practice, where Whitehall may not previously have involved the territorial administrations in the UK European policy process. Alternatively, it may be indicative of a previous decision not to devote Scottish Office resources to that policy area because of its marginal importance to Scotland.

So, although much of the work of SE (Brussels) is determined by the needs of the officials within the Executive – i.e. it is 'customer-driven' – it also has a role to play in initiating debate within the Executive in 'new' policy areas (e.g. the EU White Paper on Governance), and in bringing to the Executive's attention prospective EU policy debates that have implications for Scotland (e.g. treaty reform). As an integral part of the Executive Secretariat, SE (Brussels) utilises the normal communications machinery available to that Secretariat. Counterpart officials in Scotland are housed in the External division of the Executive Secretariat (covering European and international matters), and it is with those officials that SE (Brussels) liaises on a day-to-day basis. Further, SE (Brussels) has access to all information flowing between UK government and the Scottish Executive, including telegrams from and meetings convened within UKRep. Relations between UKRep and SE (Brussels) are covered by the relevant concordats – particularly the MoU and inter-departmental concordats when referring to EU policy issues.

SE (Brussels) also has a broader – almost ambassadorial – remit to establish contact with other regional representations and promote the general interests of Scotland to the wider community. In this guise it appears to have enjoyed considerable success. The model of Scotland House is one that has been admired by other regional delegations – a model which involves the sharing of certain resources (e.g. accommodation) by different and distinctive organisations each of which is representing some economic and/or societal aspect of Scotland. It was suggested to us that visitors to Scotland House are, subconsciously, exposed to a 'Scottish experience' the totality of which is greater than any single organisation acting alone could deliver. At the same time, of course, each organisation retains its own identity and integrity – clearly a requisite when one of the organisations concerned is a department of the Scottish Executive.

The evidence drawn from interviews suggests that SE (Brussels) has emerged as an effective and important element in the devolution arrangements. That it was a necessary adjunct to devolution is unquestionably the case. What has become clear since SE (Brussels) was established is that it has forged a constructive and mutually advantageous relationship with UKRep, while at the same time serving an increasingly important function within the domestic decisional structures. That it would succeed in these endeavours was not self-evident at the outset. However, with respect to UKRep, it is clear that both SE (Brussels) and UKRep wanted the relationship to be a successful one and that there was much goodwill and determination to make a success of matters between the offices from the very outset. With regard to domestic issues, SE (Brussels) is a key resource shared by all departments within the Scottish Executive and is likely to become more important in this role over time. As the Scottish Parliament matures and the EU dimension of Scotland's politics becomes more important, SE (Brussels) is likely to experience ever greater pressure on its currently modest resources.

6.3   Wales

6.3.1   Relations between Wales and the institutions of the EU prior to devolution

Formal institutional links

Prior to devolution, the Welsh Office carried out formal relations with the main EU executive body, the European Commission. The European Affairs Division (EAD(WO)) of the Welsh Office was responsible for European business and for maintaining relations with UKRep. Generally, the potential for a distinctively Welsh input to EU business through these formal channels had been underused. The Welsh Affairs Select Committee at Westminster (1995) reported that even where the Secretary of State for Wales had had the right to attend sittings of the Council of Ministers, this had rarely been exercised. Also, contact between the Welsh Office and UKRep had been limited, in part by lack of resources at the Welsh Office. There are indications that a Wales–Brussels link was more actively promoted through Wales's elected representatives in Brussels than through these formal and central routes. Policy actors in Wales had come to see Welsh MEPs as more important for future development in Wales than the Welsh MPs at Westminster (Loughlin 1997). In contrast, on the grounds of its institutional limitations, the CoR was not highly rated as an effective channel of Welsh local and regional interests.

Welsh representative organisations and agencies

In 1992, the Wales European Centre (WEC) was established by the Welsh Development Agency (WDA) and local authorities to promote the interests of Welsh-based organisations in Brussels. The WEC partnership has widened considerably in recent years to include most public sector organisations active in economic development and training, voluntary organisations and unions.[238] The WEC has developed a capacity in the following areas:

- extensive EU policy expertise/consultation;
- disseminating information on current EU programmes;
- maintaining contacts with the European Commission and the EP (particularly committee chairs and group co-ordinators);

- networking and arranging contacts with organisations based in other Member States;
- supporting Welsh delegations and members on the Committee of the Regions; and
- providing a Welsh focal point in Brussels by organising profile-raising events and activities, the WEC perceives itself as representing 'Team Wales'.[239]

Founded in 1995, the Wales Commercial Centre (WCC) is directly oriented to the Welsh business community. The WCC is a local office of the International Division of the WDA. It represents the Welsh private sector in Brussels, assisting Welsh firms in establishing business contacts in the EU (WDA 1998; NAWRP EAC EUR-02-99, Annex A). By promoting business opportunities offered through EU programmes to aid the restructuring of eastern European economies, the WCC has actively engaged the Welsh business community in wider EU concerns such as future enlargement and the consolidation of a pan-European economic community (WDA 1996). The WCC has been co-located with the WEC since June 1999, but remains a separate structure (NAWRP, EAC EUR-02-99: Annex A).

The involvement of Wales as a recipient region in EU funding processes has progressively enhanced the role of Welsh organisations, particularly the WDA, as *direct* – if informal – actors in EU politics. It has simultaneously involved Welsh organisations in links with EU Member State regions with similar problems and policy concerns. The WDA has participated, along with partner organisations from Austria, Eire and Italy, in the EU's 'Strategic Adaptation to a Global Economy' programme for Member States awarded grants from the Structural Funds and designed to promote sustainable and innovative economic development. Similarly, it has been involved in the EU's 'Intelligent Region' programme to promote collaboration between development agencies and university researchers to further regional economic growth. Welsh organisations, with their counterparts in other Member States, participate in parallel regional projects aiming to stimulate social and economic change through new technologies. In Wales, significant projects in this field have been the Wales Regional Technology Plan and the 'Wales Information Society' programme (Thompson 1999: 314).

The 'Wales in Europe' movement and the devolution debate

The cultural dimension had been particularly significant in Wales–EU relations prior to devolution. From the late 1980s onwards, a growing pro-EU lobby of politicians and business interests had been working outwith the formal and organisational channels noted above to establish a more autonomous Welsh influence on EU politics. Such groups were encouraged by the increasing availability of funding under various EU programmes. In addition, there was a growing recognition of the EU as a decisive forum in policy-making, particularly in economic affairs (Gray and Osmond 1997: 7; Thompson 1999: 310). During a period of uncertain central government support, EU funding made a significant contribution to the economic restructuring of areas in economic decline, particularly the South Wales Valleys, and shored up the ailing agricultural sector based in West Wales. Between 1988 and 1993 Wales received nearly £300 million in EC/EU grants (Commission of the European Communities 1998; Thompson 1999: 313). By 2000, Wales anticipated awards of over £1 billion from the EU Structural Funds alone (Gray and Osmond 1997). To these economic considerations was added a party political incentive for a more Euro-centric approach to the pursuit of Welsh policy interests. From 1979 until 1997, the Labour Party, Plaid Cymru and the Liberal Democrats all wanted to find means of checking the Conservative domination of Welsh politics through central government. This shared interest was to develop into a cross-party lobby for establishing a Welsh Assembly that could effectively side-step Westminster and promote Welsh interests in the increasingly significant context of EU politics. In this way, an early link was forged between the Welsh devolution project and the Welsh pro-Europe lobby located outside the Whitehall–Welsh Office axis. Party political and business initiatives for devolution in Wales were firmly rooted in the wider context of European integration and European policy-making.

Such organisations were successful in promoting an autonomous Welsh profile in the EU and – perhaps inevitably – clashed with UK central government over the question of competencies. In 1994, John Redwood, the Conservative Secretary of State for Wales, berated the WDA over its slogan 'Wales in Europe', reminding the WDA that Wales had no official status in the EU independent of the UK. Even so, the 'Wales in Europe' concept went from strength to strength from the late 1980s onwards, entering the political vocabulary of all the main political parties (Osmond 1997) and the general discourse on devolution in Wales. The Welsh pro-Europe lobby succeeded in giving priority to Welsh–European concerns in the Labour government's White Paper *A Voice for Wales* (1997), in which it was asserted that devolution would bring people in Wales a 'strong voice in Europe'.

6.3.2 Preparing for devolution: July 1998–June 1999

Relations between the National Assembly for Wales and the EU

The regional interest in an autonomous Welsh input into EU politics was not reflected in the formal documents establishing devolution. The fact that the UK would retain its status as Member State of the EU meant that there could be no *formal* relations between the National Assembly for Wales (NAW) and the EU.[240] The Government of Wales Act (1998) noted the Assembly's European obligations, but contained no direct reference to the role of the Welsh Assembly in the EU and made no specific mention of a future Welsh representation in Brussels. Nevertheless, the Act outlined NAW's responsibility for devolved matters, many of which are affected by European policy. The legislative framework for devolution meant that, in order to carry out its functions, NAW would have to forge informal links with the EU consistent with the pre-existing formal structures for Wales–EU relations noted above. Consistent with the Government of Wales Act, the Transfer of Functions Order did not give high priority to the EU context. In forging the necessary informal links, then, the Welsh Office/NAW would have to refer back to the White Paper for guidance.

Capacity-building

The approach adopted by the Welsh Office with respect to the future Welsh Representation in Brussels contrasted strongly with the pro-active approach adopted by the Scottish Office. The reasons for this mirrored other areas we have examined. These were: severely constrained resources which limited Welsh Office attention to those tasks immediately required by law; and a point of principle: that capacity building as well as procedural matters should be left to regulation by the new Assembly.[241]

A consultative European Strategy Group (ESG) was established under Hywel Ceri Jones's chairmanship to report on the future handling of European matters and published a report at the end of 1998 (ESG 1998). The ESG's recommendations with respect to Wales–Brussels links centred on (paragraphs cited are from ESG Report):

- The maintenance of annual visits between the First Secretary and Secretary for Europe and other key Assembly personnel and senior representatives of the EU institutions (para. 4.8).
- The active participation of members of the CoR and ECOSOC in the Wales European Forum and in providing information to the European Affairs Committee of the Welsh Assembly (paras 11.1, 10.3).

- The establishment of European Team with a core of policy staff suitably qualified to build relations with the EU (para. 4.54).

- The maintenance of active links between the Assembly and local institutions and organisations with other regions of the UK, particularly Scotland and Northern Ireland, and with other regions of the EU (paras 13.1, 13.2, 14.1, 14.3).

- A more strategic use of Assembly secondees to European institutions. In particular, the Assembly should second staff to UKRep and should establish a small core of staff within this institution; and also second staff to Directorates General within the Commission (paras 4.55, 6.3, 8.3, 8.5).

- Co-ordination of local organisations and institutions, particularly the WDA, in seeking EU funding and in seeking co-operative ventures with applicant states (paras 15.1, 15.2, 15.3, 16.3, 4.47, 4.48, 4.51) (NAWRP, EAC Eur-01-99: p. 1; EAC Eur-03-99: p. 3).

- The joint establishment of a 'Ty Cymru' (Wales Centre) by the Assembly and the members of the WEC and the development of its functions to promote a Team-Wales presence in Brussels (paras 17.1, 17.3, 17.4, 17.5).

In the months leading up to the transfer of functions, the Welsh Office made no pre-emptive provision concerning the agencies, structures, procedures and conventions which would together form the conduit for the future Welsh Assembly's dealings with EU institutions, representations and Member States. Nevertheless, the Welsh Office anticipated the establishment of a Welsh Representation in Brussels and, as a starting point, envisaged that it might be founded on the pre-existing organisational framework of the WEC.[242] Unlike the case with Scotland, then, the Welsh representation was not initially expected to be founded separately from the WEC, but instead to merge with it to create a new, multi-faceted single organisational base for the representation of Welsh interests in Europe.

Prior to the transfer of functions, a number of considerations had prevented any concrete steps towards the consolidation of the WEC as the future Ty Cymru. One was that the Welsh Office was not a member of the WEC. Further, neither the Welsh Office nor the future National Assembly could be considered for membership of the WEC under the partnership's existing legal base. Using this body for NAW representation would require a legal overhaul and the introduction of new management structures. Secondly, there had been a history of indifferent to hostile relations between the Welsh Office and the WEC membership.

The 'grassroots' promotional organisations in Wales, including those participating in the WEC, had come to view the Welsh Office as at best insufficiently pro-active in working for Welsh interests and at worst as the servant of a Wales-hostile Conservative central government.[243] This conflict was reflected in the diverging aims articulated for the future Ty Cymru by the existing members of the WEC on the one hand and the Welsh Office on the other. The WEC saw the new Brussels office as an institutional consolidation of the active pursuit of Welsh interests in the EU; the officials of the Welsh Office saw it rather as a base for members of the future Assembly visiting Brussels and also to provide information on European issues of particular relevance to Wales.[244] The difficulties were compounded by the fact that the devolution process coincided with a controversy over the leadership of the WEC which had the temporary effect of holding back progress on any merger with the future Assembly. In spite of these difficulties, it appeared that, in political terms, the WEC would have to be established as the Welsh Assembly's representation in Europe as it had featured so strongly in manifesto pledges.[245]

As part of the consultation procedure which fed into the plans being formulated for the National Assembly, the National Assembly Advisory Group (NAAG) discussed the way in which communications might be established between the Assembly and the WEC so as to provide an efficient system of information for policy-making. The NAAG group was keen to ensure a consistent flow of information from Europe; one which would not be differentiated from other British government information flows that were available to the Assembly. NAAG highlighted the potential role of a future European Committee to establish itself as a focus for liaison between all the subject committees and the WEC.[246] On 1 July 1999, responsibility for such arrangements passed to the Assembly and was delegated to the European Affairs Committee (EAC).[247]

6.3.3 Post-devolution: June 1999–February 2000

Establishing the National Assembly's representation in Europe

With Scotland, Wales's choices in elaborating its relations with Brussels-based organisations were circumscribed by the guidelines established by the MoU and supplementary agreements, part B4: Co-ordination of European Policy Issues: Common Annex (see above). At its meeting of 14 October 1999, the EAC based its deliberations on future relations with UKRep on the terms of the arrangement forged between the UK Foreign and Commonwealth Office (FCO) and the Scottish Executive earlier in 1999. While maintaining that the Welsh Assembly need not follow the Scottish model, the EAC tacitly accepted the FCO's assertion of specific elements of this model as a precedent for any Wales–UKRep arrangement.[248] These comprised the following:

- The Assembly should have a distinct identity for its representation in Brussels.
- The Assembly's representation would not have to be located with UKRep.
- Assembly staff seconded to Brussels would have diplomatic status.
- Assembly staff seconded to Brussels would have UKRep passes and access to UKRep computer and communications systems.
- Assembly staff could attend Working Group meetings as part of the UK delegation.

The EAC supported the principle that the Assembly should be separately represented in Brussels, but with its staff also formally part of UKRep. As in Scotland, under such an arrangement Assembly staff would need to ensure that their operations were consistent with the substance and presentation of UK policy by UKRep.[249] In preparing a proposal on these matters, Assembly representatives consulted with the FCO, UKRep, and with SE (Brussels). On 5 November 1999, the Scottish Office report (see above) on the representation of Member State regions in Brussels was circulated to Assembly members for information. By the time the EAC began its deliberations on the Assembly's representation in the EU, consensus had been reached that Wales would indeed seek to establish such an office and that the most likely organisation on which to base the Ty Cymru would be the WEC. On the third meeting of the EAC on 25 November 1999, a proposal detailing the establishment of a separate Welsh representation and how this might relate to the WEC was put to committee members (NAWRP, EAC EUR-03-99: p. 1; p. 2). A complementary approach to the two matters was proposed. (i) A dedicated Assembly Office within the UK's Permanent Representation to the European Union would be created. At the same time, (ii) NAW would become a partner in the WEC. The Assembly Office would be co-located with the WEC, but would operate in a 'semi-detached' way and would 'hot-desk' at the UKRep offices.

The proposal was detailed as follows:

- The Assembly's Office would formally be part of UKRep, thereby demonstrating the Assembly's commitment to working with the UK government. The Assembly's officials would have automatic access to information and policy advice from UKRep desk officers and would be able to attend relevant negotiations as part of the UK team. It might be possible for the Assembly Office to negotiate use of UKRep's administrative support services, for a fee. Assembly officials attached to UKRep would report to and receive instructions from Cardiff, they would be subject to the authority of UKRep on issues such as personal conduct and the exercise of diplomatic privileges 'and would ensure that their activities fit in with the substance and presentation of UK policy by UKRep' (NAWRP, EAC EUR-03-99: p. 1; Annex A).

- Membership of WEC would provide policy advice, support on lobbying and an enhanced profile for Wales in Europe. The work of the Assembly Office would be separate from that of WEC. 'On the occasions they do work together, activities would focus on lobbying and the provision of information' (NAWRP, EAC, EUR-03-99: p. 1; Annex A). Much of the Assembly Office's work in raising the profile of Wales in Europe would be arranged in conjunction with the publicity and events activities of the WEC. The Office would be co-located with WEC, but for reasons of security and confidentiality would be situated in a separate part of the building. It would be understood that individual members of WEC would need to preserve the confidentiality of their own particular business. The Assembly's Office would provide specific services for the Assembly which it would not be appropriate for the WEC to offer. By locating the Assembly's Office with WEC , the Assembly would be working in partnership with other Welsh organisations and would reinforce the concept of a 'Team-Wales' approach.

The proposed operation of the Assembly Office

The functions of the Assembly Office in Brussels were envisaged as follows:

- To influence EU decision-making.
- To arrange meetings for Assembly representatives (particularly Assembly Secretaries and officials) with key decision-makers within the Commission, EP and other EU level institutions.
- To participate in Commission working groups on behalf of the UK, as appropriate.
- To provide support for visiting Assembly representatives, including support for Cabinet Secretaries attending meetings of the Council of Ministers.[250]
- To facilitate the flow of information, for example: between the Assembly and UKRep; concerning the progress of proposals through the Council of Ministers in liaison with the EAD (NAW) and Assembly

policy divisions; and alerting the Assembly to key legislative proposals and Regulations/Directives which will impact on Assembly policy or subordinate legislation.

A triangular relationship was envisaged between the Assembly Office, UKRep and the WEC. The representational-promotional activities provided through membership of the WEC would complement the work of the Assembly Office, which would focus on meeting the requirements of visiting Assembly Secretaries and Members and on links with UKRep and the Council of Ministers. The Cabinet Secretariat would deal directly with the Assembly Office in the first instance. The WEC would deal directly with officials rather than with elected Assembly members. In addition to liaising with the WEC, the Assembly Office would maintain key contacts in a range of European Union institutions: Welsh representatives in the European Parliament, Committee of the Regions and the Economic and Social Committee; and the offices of other European regions located in Brussels. In the past, the four Welsh representatives on the Committee of the Regions (CoR) had been chosen from local government. Following devolution, the Assembly was now entitled to nominate two representatives of its own.[251] It was acknowledged that the forum of ECOSOC could help to maximise the representational role of the Welsh Assembly.[252] In addition, it was proposed that Wales ought in future to learn from Scotland and Northern Ireland in adopting a more strategic approach to secondments. Instead of using secondments primarily as a means of individual career enhancement, they should be used in future to have Assembly representatives placed in key positions in Europe. Secondees should be prepared in advance for their placement, and, on their return, should be placed in Assembly posts which would benefit from their experience.

The core staff for the office would be drawn from the Assembly and would consist of two officers: a middle manager and an executive officer. The cost of staffing the office, including allowances, would fall under the National Assembly's Personnel Management Division's Secondments Budget. The provisional draft budget tabled before the Assembly on 4 November 1999 proposed the establishment of a Miscellaneous European Support Services expenditure line with a provision of £0.4 m from 2000–2001 onwards. Some resources from this would contribute towards the cost of setting up and running the office and paying the rent.[253]

The Assembly applied to the WEC board to join and hoped to have the Assembly Office operational by April 2000 under the direction of

Des Clifford, supported by a middle manager.[254] Tacitly acknowledging the difficult relationship between the former Welsh Office – persisting through NAW (Officials) – and the WEC, it was noted that the Assembly's application for membership 'should not be thought of as a "take-over"'.[255] Given the strained relationships, there were fears from the outset that the Assembly's application might be rejected. Nevertheless, the strength of the Welsh consensus over the need to establish an effective representation in Brussels was expected to bring pressure to bear on the parties to reach an agreement on the membership of the Welsh Assembly.[256]

6.4   Conclusions

Having reported on the design and early operation of the Brussels-based representative offices of the devolved administrations, it remains to conclude how the Brussels dimension of the handling of UK EU policy has been affected by the devolution process to date. In this case, the logic of developments in the devolved administrations was clearly determined by the systemic changes associated with the devolution process.

While in a strict sense, the *systemic* dimension of this aspect of our question might properly be limited to the different policy competencies afforded to Scotland and Wales under the UK model of asymmetric devolution, systemic changes in effect also permeate the organisational, procedural and regulative dimensions. Regarding the establishment of new relationships with Brussels, the asymmetry of the devolution settlement was sufficient in itself to launch a differential trajectory and pace of development in Scotland and Wales respectively. This could be readily observed in the two territories' approach to establishing an independent representative office in Brussels. For Scotland, new competencies in policy fields closely interlinked with European policy were sufficient motivation to promote a keen interest in developing the capacity for a representational function which might also serve informally to promote Scottish policy interests (even where mediated through Whitehall), particularly through the crucial SE (Brussels)–UKRep relationship. This twin function was consistent with the early decision to found SE (Brussels) as a parallel organisation to the pre-existing SEL. The potential for the informal involvement of SE (Brussels) in policy development gave an incentive to found the institution at the outset, in tandem with the creation or realignment of related structures of devolution. While the EAC (Wales) saw the establishment of a Welsh representation as a priority, compared to Scotland, the more restricted ambit of a Welsh representation effectively relegated it to a secondary consideration, ranked below the consolidation of Assembly-internal structures and procedures. A relatively late start in planning for an Assembly representation meant that Wales was in a position to base its deliberations both on Scottish office internal preparations and the precedents set by its consultations with relevant central government actors. For Wales, the absence of primary legislative competencies (and therefore the absence of problems of policy overlap) meant that the establishment of an independent representation had a more clear-cut representational-promotional function and capacity-building could be restricted to this end. The pre-existing WEC could simply be expanded, incorporating the Assembly representation as a partner and thereby taking on the new representational-promotional functions implied by devolution.

Organisational change with respect to Brussels has resulted, then, in the creation of new structures in Scotland and the adaptation of existing structures in Wales. This dual approach held both for the required internal bureaucratic capacity-building and for the establishment of the new territorial representations. As described in Chapter 3, the Scottish Office created new internal structures in early 1998 in anticipation of the devolution of powers. This restructuring included an Executive Secretariat (External) to be responsible for co-ordinating the Scottish Executive's response to EU policy issues that impacted on a number of departments, and to liaise with the COES. In the Welsh Office the existing European Affairs Division was to fulfil this role. (Since the transfer of functions, the Welsh EAC's development of its own competencies suggests at least a potential role for this committee in such Wales–Whitehall–Brussels interactions.) Responding to the need for capacity-building through the establishment of independent Representations in Brussels, Scotland again took the innovative route in creating the new institution of SE (Brussels) as a branch of the Executive Secretariat (External) of the Scottish Executive. Wales opted to adapt and develop the existing organisational framework of the WEC, a process which was ongoing at the end of the period of study. Both the creation of new structures in Scotland and the adaptation of existing ones in Wales will inevitably impact on past practice in relations between the devolved territories themselves, Whitehall and UKRep. Organisational change can in turn be expected to influence both regulative and procedural matters.

Within the *regulative* dimension the introduction of a new representational function for Scotland and Wales in the EU has required the clarification and review of regulative guidelines to protect the ambit of existing institutions and organisations (UKRep, SEL, the WEC), while giving adequate scope for the development of the territorial representational function. The secured position of UKRep, as established under the MoU (B4.26), was the keystone of the regulative framework for a devolved UK's interactions with Brussels. The new territorial representations would not be permitted to encroach on the role of UKRep. Those institutions recognised as the 'voice' of Scotland and Wales, SEL and the WEC respectively, formed a second set of institutional parameters for the development of the new representations. Although the rights of these organisations to retain any aspect of their former role was not legally secured in the same way as those of UKRep, in practice, their prior 'institutional *acquis*' was respected in planning for the new territorial representations. In joining the WEC as a partner, the Assembly was not faced with the same pressures as Scotland to establish SE (Brussels) with a distinct institutional profile and remit from that of SEL.[257] Nevertheless, the proposed functions of the Assembly Office incorporate areas of potential overlap with the functions currently carried out by the WEC and a future internal division of competencies will be necessary. Preliminary work on defining the role of the Assembly Office suggests it will go down the same path as SE (Brussels) in developing an 'ambassadorial' role. Together, the establishment of Scottish and Welsh representations offers the potential for an enhanced and explicitly territorial strategic capacity in Scotland and Wales with respect to European policy-making.

Within the *process-related* (or *procedural*) dimension, both of the new territorial representations are currently negotiating their new role within the institutional parameters bounded by UKRep on the one hand and the SEL/WEC on the other. The exercise of new roles associated with the new representations can be expected to expand Scotland's and Wales's European information network: for example, the new ambassadorial role will allow for informal soundings to be taken before attempts are made to input into policy shaping. The procedural dimension can be expected to best reflect the 'semi-detached' nature of the Assembly's partnership with the WEC that has resulted from the Assembly's obligations towards UKRep and the need for clear internal guidelines perceived by all partners of the WEC. It remains to be seen whether residual hostilities between the Assembly Office and the 'historic' WEC partners will restrict the former's channels of information in the longer term (see cultural dimension, below).

In addition to the new institutional arrangements being forged with the EU in response to devolution is a new potential for strategic alliance between the devolved territories and other Member States or Member

State regions. These may be led by common functional or policy interests, such as those shared by the Scots and the Nordic countries. In future, such common interests may encourage the devolved territories possibly to bypass London in order to establish more explicit strategic alignments with other Member States and regions, or alternatively with specific partisan groups of the EP.[258] It can be surmised that Whitehall must have been well aware of the potential role, as mediating institutions, of SE (Brussels) and the Assembly Office in such a development. Such awareness might have been one factor behind Whitehall's determination to tie the incipient representations firmly into UKRep's ambit.

At this stage in the development of autonomous EU representations, the reciprocal impact of the *cultural* dimension is difficult to assess. The cultural dimension governs the spirit in which the representations are likely to approach the consolidation of their role and the conduct of their business. Of most concern to us is the degree to which SE (Brussels) and the Assembly Office are likely to uphold the '*status quo*' approach promoted by Whitehall and UKRep in UK–Brussels relations. We can surmise that territorial representation in Brussels will certainly continue to be seen as part of an integrated arrangement with UKRep. Sufficient regulatory and procedural safeguards have been put in place to entrench this cultural norm, at least for some time to come. However, under certain circumstances, new and potentially conflicting norms might impact on the role of the Representations. For example, nationalist parties might come to power in Cardiff or in Edinburgh, bringing different cultural priorities to bear on relations with London and with Brussels. Although beyond the scope of our present study, the cultural norms which informed territorial relations prior to devolution might also prove crucial for post-devolution developments. Although this is by no means certain, diverging cultural traditions in Scotland and Wales carry the potential to promote a differential dynamic in the relations surrounding SE (Brussels) and the Assembly Office.

The creation of SE (Brussels) was an explicit recognition that, in Scotland, the EU-dimension to devolution was of central significance over a wide range of policy and related matters. On the one hand, SE (Brussels) augmented an existing set of bilateral relations between officials in the Scottish Executive and their counterparts in Whitehall and the European Commission and brokered new contacts where the devolution of competencies made this necessary. On the other hand, SE (Brussels) took on the more pro-active role of informing – sometimes initiating – aspects of the EU debate in the new Executive where territorial interests were involved and which, prior to devolution, may have fallen to the Secretary of State and the Scottish Office to monitor at the prompting of Whitehall. Simply because devolution had transferred policy autonomy to the Scottish Executive and Parliament in Edinburgh, it was inevitable that the creation of SE (Brussels) could be viewed with suspicion by some parts of UK government – all the more so in the light of the importance and sensitivity of the role of UKRep in the 'new' approach to European policy heralded by the Blair administration. In the event, it seems that UKRep adapted relatively easily to the creation of SE (Brussels) and its stated aim of being regarded as a part of the broader UKRep family. It is clear that there was a determination on the part of officials in both representations to make a success of the new arrangement. It may well be that the pre-devolution tradition of close co-operation between sections of the former Scottish Office and Whitehall with respect to the territorial dimension to EU policy developments eased greatly the adjustment to this new situation.

In Wales the pro-active pre-devolution 'Wales in Europe' movement was located outside the formal channels of the Welsh Office and Secretary of State for Wales. These official channels were perceived by local groups as being passive at best and as instruments of central government at worst. As yet it is uncertain whether past hostilities will persist as 'residual conflicts' within the reformulated WEC, now incorporating the Assembly Office. It is possible that such aspects of the cultural dimension might impact on the development of relations and channels of information between the Assembly Office and former partners of WEC, establishing path dependency in conflictual or mutually suspicious exchanges. Blocked relations might in turn prompt Welsh local organisations to avoid dealing via the Assembly Office and to attempt to channel links with Brussels separately.

Of course, at this stage we can only speculate on such matters. The above scenario is not intended to represent the most likely outcome of influences within the cultural dimension, but simply to illustrate their potential scope and force.

7
Conclusion

7.1 Introduction

In this study we have examined the nature and consequences of devolved government in the UK through an analysis of the changing arrangements for handling UK European policy. The report documents the crucial preparatory and initial phases of devolution in Scotland and Wales, and importantly evaluates the degree of change that is taking place both in the governance of the UK and, more specifically, UK European policy-making. A key objective has been to assess the process of devolution in this regard. Specifically, are we witnessing a critical juncture in the handling of European policy? The previous chapters, as well as documenting what has taken place, have touched on these questions. In this concluding chapter we review our findings and we examine this question of change. We begin with a summary of the main changes that have taken place, followed by an examination of the thinking behind them, before proceeding to look at the points of tension and the potential for further development that seems inherent in the present set-up. Thereafter, we assess the degree of change involved and suggest criteria for judging its significance. We conclude with some proposals for the further reform of UK European policy-making in the light of devolution.

At a high profile level, through the media and in public debate, European policy issues have already had important political impacts on the working of the devolved governments. This has been most evident in Wales where questions concerning the seeking of extra money from the UK Treasury so as to ensure full benefit of EU structural funds partly contributed to the downfall in February 2000 of the First Secretary Alun Michael and his replacement by Rhodri Morgan. The debacle over calf processing subsidy greatly weakened the position of the then Agriculture

Secretary, Christine Gwyther. She was subject to criticism in the Welsh Assembly and the story was given much coverage in the Welsh and London media. These and other European issues which have created a high level of public and media attention provide an indication of the critical part that European policy questions have already played in shaping the pattern and content of devolution politics. They also provide a clear indication of the importance of the subject matter of our study and the extent to which it can provide revealing insights into how and to what extent the UK state is changing as a result of devolution.

Most of the aspects of European policy and devolution have not, however, been the subject of media attention. Much of the process of institution-building to handle EU business has taken place outside the glare of publicity, though is none the less important for that. As we have seen in earlier chapters, devolution has brought about a number of alterations in the handling of UK–EU policy. These are summarised below in accordance with the institutional dimensions outlined in Chapter 1 – systemic, organisational, process-related (or procedural), regulative and cultural – and drawing from the conclusions to each chapter. The initial overall impression given is that the most evident and substantial changes have taken place within the systemic and organisational dimensions. A more detailed examination reveals, however, that the pattern of change is in fact quite subtle and varied within and across each dimension.

The most significant changes have taken place within the *systemic* dimension. Indeed, change can be seen as being initiated at this level, for devolution begins by seeking to reform the framework and constitution of the state. It has engendered a shift to a form of multi-level governance more in line with the European model and involving a dispersal of authority with the allocation of functions and activities to different levels of governance. Moreover, the new sub-state structures now operate within the context of more territorially-focused electoral and parliamentary pressures – and this has implications for the centre too. Accordingly, the political situation is new: with initially a minority Labour administration in Wales (later in coalition with the Liberal Democrats), and a coalition between Labour and the Liberal Democrats in Scotland. Notably, however, change at the systemic level has only taken place in relation to certain areas of state activity. Officials in Cardiff and Edinburgh remain part of a unified British civil service and in large part the determination of revenue and the broad expenditure framework remain matters in the preserve of Westminster and Whitehall. Overall changes within the *systemic* dimension have thus been dramatic across both the representative and the political executive components of the polity, but have been far less significant within the bureaucratic one. In addition, a key feature of the new constitutional settlement is its asymmetry. The policy areas devolved to the authorities in Wales and Scotland differ; the National Assembly for Wales (NAW) is a unitary body and this creates special challenges; and the Scottish Parliament (SP) has primary law-making powers which its Welsh counterpart does not have. These three features of asymmetry have implications for the handling of EU policy which have yet to work themselves through. All in all, changes within this dimension constitute a significant re-ordering of the institutional framework within which politics takes place and policies are shaped.

Significant *organisational* changes are to be found within both the representative and political executive components of the polity. Indeed the effect of devolution has been to create a whole new set of organisations and positions, with powers and authority attached to them in the form of a 129 member Scottish Parliament and Executive and a Welsh Assembly with 60 members and a 'cabinet'. Welsh Assembly Members (AMs) have already impacted directly on the handling of European policy as the experiences of Alun Michael and Christine Gwyther show. But in truth the frequency of the involvement of AMs and Members of the Scottish Parliament (MSPs) in EU matters in the first eleven months of devolution was, as Chapter 4 makes clear, somewhat limited. The important point to note, however, is that the early phase of devolution saw arrangements for involvement put in place and they are likely to be exploited on a more regular basis in the future. The upshot has been that within the early months the task of handling European policy has been contained largely within the bureaucratic component of the polity where organisational changes have been less evident, though the degree of change in this area has varied across Whitehall, Scotland and Wales. Within Whitehall the creation of the Constitution Secretariat is a significant addition to the range and scope of co-ordination machinery and a clear recognition of the cross-departmental impact of devolution and the need to provide for its management above the level of departments. Additionally the restructuring of the roles, the authority vested in and the resources available to the Secretaries of State for Wales and Scotland and the creation of Wales and Scotland Offices marked a significant change in the organisational power map of Whitehall. Again the potential of these changes is not yet clear. Indeed, the long-term status of these Offices is open to some doubt (see below). Within the bureaucratic component of the Scottish polity the creation of the Executive Secretariat at the core of the Scottish Executive with EU policy amongst its tasks and the establishment of the European Co-ordination Group represents a potentially significant re-organisation and re-focusing of the Scottish EU effort. In Wales apart from a marginal augmenting of staff resources in the European Affairs Division (EAD(WO/NAW)), there were no substantial organisational changes within the bureaucratic component, except to contend with the novel arrangements of servicing the Assembly.

Change within the *process-related* (or *procedural*) dimension of institutional activity is, on the face of it, less evident than along the organisational one. The representative component of the newly devolved polity was not directly included in the process of EU policy-making. As Chapter 4 shows, though, the new assemblies are engaged in establishing channels of information flow within the devolved institutions in their own territory, with Westminster and with other EU Member States. The Scottish Parliament was also aiming for a measure of systematic scrutiny of EU documents. By the end of the period of this study, it had made some progress in this regard, but was hampered by under-rehearsed Parliament–Executive relations and by policy timetabling constraints. Wales, on the other hand, had seen no changes in the scrutiny of EU documents. NAW's European Affairs Committee (EAC) had concentrated instead on promoting the full deliberation of EU matters in the subject committees and in plenary. The political executive component of the devolved polity is being accommodated in the formulation of EU policy, but Whitehall maintains the upper hand. Notably, devolved ministers' involvement in Council is a matter for the lead UK minister to determine and the formal machinery (the JMC structure) for involvement of the devolved authorities is consultative only. So far as the bureaucratic component is concerned this has been accommodated by fudging the traditional rules and allowing involvement through creating arenas for meetings and means of distribution which do not fundamentally undermine the exclusive mechanisms of the UK state. Hence the greater use of *ad hocs*, informal meetings and distribution lists now through the JMC(O)EU, rather than the EQ(O), net. While these arrangements had, by and large, proved satisfactory during the period of this study, there were one or two occasions on which the devolved administrations had not received adequate notification of important policy matters, or had not been involved to their satisfaction. The most evident flaw in these procedures concerns how to deal with EU policy issues brokered between departments at the Cabinet level. As long as UK government circulates only edited Cabinet committee papers to the devolved administrations, the ability (or, as importantly, the perceived ability) of the devolved administrations to contribute independently to policy will be compromised. What has not yet happened is any conflict that has required the bringing into play of the formal procedures established in the JMC structure and a lot depends on how this formal process is actually used. In the meantime the involvement of the bureaucracies of the devolved governments in the processes for handling and determining UK–EU policy have continued to operate. Scottish and Welsh officials have continued to be drawn into the networks dealing with these tasks and to receive information about them. Importantly, however, the criteria for legitimating the devolved administrations' involvement in the network have changed. They are now members as of necessity and circumstance but not as of right as a full part of the UK government. This alteration in membership status can result, either intentionally or inadvertently, in limitations on network access and involvement. A point we explore more fully below.

Turning to the *regulative* dimension, at least so far as the rules and procedures governing the handling of European policy are concerned, change again seems to have been marginal. The concordats and rules of guidance are intended to ensure the continuation of smooth working relations between London, Edinburgh and Cardiff. In effect they codify what were good intra-administrative practices pre-devolution and transform these into sound inter-administration practices post-devolution. They are specifically aimed at the bureaucratic component of the polity but with important implications for the devolved assemblies and their executives. They indicate the grounds on which relations should be conducted and information distributed. They place most of the strongest cards in the hands of Whitehall, for, as in the case of procedural questions, these changes on the regulative dimension make clear that the devolved administrations are no longer 'insiders' with respect to Whitehall, although the concordats do attempt to provide assurances which, if met, should enable the devolved administrations to continue to play an appropriate role in UK European policy arrangements. This, coupled with the nature of the financial arrangements and the pivotal position of the Treasury in determining them, leaves the greater part of the pre-devolution arrangements still intact. Where there is a change is in the strategic capacity to plan and think ahead on European matters. In the broadest sense this remains a prerogative of central government, but the new administrations have the potential to focus more on specifically Scottish and Welsh concerns. This potential is further augmented by the new arrangements in Brussels reviewed in Chapter 6. Early indications are that both Scottish and Welsh administrations are likely to exploit these opportunities, though when and how and with what consequences remains to be seen.

It is difficult to generalise when it comes to changes in the *cultural* aspects of the institutional dimensions explored above. Changes in the norms and values underlying practice take time to emerge and to become accepted. One notable feature affecting the way things have developed so far is the underlying assumption that pre-devolution arrangements for handling EU policy-making worked well and that everything should be done to preserve these. This way of thinking has greatly affected the detailed articulation of the whole post-devolution approach to EU policy-making and the ways in which this has been put into practice. While these values and assumptions assure a high degree of continuity, new assumptions and values appertaining to the role and relationship between the tiers of government have yet to fully emerge. Indeed Whitehall does not seem to be fully aware of the implications of devolution for how they handle EU business and how they can best address the devolved administrations. For instance, the sensitive issue of how UK ministries are seen to distinguish their English from their national interests has only really been addressed by MAFF. In a devolved framework these matters need to be thought out. Those representing the devolved governments are bound to feel aggrieved if London-based ministries do not appear to act impartially when speaking for the whole of the UK in the fora of the EU. Perhaps the answer will be a form of administrative federalism where clear distinctions are made between the UK and English roles of Whitehall departments. Beyond these points, the *cultural dimension* will take much longer to become clear. The critical questions are well summarised in the conclusion to Chapter 3. Most important of the points raised there, however (and echoed in Chapter 4 on inter-parliamentary relations), is whether the values of information sharing which have underlain the formulation and articulation of a co-ordinated UK view on European policy can survive in the new world of multi-level governance. This is a matter that we return to below.

Clearly the UK approach to the handling of European policy is changing as a result of devolution though the consequences of those changes still remain hard to judge at this early stage in the process. Before examining some of the possible problems for UK European policy-making we consider the thinking behind the changes and what that implies in terms of further development.

7.2 The thinking underlying the changes in EU policy-making

As noted in Chapter 3, there was no overall master plan to guide the key players involved in formulating the post-devolution EU policy arrangements. Two considerations provided general guidance. First, the legal fact that final responsibility for policy was reserved to the UK government meant that those at the centre had the final say in setting the terms of the new arrangements. As we have seen in Chapter 3, devolution maximalists, who felt that Scotland should be able to directly represent its interests to the Commission and take the lead in the Council as of right on some areas of business, were given little shrift. The point is well illustrated in the case of agriculture where the devolved administrations pushed for the right to communicate information to the Commission, via UKRep, in those instances where they were responsible for implementing a directive, but were denied this, except in a limited number of cases: the line being settled rather through MAFF (see Chapter 5). There is thus no ambiguity here; under the new arrangements UK ministers and departments have the lead and it is they who determine the composition and strategy of any delegation. Yet, despite this reservation of power to the UK level, as a matter of practical necessity the devolved governments, as implementers of EU policy, need to be involved in the formulation of policy positions. This has necessitated the developing of an inclusive approach, but one which maintains the UK government's primary position in the process. Assuming that participation in EU policy-making by the devolved governments continues to take place in a reasonable and agreeable way, the system can be expected to work in a mutually accommodating manner. Only if things go badly wrong will the mutuality of this process need to be set aside by the UK government asserting its legal primacy over and above its devolved counterparts. Such a development was unlikely to occur in the initial period of devolution, where Labour's strong presence in all three administrations assured 'fair weather' circumstances.

This use of legal primacy as a back-stop related closely to the second source of general guidance: the implicit assumption that nothing should be done that would compromise the effectiveness of pre-devolution arrangements. As we have seen the central idea amongst ministers and officials in the run-up to devolution, which underpins the EU concordat and other EU arrangements, was that the prevailing arrangements worked well and should, as far as possible, be preserved. Concerning new procedures, if such were required, it was implicit that these should be designed to buttress the *status quo ante* rather than be regarded as an opportunity to modify or change current practice. The overwhelming preference was for continuity rather than change and the impact of this mind-set was to set in place institutional foundations for the further development of European policy-making in a devolved UK which emphasise the coherence of UK governance overall. This way of thinking was reflected in the

EU concordat, though, as argued in Chapter 3, interpreting the likely effect of this document is difficult. On the one hand it is intended to preserve the existing approach, as it makes clear that the engagement of the devolved administrations is largely on Whitehall terms (as European matters are reserved to them), yet on the other hand it can be seen as a way of avoiding any weakening of the territorial input into UK European policy. This illustrates the double-edged thinking, which underlies the development of the new arrangements.

In short the aim was to maintain, as far as possible, the established way of doing things. And a framework had to be provided for this as a matter of urgency so that the process of government could continue immediately after 'devolution day'. This codification was best assured within the bureaucratic component of the polity, but it is also worth noting that further mechanisms intended to ensure continuity and a smooth transition were to be found within the political executive and party political components of the polity. A deliberate part of the devolution strategy of the leadership of the UK Labour Party was to make sure that political control of the devolved governments was in the hands of the right party, the Labour Party, and the right personnel. This was seen at the level of UK Prime Minister and Cabinet as an essential pre-requisite for the effective establishment of devolved government during its first term of office. It produced a tendency to intervene to try to influence the selection of candidates for the devolved assemblies and especially leadership candidates. A tendency most evident in the highly publicised support for Alun Michael as Labour's candidate for First Secretary in Wales and the attempt to prevent Ken Livingstone gaining the Labour nomination for London's Mayor. This tendency to intervene is often written up as a desire to maintain control by the leadership of the Labour Party and perhaps it was, at least partly. But it was also a considered attempt to ensure the effective bedding down of devolved government. In the event the strategy was not wholly successful but it was an important and conscious part of the process for initiating and establishing devolved government in its earliest phase.

The outcome is that the design and construction of the institutional foundations established for dealing with European policy reflects a strong bias favouring the continuation of previous practice. They emphasise continuity and if anything clarify and more deeply entrench the pre-devolution approach. The result so far is that the observed strengths of the UK approach have been preserved and the means to ensure that this has the highest possible chance of continuing in the changed circumstances of devolution has been embedded in the new arrangements. Indeed, the territorial input into European policy-making has in some ways been enhanced as a result of the changes. As we have seen in Chapter 6, Scotland and Wales's lobbying efforts in Brussels have been extended. Also devolution has helped to clarify what were previously unclear lines of responsibility and to formalise and substantiate what were previously informal but uncertain points of contact. As noted in Chapter 3, the formalisation of arrangements for territorial input as a result of devolution may mean a greater allowance for and involvement by the Welsh and Scottish administrations than heretofore. Also in our case studies we noted that in those ministries where practices and procedures for dealing with the territorials were already well developed the effect of devolution was to codify and formalise them (as in agriculture), and where such practices were not especially well developed (as in DETR) the effect of devolution was to lead to some clarification and development of these relationships (see Chapter 5). However, while the initial blueprint for European policy-making in a devolved UK emphasises continuity and to some degree enhances territorial involvement, the fact of devolution still seems likely to open-up the process. There are clear points of potential tension which are already evident. A lot depends on how these play out in the years ahead.

7.3   Points of tension

The critical point about devolution so far as the handling of European policy is concerned, is that however smooth the transition, it does open up the process to new pressures and agendas and takes the issue outside the confines of the central state apparatus. In essence, European policy-making has become less exclusive and less subject to central control. The dynamic following from this weakening of the coherence of the mechanisms for handling European policy is likely to have consequences that are hard to predict. The critical change centres on the point (noted in Chapter 5) that pre-devolution UK European policy-making took place within a framework of collective responsibility to which ministers were bound. The consequence of this was that tensions that undoubtedly existed between the territories were smoothed out within the central state structure. Under devolved arrangements Scottish and Welsh ministers are under greater pressure to make public a distinctive line. In effect devolution opens up the process. It breaks the chain and the seamless web, introduces new arenas, and new points of tension and conflict. These may generate further tension and more significant further change.

Whether in fact these points of tension turn into explicit conflicts depends on a number of factors which can be enumerated if not predicted. These include changes in party control at any one of Westminster, Holyrood or Cardiff, and also the emergence of new policy issues with distinctly different implications for each of the territories of the UK (imagine how the BSE crisis might have played out under devolved government), and unforeseen events. As noted in Chapter 3, devolution has brought about a change in the environment surrounding the handling of European policy at the very same time as the process has become less homogeneous and more politicised. This new environment and more open process creates possibilities for development that were not there before. Some of these possibilities have begun to be exploited, but no clear pattern has emerged as yet. What have emerged are some potential points of tension which could become sources of conflict. These are briefly reviewed below. Whether or not the potentiality is realised depends on a number of factors: on the 'unpredictables' as mentioned above; on how sensitively matters are dealt with by the participants involved; and on the strength of precedents in the executive-bureaucratic component of the polity in which initial consolidation of the devolution process has taken place.

One potential problem is that the loss of insider status may weaken the influence that devolved administrations feel they have on the formulation of European policy (see Chapter 3). It may lead to a sense of exclusion. It is worth recalling that the old system has been adapted by some fudging of procedures, notably through a shift from the use of formal UK official cabinet committees to *ad hocs* and a reconstruction of the distribution net for European matters around the mechanism of JMC(O)EU.[259] Such informal arrangements have worked well so far but they may not survive any real difficulties. Moreover, the old process and distribution net still exists and is still used within Whitehall. Such practices, if used extensively, are bound to create some concern on the part of devolved governments that they are being excluded. As we have seen in earlier chapters exclusion can take a number of forms. Information may not get through in full or it may be slow to get through or the devolved administration may be kept out of the loop entirely, sometimes deliberately (see Chapter 5). This has further consequences for the conduct of effective parliamentary input to the policy process at the sub-state level (see Chapter 4). Of course there may be good administrative reasons for these practices. A slowing down of the flow of information on some issues (especially those with a central pertinence to devolved governments) might be because procedures in Whitehall have become more complex, perhaps involving wider consultation (with the PM and Treasury, for example). This means there is likely to be a delay as UK government may wish to get its act together before contacting the devolved administrations.

Delay and caution in distributing material is especially likely if there are different political masters at the devolved level. As revealed in Chapter 5, civil servants in Whitehall were fully aware of the importance of the fact that the Scottish Rural Affairs Minister, Ross Finnie, is a Liberal Democrat, though whether they acted on this is a different matter. They were also fully aware of the difficulties of distributing confidential information to the Welsh authorities given the corporate status of the Welsh Assembly and all that that implies in terms of who might be able to see it (see Chapters 4 and 5). Of course delays and exclusion happened under the old system; the problem is that devolution has made the matter much more sensitive. In general devolved administrations will not be privy to debates underway in Whitehall to the same extent as they were when fully in the system. To counteract the potential tensions involved here, Whitehall needs to guard against creating any sense of exclusion on the part of the devolved governments. What is at stake is the element of trust that has been central to the traditional handling of UK European policy. The old system, where it was well developed (as in agriculture), depended on sharing information and consultation, it depended on keeping the other informed about any initiatives and consulting them where necessary. The system worked on the basis of mutual trust and devolution threatens that mutual trust.

Our findings also highlight other possible points of tension. A central factor in smoothing out differences on EU policy is the role of the territorial Secretaries of State. Especially important here are their relations with the First Minister and First Secretary in the Scottish and Welsh cases respectively. The Secretary of State is the key person able to pursue the EU interests of the devolved governments in Whitehall if difficulties arise. The closeness of the relationship with the devolved governments is essential if matters are to be effectively settled and satisfactorily concluded. As we have seen the Secretary of State for Wales is in more of a position to act as a broker as s/he is involved in all policy areas as a result of involvement in the designation of the Assembly's secondary law-making powers (see Chapter 3). The possibility of there being tension between the devolved governments and their Secretaries of State is a live one, especially if there is a change of personnel and or political control at either level. A further source of potential tension arises in the Scottish case concerning the means whereby EC law will be given effect. As we have seen in Chapters 3 and 4, the Scottish Executive is responsible for presenting draft legislation to the Scottish Parliament, including legislation required to give effect to EC law in Scotland. London is especially likely to be concerned to see that Scottish legislation does not undermine the uniformity of the UK response to implementing EC directives.

This matter of seeking uniformity in approach also arises in the case of EU subsidy and support policies. The evidence presented in Chapter 5 reveals a potentially acute point of tension over different territorial requirements concerning the take-up of EU aids and support schemes. The EU requirement is interpreted such that these schemes must be applied uniformly over the territory of the Member State and that they cannot be applied in one part of the state and not in another part. Yet there are bound to be distinct territorial interests involved that devolved governments are likely to champion. This point is clearly illustrated in the calf processing and culled ewe schemes examined in Chapter 5. In both these cases the issues were finally settled at UK level, though clearly Scottish and Welsh ministers were not that happy with the outcome. While these issues may have provided devolved governments with some lessons about the limits of their competence in matters European, they also fuelled the 'independence' argument, which claimed that had Wales and Scotland been independent Member States within the EU they would have got the subsidy regime they were seeking. Given that a large proportion of devolved and transferred policy areas have an EU dimension, this highlighting of the independence argument through EU policy issues might be expected to occur more frequently in the years ahead.

A further source of tension which may lead to conflict concerns the way in which UK ministers and officials present themselves to the devolved administrations and the impartiality with which they are seen to handle UK interests as against English ones. As already noted, some UK government departments have begun to address this problem by adopting a form of administrative federalism. MAFF has on an informal basis nominated an English minister to represent English interests independently of UK ones, though the DETR has not taken this approach and has become in some ways (with its concern for the English regions) more of an English ministry post-devolution than it was before. This is a highly sensitive matter for the devolved governments and unless Whitehall develops a general policy on these questions of dual identity and impartiality it seems certain to cause difficulties and tensions.

The source of potential tension does not simply lie with Whitehall or Westminster. Some of it is built into the very fabric of the devolution settlement. The asymmetrical nature of the settlement may itself be a source of instability as AMs in Wales seek to achieve the greater powers of their counterpart MSPs in Scotland. In the matter of European policy-making this might mean seeking greater involvement in negotiations or drawing the Assembly, rather than the Secretary of State, more directly into the process of policy-making. An interesting test could be the negotiations surrounding the next round of structural funds and the designation of assisted areas, though this matter will not begin to arise until 2004. Other potential sources of conflict spring out of the extra opportunities for Scotland and Wales to shape the informal process of European policy-making in the EU that the devolution settlement affords. The extra links into Brussels outlined in Chapter 6 extend the opportunity for both countries to lobby direct and to seek allies at the supranational and regional levels of the EU in pursuit of policies which may be at variance with those favoured by the UK government. This is already a feature of the ways in which policies are shaped in the more devolved EU Member States such as Germany and Spain. In the process of shaping policy in Europe the devolved governments are to some degree certain to pursue their own agendas. The national government will need to find ways of coming to terms with this while at the same time seeking to achieve a unified national position at the end point of negotiations in Brussels.

There remains a question about how, if these and other sources of tension lead to severe conflict, such differences will be settled. The machinery for doing this at the highest level, centring on the JMC and ultimately the Judicial Committee of the Privy Council, has not yet needed to be brought into play in dispute settlement mode. There remains the question of how successfully the machinery will actually work. Given the tensions in the area it is quite probable that it will be an EU-related matter that will provide its first real test.

7.4   Measuring change: a critical juncture?

As argued in Chapter 2, the process of UK European policy-making has evolved from foundations established prior to entry and in keeping with traditional Whitehall ways of handling business. In our terms change has, between 1973 and 1999, been incremental. UK state activity in relation to Europe has expanded enormously over this period but it has been organised in keeping with and in accordance with the blueprint laid down many years before. As in the case of the UK's entry to the EU in 1973, devolution provides a critical moment for significant change to take place in the UK approach to handling EU policy. A key research question is whether this 'moment', this opportunity for significant change, has resulted in a 'critical juncture'. Moreover what does our examination of the new arrangements for handling UK European policy tell us about the significance of devolution in altering the nature of UK governance? Once again, on this broader level, is this a critical juncture?

Our analysis suggests that there have been notable alterations both in the patterns of UK governance generally and in the handling of UK European policy-making specifically, and these are most evident within the representative and political executive components of the polity and within the organisational and systemic dimensions of these. These changes are balanced to some degree, at least in so far as UK European policy-making is concerned, by strong continuities at the bureaucratic level especially in so far as procedures and ways of operating are concerned. Overall in our view, and from an institutional standpoint, these changes *do* represent a critical juncture in UK EU policy-making and, more broadly, in the nature of UK governance. This is because the effect of devolution has been to re-order the institutional framework within which European policy-making takes place. This re-ordering has created new opportunities for intervening in UK EU policy-making. Essentially, the system is opening out and a new opportunity structure is emerging. But, while the institutional framework has changed, the policy outcomes themselves have not yet been significantly affected. We must recognise that it is early days, that the new system is bedding down and that the range of critical issues that have arisen to test the new settlement have been few. Most importantly, the full implications of the changes that have taken place will not become clear until the political constellations have altered. One thing is certain, Labour will not always be the party in power at UK level as well as being the dominant partner at Scottish and Welsh levels. These contingent factors need time to play out, but the ground on which they will be played out has significantly shifted.

So far as the sources of institutional adaptation identified in Chapter 2 are concerned, devolution provides an example of domestic change at the level of the Member State driven by pressures deriving from the 'third level' of territorial politics within that Member State.[260] Decisions within the UK led to the re-structuring of the British state and these decisions were in response to pressures from within Scotland and Wales and the way these impacted on the Labour Party in Opposition. The Europeanisation effect was marginal and secondary. However, the changes that have been brought about are, notably, in keeping with European models of multi-level governance. Moreover, as a result, the opportunity for a more evident Europeanisation effect in the future is much more extensive. Especially as the devolved tiers will be more likely and more able to exploit contacts in the EU at the supranational and regional levels possibly in pursuit of interests at variance with the UK line. The questions about critical junctures in governance and EU policy-making also raise the issue of how judgement about these is to be made. For intelligent research is not just a matter of collecting the evidence, but also of how it is to be analysed and interpreted. This takes us back to the points raised in the first chapter about the nature and extent of change. How can we examine the nature of change? On the basis of what criteria can we judge whether change is significant or not? Our analysis already allows us to make some propositions about the nature and evaluation of change. First, it is worth noting that practices before devolution, especially concerning European policy-making, were often more territorially variegated than might be implied in the term unitary state. This highlights the need, expressed in Chapter 3, to be very clear about the base from which we are starting when it comes to evaluating change.

A second consideration when analysing change, which can be drawn from our report, is that it has to be evaluated in a way that respects its multi-dimensional nature. The significance of change varies over time and across institutional dimensions and components of the polity. It also, as we have seen, varies across territory. Change, for example, at the executive level in Scotland has been greater than in Wales. In part this reflects the asymmetrical nature of devolution and the working through in practical terms of the differences between the settlements in Scotland and Wales. Change also varies across policy areas. In agriculture, for instance, there has traditionally been more consultation and involvement on a regular basis, in environment this has been less the case and the territorials were often not fully consulted. Indeed we make the point that devolution has provided both a critical moment and juncture for the handling of environment policy in Scotland (Chapter 5).

There remains the question as to how we assess degrees of change? What criteria might we use to evaluate whether change is significant or not? What we have done is develop an approach that can accommodate and even utilise the multi-dimensional character of change. Our approach offers a useful starting point to analyse constitutional reform. To take the analysis further requires distinguishing degrees of change along these dimensions and components (as set out in Chapter 1, Table 1.1). A useful approach, suggested by Hall (1993),[261] is to employ a sliding scale when examining policy change. This would enable distinctions to be made between the least and most radical changes. We can adapt Hall's policy approach to that of institutional analysis by proposing that first order changes involve significant alterations within one institutional dimension and not others. Second order changes involve significant alterations within two dimensions and not others. Third order changes involve alterations within three dimensions, and so on. Along this scale fourth order changes are the most radical. Change is even more radical along each dimension and cumulatively across them if it reveals significant changes in culture, that is in the norms and values that affect the operation of the institution. Finally, we need to consider the variation of change across the various components of the polity such as the representative, the political executive and the bureaucratic. This would allow us to plot the significance of change within an institutional framework which recognises both the dimensions of institutions and the components of the polity in which they are located. Viewed from this perspective, an extreme example of radical change would involve alterations across all 15 elements (components and dimensions) making up the model.

It is also important to remember the connections within the model. These dimensions and components are often closely inter-linked; consequently change in one element may need to be accommodated by change in another. What we have seen in our report is that the creation of new political components, notably Scottish and Welsh elected assemblies and executives, introduces a dynamic into the process of British politics, which previously did not exist. That is why we consider it to be a critical juncture. This dynamic of devolution will drive change in ways that cannot be foreseen.

Moving from the lofty heights of theory to the more grounded level of practice, we conclude this report by putting forward some proposals for reforming the process of European policy-making as it has emerged in the initial period of devolution.

7.5 Proposals for the further reform of European policy-making

Our analysis suggests that the manner in which potential points of difficulty are addressed could do a good deal to ensure that the smoothness of the evolution of UK EU policy-making under devolution. There are a number of practical policy points that arise. Some apply to the UK government others to the devolved authorities.

UK government
- Create a devolution section with a Cabinet minister (possibly located in the Cabinet Office) and incorporate within it the Scotland and

Wales Offices. The particular functions of the Welsh Secretary of State under devolution will have to be safeguarded, albeit in another form. The Northern Ireland Office, given the sensitive nature of the situation there, should for the moment remain a separate entity.

- Ensure UK ministries carefully distinguish their UK and English roles. There needs to be a consistent policy on this matter. We would recommend an approach in line with that adopted informally by MAFF in appointing a junior minister as the English minister.
- An information and awareness programme should be launched to make Whitehall civil servants fully aware of the implications of devolution for the work they do and in particular devolved matters should be included as part of EU training curricula.
- Monitor and ensure the continuing regular interchange between officials in the devolved administrations and those in Whitehall. The essential element of contact which allows the development of mutual understanding and trust – on which the effective operation of the bureaucratic component of the polity depends – needs to be watched over and nurtured.
- Provide some clarification and uniformity of the process across Whitehall for formulating secondary executive powers for the National Assembly for Wales.

Wales and Scotland

- Explore in full the new opportunity spaces that devolved governments might exploit. The formalisation of procedures has given them a clear indication of where they can fit in to EU policy-making. Are they fully exploiting these opportunities?
- Scottish and Welsh administrations should plan to maintain (Scotland) and expand (Wales) placements in Brussels and to provide comprehensive training on the EU for all their officials.
- Potentialities of lobbying so as to influence both the UK position and the EU position should be carefully examined and a plan for exploiting this potential should be drawn up.
- The mechanisms for handling European policy in the National Assembly for Wales and its executive should be clarified and streamlined.
- There should be closer co-ordination of European policy strategy between devolved administrations – in particular they should exploit links with English regions and with other EU regions.

As these suggestions indicate, the Scottish and Welsh devolved authorities have new opportunities to project themselves into the EU arena:
whether through Whitehall or through the more limited direct options
to Brussels itself. Both must be taken into account. These opportunities
must be seized in order to make devolution work. If a more passive role
were adopted – i.e. a mere acceptance of the 'reception' of EU business
as passed down via the Whitehall channel – the authorities would
scarcely be living up to the new possibilities offered by the 'new',
devolved Britain.

Notes

1 See Chapter 4.

2 This structure changed in October 2000 when the NAW was put onto a quite different footing following the formation of a coalition government between Labour and the Liberal Democrats. One element in these reforms was that Assembly Secretaries were to be called Ministers, with the First Secretary becoming the First Minister. For an interpretation of these recent changes see Osmond (2000a,b).

3 It is difficult to judge the importance of the changes brought about by devolution in resource terms, for while new representative assemblies have taken over functions and personnel, there has been no significant transfer of staff, functions or finance to Scotland and Wales *per se*. Importantly, the determination of the overall spending framework within which devolved governments are obliged to work remains the responsibility of the UK Treasury. And the distribution of funding within the UK total is still determined by the 'Barnett formula' that has governed dispensations to Wales and Scotland over the period since its inception in 1978 (Thain and Wright 1995: 307–27).

4 McLeish resigned as First Minister on 8 November 2001 and was succeeded by Jack McConnel, MSP.

5 The relevant documents include the standing Orders for both assemblies, Scotland's Consultative Steering Group (CSG) Report, for Wales the NAAG and the Wales in Europe reports, the concordats and devolution guidance notes. See, National Assembly Advisory Group 1998; Welsh Office 1999; National Assembly for Wales 1998; Cabinet Office 1999.

6 Some multi-levelledness existed in respect of the handling of the EU structural funds but devolution would reinforce this feature and extend it to a range of additional policy areas.

7 Schedule 5, Part I, 7(1), Scotland Act 1998 states that relations with the European Communities and their institutions are matters reserved to Westminster; see also Welsh Office 1997, para. 3.46.

8 For summary outlines of historical institutionalism see Hall and Taylor (1996) and Peters (1999). For discussion in connection with UK European policy-making, see Bulmer and Burch (1996).

9 On the Cabinet Office secretariats, see Burch and Holliday (1996), pp. 32–5.

10 The standard procedure is that there is contact between permanent secretaries or their nominees and shadow ministers in the months running-up to the election, at least to the extent that the date of that can be predicted. In the run-up to the 1997 election the period of consultation was more extensive covering a period of more than six months and the extent of contacts, though still limited, between officials on both sides was more extensive than heretofore. This was done with the permission, indeed at the behest of, the then Prime Minister, John Major.

11 Interview November 1999.

12 This committee was renamed Devolution Policy (DP) following the 1998 Good Friday agreement when responsibility for devolution in Northern Ireland was removed from the ambit of the Cabinet's Northern Ireland Committee and combined with the remit of DSWR.

13 Interview November 1999.

14 In the Welsh case no mention of a scrutiny committee is to be found in the White Paper or the legislation, though there is, in Section 57 of the Government of Wales Act 1998, mention of a general requirement for the 'Assembly to establish committees with responsibilities in the fields in which the Assembly has functions'.

15 Implementation is mentioned in the Government of Wales Act 1998, see Section 106, following the stipulation that the Assembly cannot act contrary to Community law. The Act makes one other mention of European Union matters in Section 29 empowering the Assembly to implement Community matters under the European Community Act 1972. For the Scottish case see Section 57, Scotland Act 1998.

16 There is a rich literature dealing with third-level governance in other states or comparatively within an EU context. We do not engage with this literature in this report, although we plan to do so in other work. For examples of this literature, see Jeffery (1997; 2000).

17 We recognise there is some artificiality in isolating these parts of UK governance, especially in connection with such an issue as European policy-making, where both main UK political parties have experienced serious problems in adapting to Europe; see Baker and Seawright (1998).

18 We exclude globalisation from consideration as a level here, although it plays a prominent role in the analysis of policy change.

19 Our analysis of third-level change excludes local government, although we recognise it is both affected by the EU and has been subject to considerable institutional change under the governments of John Major and Tony Blair.

20 Thanks to Andrew Jordan for alerting us to this point.

21 Radaelli's actual definition is: 'A set of processes through which the EU political, social and economic dynamics become part of the logic of domestic discourse, identities, political structures and public policies' (Radaelli 2000: 4). Our quibble is about EU dynamics becoming *part of* the domestic logic. That implies a top-down impact as well as implying that domestic adjustment does take place. Both are matters that we would consider to be for empirical exploration. A later version of this paper is available as a *European Integration on-line Paper* at:
http://www.eiop.or.at/

22 We use the term 'territorial' at times throughout this report: e.g. when referring to the territorial ministries (the Scottish and Welsh Offices) in the pre-devolution era. This term is used as shorthand; we acknowledge that it is a rather value-laden term, especially in the post-devolution era.

23 For more on this, see Smith (2001).

24 For an inside review of the arrangements in the House of Commons as of 1999, see House of Commons (1999).

25 The European Standing Committees – see also Chapter 4 of the Report.

26 For example, where a number of interlocking policy proposals are concerned, e.g. the EU's Agenda 2000 programme of policy reform (European Commission 1997).

27 Prior to devolution constraints of time and personnel meant that the territorial offices would tend to play a lesser role where this policy pathway operated. Moreover, where the issue touched on matters of national strategic importance a territorial involvement was, arguably, of less relevance.

28 The DSWR committee was serviced by an official-level committee, designated DSWR(O).

29 Reflecting on the failure of devolution in the 1970s, one interviewee attributed part of the reason to the lack of 'ownership of that scheme by the territorial departments ...'. Interview November 1999. Devolution at that time was managed entirely from the centre of UK government.

30 For the overarching EU concordat, see Appendix I. For excerpts of the MAFF–Scottish Executive concordat, see Appendix II.

31 There have been a number of instances of this type of contagion occurring post-devolution e.g. student fees, teachers' pay, and the provision of care for the elderly.

32 Interviews April 1999.

33 The notion of 'provisions' implies something more interpretative (and so flexible) than 'rules' – closer to what one would expect to be included in a 'treaty' where success or failure is assessed according to achieving the overall objectives of the settlement, rather than whether specific procedural rules are or are not being observed.

34 For many years a controversial subject owing to concerns that one territorial (now devolved) administration could outbid another for much valued inward investment projects.

35 Although both the Scottish and Welsh administrations also would be required to service the EU-related work of the newly created assemblies, which was strictly a matter for those assemblies rather than for negotiation with Whitehall, in reality the work of both assemblies would need to dovetail with the UK system if it was going to have an impact on the UK policy process.

36 In reality the COES had been closely involved in the EU side since the outset.

37 Subsequent events in Wales demonstrated the way in which devolution increased the political sensitivity of the Treasury's EU-related public spending arrangements when the First Secretary, Alun Michael, was put under pressure in Cardiff to demonstrate an ability to secure matching funding from the Treasury for EU Objective 1 funding (see Chapter 7).

38 On some EU fisheries issues the Scottish Office had effectively 'led' the UK delegation, while in other areas it had played an integral part in the UK delegation.

39 It is not intended to give an impression that neither the Scottish or Welsh Offices were never consulted on, say, UK policy towards EU environmental policy proposals. Nonetheless, our impression is that DETR tended to regard EU issues as something to be discussed within the confines of Whitehall.

40 In the Scottish Office this included personnel who had previously been seconded to UKRep or the European Commission.

41 The ESU had been established in the wake of the 1991 management review of handling EU business initiated by Ian Lang, the then Scottish Secretary of State, and had responsibility for EU policy issues which had no single departmental 'home'.

42 The EAD(SO) provided advice to the parliamentary Constitutional Steering Group as to how EU issues might be handled by the Parliament.

43 Accordingly, the Scottish Office Department of Agriculture, Environment and Fisheries (SOAEFD) – later the Scottish Executive Rural Affairs Department (SERAD) – worked in conjunction with MAFF, while officials responsible for EU structural funds and environmental policy were engaged in a similar task with colleagues from the DTI and DETR respectively.

44 As we discuss in detail below, the overall structure and content of the inter-administration concordats (which incorporated the dispute settlement machinery) emerged only after devolution had been endorsed.

45 This point was made particularly with regard to the structural funds (where the DTI would continue to be the 'lead' UK department), and to agricultural policy where SERAD (the Scottish Executive Rural Affairs Department) would remain as the Scottish department responding to MAFF lead. Multiple bilateral mode applies where there are bilaterals with more than one of the devolved executives: something which depends on the subject matter in the UK's asymmetrical devolution.

46 For a detailed description of the UK policy process, see 'The Guide to Better European Regulation' published by the Cabinet Office.

47 Officials from the Scottish and Welsh Offices did not attend all such meetings, but would attend where there was a distinctive territorial interest.

48 Although devolution did not change the Cabinet status of the territorial Secretaries of State, it was assumed that these offices would lose much of their standing after devolution – at least with respect to EU policy – and that responsibility for territorial representation instead would default to the devolved administrations.

49 The genesis and arrangements for the JMC are discussed below. The creation of a JMC is anticipated by para. 5.4 of the Government White Paper, *Scotland's Parliament* (Scottish Office 1997).

50 In the case of devolved matters, the expectation was that it would be the Scottish Executive that would implement EC law although, as a shared power, the UK government retained the power to do so. Some concordats – e.g. agriculture – include specific guidance on implementation arrangements.

51 The Northern Irish Executive Committee was also a signatory to concordats.

52 One interviewee described the function of concordats as '... ultimately all they are designed to do is set out good administrative practice post-devolution'. Interview April 1999.

53 *Scotland's Parliament*, para. 4.13.

54 Were they so to do, they would be elevated to a constitutional status and could become justiciable.

55 This was very much in keeping with the UK/Whitehall approach to governance which prefers codes and procedures rather that the juridification associated with many forms of constitutionalism.

56 Notwithstanding this, however, paras 13 and 14 of the MoU restate the constitutional position that the UK government has the authority to legislate on any matter, whether devolved or not.

57 The fact that, in the event, the concordats were not published until late in 1999 does suggest that they simply were not ready sooner rather than their being caught up in a pre-election purdah. An added complication during this period was the lack of progress being made with the devolution settlement in Northern Ireland which may have contributed to this delay.

58   For example the concordat between MAFF and SERAD included considerable commentary on EU policy.

59   This was necessitated because of the asymmetry in the devolution settlements (with the Assembly being a corporate body), including the different terms that applied to the devolved administrations in the respective territories. Otherwise, in terms of substantive content, the Scotland and Wales elements of the concordat are identical.

60   Under the Scottish variant of devolution the Executive would be accountable to a Parliament for all policy outcomes. Accordingly, it would seek to maximise its influence over reserved matters which impacted significantly on Scotland, such as UK EU policy. A failure of UK government to endorse a Scottish position could be construed as a failure of the governing party in Scotland, or – worse still – a failure of devolution. Under the Welsh variant, on the other hand, because the Assembly was in effect the executive organ, there was not the same degree of political exposure or accountability for any party in the event of a Welsh position on a reserved matter (e.g. EU policy) not being endorsed by UK government.

61   Part of the significance assigned to EU policy derived from the fact that for many years the SNP had asserted that Scotland would be better served by having an independent representation at EU level as did other nation-states. How the devolved government performed with respect to Scottish EU interests was, therefore, a politically sensitive matter.

62   As with other concordats, the EU concordat covered, *inter alia*, consultation arrangements between UK and the territorial government(s), exchange of information, joint working provisions, confidentiality within the arrangements, and dispute settlement.

63   This tradition of 'singing from the same hymn sheet' reflected not only the efficiency of the Whitehall machinery whereby an inter-departmental consensus on putative EU policy was reached, but also, crucially, the role of collective Cabinet responsibility for supporting the position adopted subsequently (see Chapter 2).

64   This consideration applied particularly to Scotland because of the Scottish Parliament's competence for passing primary legislation over devolved matters. In Wales, the issue revolved around a different problem of implementation.

65   The example was given of salmon fish farming – where only Scotland has an EU-related policy interest – although the general principle could be extended to other areas of agriculture, forestry and fishing.

66   EU concordat paras B4.12–B4.15.

67   Lords Hansard, 28 July 1998, Column 1489.

68   Memorandum of Understanding, Part II: Supplementary Agreements, A1: The Joint Ministerial Committee, at A1.9.

69   Memorandum of Understanding, Part II: Supplementary Agreements, point A1.10 states '... [the JMC] will reach agreements rather than decisions. It may not bind any of the participating administrations ...'.

70   The Liberal Democrat leader in the Welsh Assembly observed that: '... the tone of the document [MoU] could sometimes be seen as treating us as country cousins'. 'Take note' debate on the MoU, National Assembly for Wales Record of Proceedings, 7 October 1999 (AM): p. 31.

http://www.wales.gov.uk/assemblydata/3801C7A500000ACF000000980
0000000.pdf

71 The Scottish Executive insisted that the Parliament had no standing in the terms of the concordats as these were agreements between the Executive and UK government which did not alter the constitutional arrangements set out in the Scotland Act. Instead they prescribed good inter-administration co-operation and co-ordination arrangements.

72 See Chapter 4 for an account of the role of the assemblies in the EU policy arrangements.

73 One response to this has been the emergence of informal, or *ad hoc*, meetings between officials in the respective administrations to discuss matters of common interest but which lie outside the formal machinery of UK government and its relations with the devolved administrations. So, while officials from the devolved administrations are not part of the EQ(O) network, they nonetheless retain close connections with that network through informal channels.

74 The remaining DGNs are UK government documents, although the devolved administrations saw their contents and 'noted their terms'. The DGNs are accessible at:
http://www.cabinet-office.gov.uk/constitution/devolution/guidance/dgn.index.htm

75 The nature of Cabinet committee deliberations inevitably will reflect disagreements between government ministers – reconciling different ministerial views and achieving a unified government policy line is, after all, a primary function of Cabinet committees. Our italics.

76 In this case, (E)DOP.

77 At the time of writing, Peter Hain holds this ministerial office.

78 The roles of the Secretaries of State for Scotland and Wales are the subject of Devolution Guidance Notes (DGN) 3 and 4 respectively.

79 The Wales Office numbers approximately 35 and the Scotland Office about twice that number.

80 The BSE crisis would have raised precisely these questions had it occurred post-devolution. As it is, one can envisage additionally environmental policy questions of this sort being raised.

81 For the composition and terms of reference of the JMC(EU) as of February 2000 see Appendix III.

82 In a speech delivered on 19 July 1999, Dr Reid stated that, 'My role is to represent Scottish interests within the UK *and* to defend the integrity and the framework of the United Kingdom' (Scotland Office press release).

83 The extent to which the Scotland Office takes its cue from the Scottish Executive is difficult to determine. On the one hand, by necessity it retains extremely close links with officials inside the Executive and so will be well aware of their views. On the other hand, as a department of UK government, it has equally well-developed links with other territorial offices of UK government and Whitehall departments via the Cabinet committee net. Finally, there is a clear intention by Scotland Office officials to incorporate their own views when offering ministerial advice. Significantly the Scotland Office has appointed an EU expert. It is that official who attends EQ(O) meetings, and briefs the SoS for meetings of (E)DOP. Interview January 2000.

84 Some evidence of the communication between the Scotland Office and the Scottish Executive with respect to EU policy issues is provided by the fact that the announcement that the European Commission had approved Objective 2 funding for Scotland was delivered jointly by Jack McConnell, MSP, (then the Scottish Executive's Minister with responsibility for Europe) on behalf of the Scottish Executive and Brian Wilson, MP, from the Scotland Office.

85 See DGN4, point 5. It continues, 'He [sic] will not be a mouthpiece for the Assembly but he will need to know the views of the Assembly Cabinet before deciding his own line. This is particularly important in relation to proposals for primary legislation that affect Wales.'

86 The SoS for Wales has a right to attend the Assembly (though not to vote) and is required, under the terms of the Government of Wales Act (1998), to consult with the Assembly on the UK government's legislative programme. There is no equivalent requirement for the Scottish SoS under the Scotland Act (1998).

87 The Scotland Office has no direct links to the Scottish Parliament: officials deal only with the Scottish Executive.

88 Although strenuously denied by officials, late in 1999 the Scottish press carried reports of a 'turf war' between the Scottish SoS and the First Minister.

89 In an article in *The Herald* which appeared on 20 March 1999, Sir William Kerr Fraser, former Permanent Secretary at the Scottish Office, predicted that the Scottish SoS would find him/herself marginalised within those Cabinet committees that dealt with issues that had been devolved to Scotland. Indirectly this raises problems with respect to EU policies to the extent that UK can steer the UK government ministers' EU policy position in a direction consistent with departmental policy aims – policy aims that may not be reflected by putative Scottish legislation on devolved matters.

90 Because of this, the Secretariat has close relations with the FCO in Whitehall and collaborated closely with the DAD of the FCO before its abolition.

91 This could be termed *ex post* consultation rather than involvement in a decision-making process.

92 In such a case, of course, the UK government could point to the involvement of the Scottish SoS in the Cabinet committee and argue that Scotland's interests have been taken into account.

93 Some Whitehall departments appear to regard the 'reserved' status of UK European policy as meaning that they have no requirement to involve the devolved administrations in the policy process – merely to inform them of decisions reached and expect their support for these decisions. Clearly this is not how the devolved administrations see matters.

94 It is clearly not in the interests of UK government to have the devolved administrations publicly claiming inadequate involvement in UK European policy-making. Not only would this threaten to destabilise the devolution settlement, it could undermine UK negotiators within the context of EU policy debates.

95 The JOC is chaired by the Head of the Constitution Secretariat in the Cabinet Office, and includes officials from the territorial Offices as well as the devolved administrations.

96 That department will, for instance, incorporate these views into the Scottish response to UK government with respect to the proposed EU legislation. There is, of course, no Scottish reserve on Westminster business.

97 See Chapter 6 for further details.

98 The frequency of attendance of Scottish Executive Ministers at the Council of Ministers has become a politically sensitive matter, with SNP MSPs regularly asking the Executive to report on the number of such attendances. The impression given is that attendance is the only mechanism to ensure Scottish interests are being noted by 'Brussels'. In fact, assuming that inter-administration policy co-operation and co-ordination over UK European policy is proceeding, it is possible to argue that Scottish interests are always being represented in 'Brussels', regardless of the composition of the negotiating team.

99 As the number of UK delegates to a Council meeting is restricted, any Scottish 'bid' for attendance will have to considered alongside a bid from either Wales or Northern Ireland. No quota mechanism on attendance operates between the devolved administrations.

100 A number of the Chairpersons of Assembly Committees are not members of the Labour Party, and – for obvious reasons – this complicates the relationship between Whitehall and the National Assembly.

101 In effect, the work of the Committees interfaces with the officials of the Assembly through the Assembly personnel. For instance, speeches for Committee Chairs are written by the Committee Clerks, albeit with advice if necessary from officials of the Assembly. In this way the integrity of privileged communications between officials of the Assembly and the First Secretary and the Assembly Secretariat is protected.

102 National parliaments across the EU hold no formal role in the EU policy process. A national parliament's input is determined in large measure by the national constitutional settlement. Given the diversity of constitutional practice across the EU, the way in which national parliaments have interacted with the EU is highly complex. This notwithstanding, some common approaches can be observed. See Rometsch and Wessels (1996); Maurer and Wessels (2001).

103 In Finland, for example, all standing committees are involved with EU business and the Grand Committee and the Committee for Foreign Affairs are the main committees which handle EU matters. See Raunio and Wiberg (2000a).

104 For example, the government publishes a White Paper every six months on developments at EU level; the agenda for Council of Ministers' meetings are forecast on a monthly basis; and two days each session are put aside for plenary debates prior to European Council meetings (Munro 1999: 209).

105 The European Scrutiny Committee was established in 1974 as the European Legislation Committee.

106 The EM must be sent within 10 working days of deposit of the EU document.

107 Interview April 1999.

108 Committee A considers documents referred to it by the ESC on agriculture and fisheries: Committee B considers documents on social security and home affairs; and Committee C considers trade and industry. See also Chapter 2.

109 COSAC is a forum for debate and exchange of information between European committees and the EP – its decisions are not binding on either the supranational institutions or on the national parliaments. See Raunio and Wijberg (2000b: 149).

110   Negotiations were conducted to establish informal arrangements to handle information flow between the ESC and the new Scottish European committee. These are discussed below.
111   Interview November 1999.
112   The Scottish committees were also to have powers to scrutinise financial proposals and administration of the Executive; to conduct inquiries; to consider and report on the policy and administration of the Scottish Administration and to scrutinise procedures relating to the Parliament and its Members.
113   In response to similar considerations at UK level, standard Westminster convention had it that the Chair of the European Scrutiny Committee was a member of the Opposition Party. However, both the 1997–2001 and the 2001– committees broke with this tradition.
114   Both primary and secondary Scottish legislation can be used to implement Directives.
115   The remit of the JCSI is to consider and, if necessary, report delegated legislation to both Houses, not with respect to its merits but only on technical grounds.
116   Interview April 1999.
117   Interviews May, June 1999.
118   Subject committees were to exercise the following functions – evidence taking; scrutiny of the Assembly Secretary; scrutiny of Non-Departmental Public Bodies (NDPBs) and other outside bodies funded by the Assembly; discussion (of policy development, etc.); consideration (of legislation and formal resolutions); the establishment of effective support for individual Assembly members; and the overall authority to be retained by the full Assembly (NAAG 1998: 7).
119   Notwithstanding the fact that the negotiation of EU matters is reserved, both Scotland and Wales expected to be involved in the formulation of UK policy.
120   'The Scottish Parliament will be able to scrutinise EU legislative proposals and ensure that Scotland's interests are properly reflected' see *Scotland's Parliament* (1997: 5.7).
121   There was limited discussion in Scotland on the relation between the SEC and the House of Lords. Discussion on the reform of the House of Lords did however consider the issue of territorial representation. See Royal Commission (1999).
122   'Westminster has 25 years of experience of examining EU proposals. Although the Scottish Parliament may not adopt all of the same practices, there remains considerable scope for co-operation and liaison. Much of this may occur at the working level (e.g. between committee clerks): but there may also be value in members of the European committee, and its Convenor and reporters, meeting their counterparts to discuss issues of mutual interest' (SO 1998b: point 26).
123   Interview April 1999.
124   Interview April 1999.
125   See Chapter 3.
126   'The European Committee of the Parliament will also have a broader and arguably more important role in conducting general debates on matters of EU relevance, which extend beyond the technical scrutiny of legislative proposals' (SO 1998b: point 29).

127 COSLA – Convention of Scottish Local Authorities; STUC – Scottish Trade Union Congress; SCVO – Scottish Council of Voluntary Organisations.

128 'Like Parliament, the Assembly will have the opportunity to scrutinise relevant proposals coming before the Council of Ministers as well as other important European documents. In this way, it will have the opportunity to ensure that their implications for Wales are fully understood and taken into account' (*A Voice for Wales* 3.48).

129 Interview April 1999.

130 Interview April 1999.

131 Interview April 1999.

132 Interview April 1999.

133 See summary report in Eur-01-99: p. 1.

134 Interview April 1999.

135 NAAG had been charged particularly with developing standing orders for the new Assembly. In its report, it took pains to reflect these themes even though they would not come under the scope of standing orders, but would be realised by other means (NAAG, 1998, *passim*).

136 One newspaper referred to him as a 'control freak', see *Wales on Sunday*, 31 October 1999.

137 Committee membership is determined by the Parliamentary Bureau.

138 The Committee was expected to be served by three full-time staff (including a senior assistant clerk) and have more policy and legal support.

139 Interview February 2000.

140 Interview November 1999.

141 This departed from the NAAG report's recommendation that each subject committee appoint one of its members to act as European co-ordinator.

142 The questions and suggestions put forward by members at the July 1999 meeting reflected numerous concerns relating to capacity-building, both outside the Assembly and within it. They included questions about National Assembly representation at the Council of Ministers; progress in establishing the proposed Council of the Isles; the Assembly's input into the European policy-making process and the need for the Assembly to be kept informed about developments in Europe; the subject committees' consideration of the European dimension of their respective policy areas; relations and active co-operation with the Welsh European Centre; and concerns about the resource implications of implementing the ESG's recommendations.

143 Following a recommendation of the ESG Report (ESG 1998: para. 4.15), Michael noted explicitly that the EAC should not concern itself with discussion on the structural funds, since this was to be dealt with by the Economic Development Committee.

144 We note that without the advantage of extensive prior planning as in Scotland, the EAC was faced with having to develop its competences and remit simultaneously with the conduct of business. One result of this was that many projects embarked on by the EAC remained relatively underdeveloped throughout the period of the study.

145 The Committee met three times during the second phase of the period of study: 1 July 1999 (Eur-01-99), 14 October 1999 (Eur-02-99) and 25 November 1999 (Eur-03-99).

146 Interview November 1999.

147   Interview November 1999.
148   Interviews November 1999; February 2000.
149   Interviewees explained that a formal arrangement existed and that the Scottish Parliament received two complete sets of everything received by Westminster: one set for the SEC and one set for reference sent to the library in the Scottish Parliament. Interview February 2000.
150   Interview December 1999.
151   Interviews December 1999; February 2000.
152   This early consensus position included the views of the Conservative members.
153   An innovation of the second First Minister, Henry McLeish, was to create a ministerial portfolio which included Europe within its remit (Education, Europe and External Affairs, although this was abolished in a later reorganisation).
154   Interview February 2000.
155   In contrast to Scottish Office recommendations.
156   Interview November 1999.
157   Interview December 1999.
158   See 'Take note' debate on the Memorandum of Understanding, *National Assembly for Wales Record of Proceedings*, 7 October 1999 (AM); pp. 28–9.
159   Interview May 1999.
160   Committees were later asked to report by March 2000 (Eur-03-99: p. 4.5).
161   See Chapter 6.
162   The terms Welsh and Wales are used interchangeably in these minutes.
163   The fact that the administrative branch of the Assembly must operate with very limited resources can be expected to promote the interpretation preferred by the political leadership.
164   This finding is in keeping with general diversity of domestic parliamentary practice in the EU policy process across the EU.
165   See Carter (2000) for full discussion of this point.
166   Interview November 1999.
167   This section draws on a series of confidential interviews conducted in the Scottish and Welsh Offices in 1997, in MAFF (1996 and 1999), UKRep (1997), the Welsh Office/Assembly (1999) and the Scottish Executive in 1999 and 2000. Those interviews dating from 1996 and 1997 were undertaken by Bulmer/Burch within their ESRC Whitehall Programme project (L 124251001). We exclude fisheries policy from our core concerns.
168   Data and quotes from interview November 1996.
169   Information as of late 1996 (following reorganisation on 1 October 1996).
170   Additionally, food issues are dealt with in the Internal Market Council.
171   Prior to 1995/6, when environment was brought in from the Development Department to create the SOAEFD, the department had been concerned only with agriculture and fisheries, and was known by the acronym DAFS.
172   Other fisheries issues were dealt with by a separate chain of command.
173   It is worth mentioning that the official first charged with this task, Kenneth MacKenzie, had formerly been head of DAFS, and was a key official handling the territorial politics of the BSE crisis. He then became the first head of the Cabinet Office Constitution Secretariat immediately after Blair's election and then Head of the Scottish Executive Development Department: see http://www.scotland.gov.uk/who/senior.asp

174 Strikingly, an interview (January 1997) in the Welsh Office's Department of Agriculture played down the importance of UKRep as a source of information, interview, but this discrepancy may reflect that the SOAEFD played a greater role in pressing for the 1995 arrangements in the first place.

175 The BSE crisis had a higher proportional impact on Scottish compared to English agriculture because of the former's greater orientation towards livestock. Moreover, some 80 per cent of Scottish beef came from specialist herds compared with only around 20 per cent in England, the remainder being dairy herds (interview January 1997). Exceptionally, junior ministers from the Welsh and Northern Irish Offices also attended some Councils during the BSE crisis.

176 Interview January 1997. Another policy participant – from outside government – has pointed out that Scottish Office officials were known to try on occasion to 'pull one over' MAFF to Scotland's benefit with the connivance of outside organisations (correspondence with S. Bulmer, September 2000).

177 Interview January 1997.

178 Interview January 1997.

179 Multi-functionality was seen in Wales as a positive advantage when compared with the fragmentation of policy areas experienced in Whitehall. A good illustration could be found in the rural White Papers produced for England and Wales under the Conservatives. In the case of England, the lead department, the DoE, worked in consultation with MAFF but dominated the terms under which the document was formulated. In contrast, Wales established a central co-ordinating unit to draw together the White Paper across the various parts of the Welsh Office, resulting in a Welsh White Paper that was felt in Cardiff to be better integrated and a more definitive statement of policy than its English counterpart (Interview January 1997).

180 Amongst the 'territorial issues' were: the higher number of cases in the English dairy herd compared to Scotland and the introduction of a different system of tracing infected cattle in Northern Ireland (which raised the possibility of special arrangements for lifting the EU's beef export ban for Northern Ireland and the Republic). The latter opened up the issue of a special arrangement for Scotland, but this was rejected by the then Secretary of State in the Major government, Michael Forsyth.

181 Proceedings relating to improper implementation can only be initiated against EU Member States – and not against 'third-level' administrations. The ultimate sanction permits fines imposed by the European Court of Justice (ECJ), which neither the Treasury nor MAFF would wish to pay for if they arose from transgressions committed by the devolved administrations. In addition, following the 1992 *Francovich* ruling of the ECJ private parties can take action in the courts to secure damages against government for improper compliance with EU obligations, causing similar concerns on who would 'pick up the tab' where the impropriety was found to be at subnational level (Case C-6/90 and C-9/90 *Francovich and Bonifaci* v. *Italy* (1991) ECR I-5357).

182 Interview April 1999.

183 Deputy Secretary level in MAFF means the level beneath Permanent Secretary. There were two Deputy Secretaries: one heading the Agricultural Crops and Commodities Directorate, the other heading the Food Safety and

Environment Directorate. Fisheries arrangements were being provided for separately and are covered by a separate concordat. In SOAEFD (later, the Scottish Executive Rural Affairs Department – SERAD), and WOAD the counterpart would be the senior official responsible for agriculture.

184   Whilst this was not an entirely new situation, the existence of administrations of different political colourings meant that differential implementation might now be preferred for reasons of party politics or policy competition.

185   For a report on one of the first meetings – including Nick Brown, Ross Finnie, Christine Gwyther and Lord Dubbs (of the non-devolved Northern Ireland Office), see 'Agriculture ministers meet to make devolution work', MAFF News Release 306/99, at http://www.maff.gov.uk/

186   As noted elsewhere, the EQ(O) machinery would exclude representation from the Scottish Executive and the Welsh Office, although an official from the (UK government's) Scotland or Wales Office could attend.

187   Interview April 1999.

188   By June 2000 there was still no MAFF concordat with the Welsh Assembly.

189   *The Herald* (City Edition), 9 January 1998, 'London to Retain Scots Farm Veto' (Murray Ritchie, Scottish Political Correspondent).

190   *The Herald* (City Edition), 9 January 1998, 'London to Retain Scots Farm Veto' (Murray Ritchie, Scottish Political Correspondent).

191   Under First Minister Henry McLeish, who succeeded Donald Dewar following the latter's death on 11 October 2000, Finnie remained as Rural Affairs Minister; Rhona Brankin succeeded Home Robertson as Finnie's Deputy (with fisheries responsibilities). Sarah Boyack's portfolio was split (see below).

192   A potential issue in future is what will happen if ministers from all the devolved administrations wish to attend a Council session, and agriculture is a likely candidate. In such a case the devolved administrations will probably have to find some agreement amongst themselves, since it would be in none of their interests to precipitate trouble with MAFF.

193   Interview June 2000.

194   Interview June 2000.

195   Interview June 2000.

196   'Ewe cull – Finnie hits out at EC rules', at http://www.scotland.gov.uk/ news/1999/10/se0846.asp

197   Interview December 1999.

198   Non-attributable interview.

199   Interview December 1999.

200   This section draws on a series of confidential interviews conducted in the Scottish Office in 1997 and 1998, in the Department of the Environment in 1996 and the Scottish Executive in 1999 and 2000. Those interviews dating from 1996 and 1997 were undertaken by Bulmer/Burch within their ESRC Whitehall Programme project (L 124251001).

201   See European Commission, *Annual Report on Monitoring the Application of Community Environmental Law*, Brussels, various years. A comparison with the UK's better performance on applying single market legislation is instructive, although the differences have narrowed.

202   In the DETR, EU co-ordination functions are undertaken in the European Environment Division, located within the Environmental Protection and International Directorate of the Environmental Protection Group.

203 Interview June 2000.

204 Also see Sharp (1998: 40–1) for an insider's view on this episode.

205 Interview June 2000.

206 To secure participation the Scottish minister has to follow a procedure of writing to the Secretary of State, John Prescott. Assuming this request is approved – and there is the possibility that other devolved ministers might wish to attend thereby creating a space problem – the minister would meet with the Environment Minister, Michael Meacher, prior to the Council session itself.

207 Following the ministerial reshuffle associated with Henry McLeish succeeding Dewar on the latter's death, Boyack's portfolio was divided. She retained the transport brief, and Sam Galbraith (Labour) became Minister for Environment, Sport and Culture.

208 It should be noted that under the Conservatives Lord Lindsay had a higher rate of attendance at the Environment Council; the personal relationship between him and Gummer was better than that between Sewel and Michael Meacher, the UK environment minister.

209 Two meetings had taken place in the first 12 months of the Scottish Executive.

210 The head of the European unit had himself been on secondment in Brussels for three years until 1999.

211 Interview June 2000.

212 Placing national experts in EU institutions is a long-standing practice and provides an important source of expertise to those institutions in developing policy. In addition, these officials return home with invaluable experience of EU arrangements and policy processes.

213 Point 5.10 of the White Paper stated that, 'It [SE (Brussels)] would complement rather than cut across the work of UKRep ...': see Scottish Office (1997).

214 Scotland Europa is a wholly owned subsidiary of Scottish Enterprise, and the majority of its budget is provided by Scottish Enterprise. The last two Chief Executives of Scotland Europa (Charlie Woods and Donald McInnes) were, on their appointment, members of the senior management team of Scottish Enterprise.

215 At the time of writing, there were some 45 subscribing members to Scotland Europa receiving a range of services. Membership is distributed by type as follows: local authorities 12%; industry 36%; educational bodies 31%; public sector bodies 17%; trade unions 2%; voluntary sector 2%.

216 This review was initiated by Donald McInnes immediately on being appointed as Director of Scotland Europa in February, 1998. In a separate exercise, there was in practice close co-ordination between Scotland Europa and the Scottish Office to assess how best the wide range of Scotland's interests could be served once devolution took effect.

217 These issues were the subject of a number of internal briefing documents, two of which – *A Representative Office for the Scottish Executive in Brussels*, and *The Relationship with Scotland Europa* – are directly pertinent to our research.

218 This involved a review of 24 regional representations already functioning in Brussels, covering most of the EU Member States.

219 The review concentrated on regional offices from Member States with relatively autonomous sub-national governments, such as Germany,

Austria and Spain, as these were considered the relevant comparators for the future UK situation.

220   Some regions occasionally represented their interests directly to their Brussels permanent representations.

221   In particular, the development of relationships with other Brussels-based regional representative offices.

222   It was mooted by Donald McInnes, Executive Director of SEL, that in the future SEL might take on a greater strategic role in promoting Scotland's business interests in Europe.

223   Early on this raised some concerns of propriety, in that the nature of SE (Brussels) activities meant that it needed to be completely separated from SEL. In the event, this proved not to be problematic and, although sharing a common address, SE (Brussels) and SEL are entirely separated entities.

224   For instance, to attend meetings within the Commission or UKRep which did not justify an Edinburgh-based official making the trip to Brussels.

225   All UK members of ECOSOC are proposed by the UK government, and this would continue to be the case post-devolution. However, it was understood that Scottish members would be proposed by the Scottish Executive subject to ratification by the FCO. This is very much how the system worked prior to devolution in any event.

226   This would hold if members were to be drawn in the future from the Scottish Parliament. Under the current arrangements where members are local authority representatives, COSLA remains the appropriate supporting organisation.

227   The full text of this speech is available at the following website: http://www.scotlandeuropa.com/dewar2.htm

228   One interviewee defined the role of SE (Brussels) as '... mak[ing] sure that those [in Scotland] who are expert in the dossiers are fully up to speed in what is happening [in Brussels] ...' Interview December 2000.

229   See Scotland and the European Union, http://www.scotland.gov.uk/euoffice/scot_eu1.asp#1

230   As reported in *The Herald*, 1 July 1999: 10.

231   Interview December 2000.

232   See MoU, para. B4.27 which states that Brussels offices of the devolved administrations '... will work closely with, and in a manner complementary to, UKRep which remains responsible for representing the view of the UK to the European institutions ...'.

233   An innovation of the second First Minister, Henry McLeish, was to create a ministerial portfolio which included Europe within its remit (Education, Europe and External Affairs, although this was abolished in a later reorganisation).

234   See MoU, paras. B4.14 and B4.15.

235   It is estimated that 80 per cent of devolved competencies have an EU-policy dimension.

236   Nonetheless officials from SE (Brussels) may buttress these contacts by attending Commission or Council meetings on behalf of another SE department.

237   Interview December 2000.

238   In April 1998 the WEC was registered as a company limited by guarantee with three categories of members: the WDA, local government and other organisations. At this time its annual budget was in the region of about

£650 000, to which the WDA contributed some £263 000; local government £189 000 and other organisations £198 000, see NAWRP, EAC, EUR-02-99: Annex A.

239 Its formal role does not extend to lobbying on behalf of specific Welsh interests, but see Welsh Affairs Select Committee (1995); Gray and Osmond (1997).

240 Amendments were tabled at Westminster by all three opposition parties to the effect that Wales *should* have a formal seat, but all were resisted by ministers. Interview April 1999.

241 Interview April 1999.

242 Interviews April 1999.

243 Interviews May 1999; November 1999. This view of the Welsh Office was symptomatic of a wider perception of a 'democratic deficit' in Wales under the Conservatives (Thomas 1999: 293).

244 Interviews April 1999; May 1999.

245 Interview April 1999.

246 The subsequent consultative Assembly Preparations Group (APG) did not contribute anything further to the NAAG recommendations on European business. The APG was established as a *reactive* group, to deal with unresolved issues referred to it by Ron Davies/Alun Michael. It met only four or five times, which was in part a reflection of the new leadership style with respect to outside consultation (Interview May 1999).

247 Government of Wales Act (1998) 62.-(1) (a).

248 Thus: 'the Foreign Office have highlighted certain elements of the agreement which would provide the basis for any agreement with the Assembly' (NAWRP, EAC EUR-02-99: p. 2).

249 They would be subject to UKRep's authority regarding issues of personal conduct, issues of diplomatic privilege etc (NAWRP, EAC EUR-02-99: p. 2). As anticipated prior to devolution, the European Concordat noted that staff of the devolved administrations would continue to be eligible for secondment to UKRep and to the institutions of the EU (MoU, B4.28).

250 Services would be provided for all Assembly members, but the level and nature of these would depend on the status of the representative and the nature of his or her business.

251 Along with Scotland and Northern Ireland, the European Concordat established that the devolved administrations would each nominate their respective share of representatives within the COR and ECOSOC. Nominations would be passed to the FCO. The final decision on proposals for UK appointments would continue to be made formally by the Foreign Secretary, with the agreement of the Prime Minister, after co-ordination by the FCO and Cabinet Office (MoU, B4.29).

252 The Chair of the EAC asked officials to consider how ECOSOC members might access the WEC website for information about the drafting of EU decisions and amendments to them.

253 These arrangements were to be reviewed and possibly adjusted a year after the office began its operations.

254 The formal application was made on the occasion of the EAC's visit to Brussels 2–3 March 2000, which lay just outside our period of research (NAWRP, EAC EUR-01-00: p. 1). The Assembly Office began operations in

May/June 2000 (NAWRP, EAC EUR-02-00: p. 1). At the end of February 2000, the WEC relocated to a more prestigious and high-profile premises in Brussels (Osmond 2000: 41).

255   NAWRP, EAC EUR-03-99, min. 2.2; a reciprocal awareness was also evident in the recommendation of the WEC Board Meeting 22 November 1999: '... there is some sensitivity that the Assembly should not become a dominant presence in WEC' (NAWRP, EAC EUR-03-99, Annex B).

256   Interviews May 1999; November 1999.

257   Shortly after the end point of our study, the Chair of the European Affairs Committee reported that, in making arrangements for a Welsh representation, the approach taken by the Scottish Parliament to establish a separate office had been considered. However, it was felt that the Assembly would benefit greatly from its partnership with the WEC (NAWRP, EAC EUR-01-00: 1 Agenda Item 1: Chair's report Paper).

258   Interview April 1999.

259   The latter practice is explicitly allowed for in DGN 6 (see Chapter 3).

260   We should note here that the UK framework for EU policy-making was not static during the research period, but was subject to other sources of change. First, the Blair government sought to pursue a more constructive European policy, and this led to some changes in the machinery, including the establishment of MINECOR (see Chapter 3) and some strengthening of the Cabinet Office European Secretariat. Second, new commitments on security and defence cooperation at EU level, notably those agreed at the 1999 Helsinki European Council, led to the Ministry of Defence becoming a more important player in UK EU policy-making.

261   See also Daugbjerg (1997).

List of Appendixes

Appendix I: Concordat on Co-ordination of European Union Policy Issues (*Source*: Devolution: Memorandum of Understanding and supplementary agreements, Cm 4806, July 2000).[1] Available at:
http://www.cabinet-office.gov.uk/constitution/devolution/

Appendix II: Excerpt from Main Concordat between the Ministry of Agriculture, Fisheries and Food and the Scottish Executive. Available at:
http://www.maff.gov.uk/

Appendix III: Joint Ministerial Committee on the European Union: Composition and Terms of Reference (February 2000). Available at:
http://www.cabinet-office.gov.uk/constitution/devolution/

---

1   The MoU was first issued as Command Paper, Cm 4444, on 1 October 1999. At that stage only Scotland and Wales were signed up to the agreement as devolution to Northern Ireland had not taken place. Cm 4804 reflects the Northern Ireland Executive Committee's decision to become a party to the Agreement, and consequent minor amendments.

Appendix I: Concordat on Co-ordination of European Union Policy Issues

B1: Concordat on Co-ordination of European Union Policy Issues: Scotland
B2: Concordat on Co-ordination of European Union Policy Issues: Wales
B3: Concordat on Co-ordination of European Union Policy Issues: Northern Ireland
B4: Co-ordination of European Policy Issues: Common Annex

B1: Concordat on Co-ordination of European Union Policy Issues: Scotland

B1.1 This document and the common Annex (B4) are to be read in conjunction with the Memorandum of Understanding (MoU) between the UK government, Scottish Ministers, the Cabinet of the National Assembly for Wales and the Northern Ireland Executive Committee and the enabling legislation establishing these administrations. Reference to devolved or non-devolved matters will be construed in accordance with the MoU.

B1.2 This concordat is an agreement between the Scottish Ministers and the UK government. This concordat is not intended to constitute a legally enforceable contract or to create any rights or obligations which are legally enforceable. It is intended to be binding in honour only.

This concordat sets out the mechanisms between UK government and the Scottish Executive for the handling of EU business. Specifically, the concordat covers:

- provision of information;
- formulation of UK policy;
- attendance at Council of Ministers and related meetings;
- implementation of EU obligations; and
- infraction proceedings.

There are a wide range of interfaces with the EU and the practicalities attached to developing and presenting UK policy are to be handled in line with the general principles set out in this paper. Other concordats may set out the procedure in more detail as appropriate.

General

B1.3 As all foreign policy issues are non-devolved, relations with the European Union are the responsibility of the Parliament and government of the United Kingdom, as Member State. However, the UK government wishes to involve the Scottish Executive as directly and fully as possible in decision-making on EU matters which touch on devolved areas (including non-devolved matters which impact on devolved areas and non-devolved matters which will have a distinctive impact of importance in Scotland). In general, it is expected that consultation, the exchange of information and the conventions on notifications to EU bodies will continue in similar circumstances to the arrangements in place prior to devolution.

B1.4 Participation will be subject to mutual respect for the confidentiality of discussions and adherence by the Scottish Executive to the resulting UK line without which it would be impossible to maintain such close working relationships. This line will reflect the interests of the UK as a whole. In accordance with these general principles, the co-ordination mechanisms should achieve three key objectives:

- they should provide for full and continuing involvement of ministers and officials of the Scottish Executive in the processes of policy formulation, negotiation and implementation, for issues which touch on devolved matters;
- they should ensure that the UK can negotiate effectively, in pursuit of a single UK policy line, but with the flexibility that fast-moving negotiations require; and
- they should ensure EU obligations are implemented with consistency of effect and where appropriate of timing.

Such mechanisms should also ensure that the Scottish Executive and the UK government inform each other of any relevant policy proposals which might impact on either existing or new EU proposals or requirements. They should also ensure that, when required by EC legislation, relevant obligations or initiatives are reported to the Commission and when necessary the other Member States.

The arrangements in the common Annex (B4) are intended to be adaptable to suit the differing circumstances of individual cases.

B2: Concordat on Co-ordination of European Union Policy Issues: Wales

B2.1 This document and common Annex (B4) are to be read in conjunction with the Memorandum of Understanding (MoU) between the UK government, Scottish Ministers, the Cabinet of the National Assembly for Wales and the Northern Ireland Executive Committee and the enabling legislation establishing these administrations. Reference to devolved or non-devolved matters will be construed in accordance with the MoU.

B2.2 This concordat is an agreement between the Cabinet of the National Assembly for Wales (hereinafter referred to as the Assembly Cabinet) and the UK government. This concordat is not intended to constitute a legally enforceable contract or to create any rights or obligations which are legally enforceable. It is intended to be binding in honour only.

This concordat sets out the mechanisms between UK government and the Assembly Cabinet for the handling of EU business. Specifically, the concordat covers:

- provision of information;
- formulation of UK policy;

- attendance at Council of Ministers and related meetings;
- implementation of EU obligations; and
- infraction proceedings.

There are a wide range of interfaces with the EU and the practicalities attached to developing and presenting UK policy are to be handled in line with the general principles set out in this document. Other concordats may set out the procedure in more detail as appropriate.

General

B2.3 As all foreign policy issues are non-devolved, relations with the European Union are the responsibility of the Parliament and government of the United Kingdom, as Member State. However, the UK government wishes to involve the Assembly Cabinet as directly and fully as possible in decision-making on EU matters which touch on devolved areas (including non-devolved matters which impact on devolved areas and non-devolved matters which will have a distinctive impact of importance to Wales). In general, it is expected that consultation, the exchange of information and the conventions on notifications to EU bodies will continue in similar circumstances to the arrangements in place prior to devolution.

B2.4 Participation will be subject to mutual respect for the confidentiality of discussions and adherence by the Assembly Cabinet to the resulting UK line without which it would be impossible to maintain such close working relationships. This line will reflect the interests of the UK as a whole. In accordance with these general principles, the co-ordination mechanisms should achieve three key objectives:

- they should provide for full and continuing involvement of Assembly Secretaries and officials in the processes of policy formulation, negotiation and implementation, for issues which touch on devolved matters;
- they should ensure that the UK can negotiate effectively, in pursuit of a single UK policy line, but with the flexibility that fast-moving negotiations require; and
- they should ensure EU obligations are implemented with consistency of effect and where appropriate of timing.

Such mechanisms should also ensure that the Assembly Cabinet and the UK government inform each other of any relevant policy proposals which might impact on either existing or new EU proposals or requirements. They should also ensure that, when required by EC legislation, relevant obligations or initiatives are reported to the Commission and when necessary the other Member States.

The arrangements in the common Annex (B4) are intended to be adaptable to suit the differing circumstances of individual cases.

B3: Concordat on Co-ordination of European Union Policy Issues: Northern Ireland

B3.1 This document and the common Annex (B4) are to be read in conjunction with the Memorandum of Understanding (MOU) between the UK government,

Scottish Ministers, the Cabinet of the National Assembly for Wales and the Northern Ireland Executive Committee and the enabling legislation establishing these administrations. Reference to devolved or non-devolved matters will be construed in accordance with the MOU.

B3.2 This concordat is an agreement between the Northern Ireland Executive Committee and the UK government. This concordat is not intended to constitute a legally enforceable contract or to create any rights or obligations which are legally enforceable. It is intended to be binding in honour only.

This concordat sets out the mechanisms between UK government and the Northern Ireland Executive Committee for the handling of EU business. Specifically, the concordat covers:

- provision of information;
- formulation of UK policy;
- attendance at Council of Ministers and related meetings;
- implementation of EU obligations; and
- infraction proceedings.

There are a wide range of interfaces with the EU and the practicalities attached to developing and presenting UK policy are to be handled in line with the general principles set out in this paper. Other concordats may set out the procedure in more detail as appropriate.

General

B3.3 As all foreign policy issues are non-devolved, relations with the European Union are the responsibility of the Parliament and government of the United Kingdom, as Member State. However, the UK government wishes to involve the Northern Ireland Executive Committee as directly and fully as possible in decision making on EU matters which touch on devolved areas (including non-devolved matters which impact on devolved areas and non-devolved matters which will have a distinctive impact of importance in Northern Ireland). In general, it is expected that consultation, the exchange of information and the conventions on notifications to EU bodies will continue in similar circumstances to the arrangements in place prior to devolution.

B3.4 Participation will be subject to mutual respect for the confidentiality of discussions and adherence by the Northern Ireland Executive Committee to the resulting UK line without which it would be impossible to maintain such close working relationships. This line will reflect the interests of the UK as a whole. In accordance with these general principles, the co-ordination mechanisms should achieve three key objectives:

- they should provide for full and continuing involvement of ministers and officials of the Northern Ireland administration in the processes of policy formulation, negotiation and implementation, for issues which touch on devolved matters;
- they should ensure that the UK can negotiate effectively, in pursuit of a single UK policy line, but with the flexibility that fast-moving negotiations require; and

- they should ensure EU obligations are implemented with consistency of effect and where appropriate of timing.

Such mechanisms should also ensure that the Northern Ireland Executive Committee and the UK government inform each other of any relevant policy proposals which might impact on either existing or new EU proposals or requirements. They should also ensure that, when required by EC legislation, relevant obligations or initiatives are reported to the Commission and when necessary the other Member States.

The arrangements in the common Annex (B4) are intended to be adaptable to suit the differing circumstances of individual cases.

North/South arrangements

B3.5 As required by the Belfast Agreement, the North/South Ministerial Council brings together those with executive responsibilities in Northern Ireland and the Irish government to develop consultation, co-operation and action within the island of Ireland on matters of mutual interest within the competence of the administrations. This includes consideration of the European Union dimension of relevant matters, including the implementation of EU policies and programmes. The Special EU Programmes Body has a clear operational remit as set out in the North/South Co-operation (Implementation Bodies) (Northern Ireland) Order 1999. This concordat applies to the Northern Ireland Executive Committee's participation in North/South arrangements. In accordance with paragraph 17 of Strand II of the Belfast Agreement, arrangements are to be made to ensure that the views of the North/South Ministerial Council are taken into account and represented appropriately at relevant EU meetings.

B4: Co-ordination of European Policy Issues: Common Annex

Definitions

B4.1 In this document,

- 'devolved legislature' means the Scottish Parliament, the National Assembly for Wales, or the Northern Ireland Assembly;
- 'devolution legislation' means the Scotland Act 1998, the Northern Ireland Act 1998, and the Government of Wales Act 1998;
- 'devolved administration' means the Scottish Executive, the Cabinet of the National Assembly for Wales or the Northern Ireland Executive Committee;
- 'Ministers of the devolved administrations' means Scottish Ministers, Welsh Assembly Secretaries and Northern Ireland Ministers.

Provision of information

B4.2 In order to contribute effectively to the United Kingdom's decision-making on European Union (EU) matters, the devolved administrations will need to have information on relevant EU business. The UK government will therefore provide the devolved administrations with full and comprehensive information, as early as possible, on all business within the framework of the European Union which appears likely to be of interest to the devolved administrations, including notifications of relevant meetings within the EU. This is likely to mean all initiatives within the framework of the EU which appear to touch on matters which fall within the responsibility of the devolved administrations. The same policy will be followed by the devolved administrations on such issues likely to be of interest to the UK government.

B4.3 These arrangements will rely for their effectiveness on mutual respect for the confidentiality of information (including statistics) exchanged. Complete confidentiality is often essential in formulating a UK negotiating position in the EU and in developing tactical responses.

Participation in formulation of UK policy (including resolution of differences)

B4.4 It is the government's intention that ministers and officials of the devolved administrations should be fully involved in discussions within the UK government about the formulation of the UK's policy position on all issues which touch on matters which fall within the responsibility of the devolved administrations. The arrangements outlined below assume maximum co-operation on both sides, although they will also need to work effectively when such co-operation is not forthcoming.

Ministerial involvement

B4.5 Many issues will be capable of being dealt with bilaterally between the lead Whitehall department and the devolved administrations.

B4.6 Even where EU issues require wider inter-departmental consultation, it may often be possible (as at present) to resolve the matter through correspondence; and the arrangements described in this document for copying papers widely to the devolved administrations will help to ensure that matters are resolved in this way wherever possible. EU business operates to an externally imposed timetable and the UK will need to determine its negotiating position in good time. Potential areas of contention will therefore be identified as early as possible, and every effort made to resolve them without escalating discussions to senior levels.

B4.7 Where it is not possible to resolve matters bilaterally or by correspondence as described above, the government envisage that such EU issues will be considered by the Joint Ministerial Committee in European format (paragraph A1.9 of the supplementary agreement on the JMC), which will bring together UK ministers and ministers of the devolved administrations to discuss non-devolved matters which touch on matters which fall within the responsibility of the devolved administrations, and where appropriate the treatment of matters falling within the responsibility of the devolved administrations in different parts of the UK. In the case of EU matters, the JMC will be the forum for seeking to resolve differences between the UK government and the devolved administrations. The procedure to be followed for handling EU business within the JMC is laid down in the supplementary agreement on the JMC.

B4.8 In the case of implementation of European Community (EC) obligations, the wider provisions for resolution of vires disputes through reference to the Judicial Committee of the Privy Council will apply, with the UK Parliament and UK ministers retaining the power, as provided under the devolution legislation, to legislate to implement EC obligations throughout the UK.

Official involvement

B4.9 In line with paragraphs B4.2 and B4.3 above, lead Whitehall departments and UKRep (within its normal reporting responsibilities) will inform officials of the devolved administrations of developments in EU business which touch on matters which fall within the responsibility of the devolved administrations. Such information will be shared both with the devolved administrations and with other interested government departments from the outset. Officials of the devolved administrations will have access to relevant papers (including telegrams) which are copied inter-departmentally by UKRep and lead Whitehall departments.

B4.10 The EU official sub-committee of the JMC will provide an important forum for discussing EU issues. In addition, informal communications and meetings at official level will continue to make a major contribution to the resolution of EU issues. Officials of the devolved administrations will be included in these contacts.

B4.11 Clearly, the nature of consultation procedures in individual cases will depend on the nature of the issue, on previous practice and on the degree of urgency. Depending on the circumstances, issues might be dealt with bilaterally between the lead Whitehall department and the devolved administrations without the need for wider inter-departmental consultation. In cases where wider inter-departmental consultation is necessary, individual departments could choose to consult bilaterally with their opposite numbers in the devolved administrations on a particular subject, before consulting more widely on the basis of an agreed approach. In other cases, they could include the devolved administrations from the outset in a multilateral consultation process.

Attendance at Council of Ministers and related meetings

B4.12 Ministers and officials of the devolved administrations should have a role to play in relevant Council meetings, and other negotiations with EU partners.

B4.13 Decisions on ministerial attendance at Council meetings will be taken on a case-by-case basis by the lead UK minister. In reaching decisions on the composition of the UK team, the lead minister will take into account that the devolved administrations should have a role to play in meetings of the Council of Ministers at which substantive discussion is expected of matters likely to have a significant impact on their devolved responsibilities.

B4.14 Policy does not remain static in negotiations and continuing involvement is a necessary extension of involvement in formulating the UK's initial policy position. The role of ministers and officials from the devolved administrations will be to support and advance the single UK negotiating line which they will have played a part in developing.

The emphasis in negotiations has to be on working as a UK team; and the UK lead minister will retain overall responsibility for the negotiations and determine how each member of the team can best contribute to securing the agreed policy position. In appropriate cases, the leader of the delegation could agree to ministers from the devolved administrations speaking for the UK in Council, and that they would do so with the full weight of the UK behind them, because the policy positions advanced will have been agreed among the UK interests.

B4.15 Attendance by officials of the devolved administrations at EU meetings will continue, as at present, to be agreed bilaterally with the lead Whitehall department. Such agreement would also cover attendance at Presidency and Commission chaired meetings, including those discussing implementation matters. The role of officials from the devolved administrations will be to support and advance the single UK negotiating line which they will have played a part in developing.

Implementation of European Union obligations

B4.16 It will be the responsibility of the lead Whitehall department formally to notify the devolved administrations at official level of any new EU obligation which concerns devolved matters and which it will be the responsibility of the devolved administrations to implement in Scotland, Wales or Northern Ireland (although the arrangements for policy formulation and negotiation described above should ensure that the devolved administrations are already aware of new obligations). In addition, Whitehall departments will, as necessary, liaise closely with the devolved administrations about the implementation by UK legislation of obligations in non-devolved areas, particularly where these could touch on areas which fall within the responsibility of the devolved administrations.

B4.17 For matters falling within the responsibility of the devolved administrations, it is for the devolved administrations to consider, in bilateral consultation with the lead Whitehall department, and other departments and devolved administrations if appropriate, how the obligation should be implemented and administratively enforced (if appropriate) within the required timescale, including whether the devolved administrations should implement separately, or opt for GB or UK legislation. Where a devolved administration opts to implement separately, it will have a responsibility to consult the lead Whitehall department bilaterally, and other departments as necessary, on its implementation proposals, to ensure that any differences of approach nonetheless produce consistency of effect and, where appropriate, of timing. The same official and ministerial mechanisms as for policy formulation will operate where wider inter-departmental discussion is necessary.

B4.18 Following the consultation referred to in paragraph B4.17, notification to the European Commission of such separate implementation should be sent through UKRep, involving the lead Whitehall department as necessary, and copying to them in any event. In cases where there is a need for a consolidated UK communication to the European Commission, this should be co-ordinated by the lead Whitehall department and copied to the devolved administrations, but without prejudice to the devolved administrations' responsibility for implementation. Areas which require such co-ordination may be specified in the relevant bilateral concordats.

B4.19 Where EU legislation provides, in relation to matters falling within the responsibility of the devolved administrations, for the possibility of local measures or derogations within Member States, subject to Commission approval, and where such legislation is being implemented separately in Scotland, Wales or Northern Ireland, the relevant devolved administrations will first consult the lead Whitehall department on whether there are wider UK policy implications. Whitehall departments will also inform the devolved administrations of any similar plans they might have. If, following such consultation, a devolved administration wishes to proceed with such local measures, the request for approval will be routed through UKRep, involving the lead Whitehall Department as necessary, and copying to them in any event.

B4.20   Under the devolution legislation, UK ministers may split a quantitative EC obligation on the UK, such as a quota, to facilitate the transfer of part of it to the Scottish ministers, Northern Ireland ministers or departments and the National Assembly for Wales. The devolved shares can be enforced as a devolution issue on the same basis as any other function of observing and implementing a Community obligation. The size of the devolved share should be equitable, taking into account the extent of the powers of the devolved legislatures and executives and the possibility that the range of measures which can be taken to fulfil an obligation could lie across both non-devolved and devolved areas. UK ministers will consult the devolved administrations before any order is made to apportion the devolved share of such an obligation, and the UK government has made it clear to Parliament that it would do its best to reach agreement with them.

Enforcement of European Union obligations

B4.21   Where they have devolved responsibilities for the enforcement of EC obligations, the devolved administrations will co-operate fully with the relevant lead Whitehall department. The devolved administrations and lead Whitehall department will, in such cases, consult and inform each other of their chosen methods of enforcement of Community and other EU instruments. They will also consult with each other on any enforcement difficulties before they are discussed with the European Commission, and on any corrective action demanded by the Commission.

Infraction proceedings

B4.22   Where the European Commission instigates informal or formal proceedings against the UK for alleged breaches of EC law, the Cabinet Office will commission and co-ordinate the UK response, which will be sent by UKRep on behalf of the UK government.

B4.23   Where a case relates solely to implementation in Scotland, Wales or Northern Ireland in relation to a matter falling within the responsibility of a devolved administration, the draft reply will be prepared by the appropriate devolved administration and agreed at official, and where necessary ministerial, level with interested Whitehall departments. It will be submitted through UKRep in the normal way as outlined in paragraph B4.19. Where a case partly concerns implementation of a devolved matter in England and one or more of the devolved regions, the lead Whitehall department will prepare the draft reply in bilateral consultation, at official or ministerial level as appropriate, with the relevant devolved administrations. Such a procedure will also be followed where a case concerns implementation in Scotland, Wales or Northern Ireland in relation to a non-devolved matter.

B4.24   Where a case partly or wholly involving implementation by a devolved administration is referred to the European Court of Justice, the devolved administration will contribute to the preparation of the UK's submissions to the Court. The devolved administration would take the lead in doing so for cases wholly concerned with implementation in relation to a matter falling within its responsibility, agreed as appropriate with the relevant Whitehall departments. The Cabinet Office and the Treasury Solicitors Department will co-ordinate the UK's submissions to the Court.

B4.25   To the extent that financial costs and penalties imposed on the UK arise from the failure of implementation or enforcement by a devolved administration on a matter falling within its responsibility, or from the failure of a devolved administration to meet its share of an EC quota or obligation, responsibility for meeting these will be borne by the devolved administration. These provisions are without prejudice to the continuing operation of standing arrangements in respect of EU programmes funded as Annually Managed Expenditure (AME).

Representation in Brussels and links with European Union institutions

B4.26   The status and functions of the UK Permanent Representation in Brussels as the institution representing the United Kingdom within the European Union will continue unchanged.

B4.27   The devolved administrations will be able to take part in the less formal discussions with the institutions of the EU and interests within other Member States. Subject to paragraph B4.26 above, the devolved administrations may choose to establish an office in Brussels, to assist direct relationships with other regional governments and with the institutions of the European Communities, so far as this serves the exercise of their powers and the performance of their functions as laid down in the devolution legislation and so far as it is consistent with the responsibility of the UK government for relations with the EU. If such an office is established, it will work closely with, and in a manner complementary to, UKRep which remains responsible for representing the view of the United Kingdom to the European Institutions, and will respect the responsibility of the UK government for non-devolved areas, including overall responsibility for relations with the EU. Both UKRep and any office of the devolved administrations will develop working procedures which reflect the need to balance the interests of all parts of the UK.

B4.28   Staff of the devolved administrations will continue to be eligible for secondment to UKRep and to the institutions of the EU.

Nominations of representatives

B4.29   The devolved administrations will be responsible for nominating their established share of representatives within the Committee of the Regions and the Economic and Social Committee. Such nominations will then be forwarded to the FCO. The final decision on proposals for UK appointments will continue to be made formally by the Foreign Secretary, with the agreement of the Prime Minister, after co-ordination by the FCO and Cabinet Office.

B4.30   The devolved administrations will be consulted by the UK government on appointments to other European Institutions where appropriate.

Scrutiny of EU legislation

B4.31   The devolved legislatures may wish to set up a procedure to allow them to scrutinise EU issues relating to devolved matters to ensure its interests are properly reflected.

B4.32   The lead Whitehall department will liaise as necessary with the devolved administrations in the preparation of Explanatory Memoranda relating to such matters, and will keep them informed. The UK department will send the finalised Explanatory Memorandum to the devolved administrations at the same time that it is submitted to the UK Parliament.

B4.33   Officials of the devolved administrations will pass on to their Whitehall counterparts the views of the devolved legislatures as soon as these are known. Where timing allows, the UK government undertakes to take account of these views in formulating the UK's negotiating position, which will continue to balance the interests of all parts of the UK.

Appendix II: Excerpt from Main Concordat between the Ministry of Agriculture, Fisheries and Food and the Scottish Executive

European Union Policy

General

9. MAFF and SE agree to work together constructively for common interests, taking into account the range of devolved and non-devolved functions involved in the formulation, negotiation, implementation and enforcement of EU-related policies and rules. This section of the Concordat is consistent with, and amplifies, the Concordat on Co-ordination of European Union Policy Issues. The latter provides the overarching framework for all relevant aspects, including representation in Brussels, links with European Institutions, scrutiny of EU legislation, implementation of EU obligations, and arrangements for handling infraction proceedings.

10. As foreign policy issues are a non-devolved matter, relations with the EU are the responsibility of the UK Parliament and government. MAFF consequently retains overall policy responsibility for the formulation of UK policy towards European Union (EU) initiatives, but will involve SE as directly and fully as possible in decision-making on EU matters which touch on devolved areas and non-devolved areas which have a distinctive impact of importance in Scotland.

11. These arrangements will rely for their effectiveness on mutual respect for the confidentiality of discussions and information (including statistics) exchanged.

Provision of Information and Policy Formulation

12. SE will be fully involved in discussions with MAFF about the formulation of the UK policy position on all issues which touch on devolved matters. In order to contribute effectively to the UK's decision-making on EU matters, SE will need to have information on relevant EU proposals. MAFF will therefore provide SE with full and comprehensive information, as early as possible, on all new developments and initiatives within the framework of the EU which may be relevant to SE, including notification of relevant meetings within the EU. MAFF will also provide information to SE on any direct contacts from any other Member States or third countries which concern SE responsibilities.

13. SE would not normally expect to receive direct approaches from the Commission relating to new policy initiatives. Should it do so, it will inform MAFF as soon as possible of such approaches and will pass on to MAFF its views in good time for them to be taken into account. Equally, SE will provide information on any direct contacts with other Member States or third countries.

14. The sharing of information relating to policy formulation will be undertaken with a view to reaching agreement between the administrations. Most issues will be capable of being dealt with bilaterally between MAFF and SE or through correspondence.

15. Following consultation and in collaboration with SE, MAFF shall notify the Commission (via UKRep) of any matters where requirements to pass on information are laid on the Member State or its competent authority, e.g. State Aids and information requirements in sectoral regulations. SE will make relevant information available to MAFF as is necessary for it to meet its obligations. In the following areas, however, and following consultation with MAFF, SE will normally notify such information direct to the Commission (via UKRep):

   i Hill Livestock Compensatory Allowances (HLCAs) returns;
  ii Information on the financial structure and incomes of farm businesses in Scotland (Farm Accountancy Data Network);
 iii Data relating to the implementation of Rural Development Programmes under the Rural Development Regulation; and
 iv Notifications under the Technical Standards Directive.

Unless agreed to the contrary, this arrangement relates to both current and successor instruments. In every case, the party notifying the Commission will send a copy to the other.

EU Negotiations and Attendance at Council of Ministers and Related Meetings

16. These principles apply to the Council of Ministers (in full or restricted session), SCA, COREPER, Working Groups, Management Committees, representation to the European Parliament and any ad hoc meetings, including those with other Member States.

17. MAFF retains overall responsibility in the agriculture, fisheries and food areas for the pursuit of UK policy in multilateral and bilateral negotiations, and in formulating a UK response.

18. As stated in the White Paper 'Scotland's Parliament', ministers and officials of SE have the right to attend relevant meetings chaired by the Commission and relevant Council meetings and other negotiating meetings with EU partners. The role of Scottish ministers and officials will be to support and advance the single UK negotiating line which they will have played a part in developing. The emphasis in negotiations has to be on working as a UK team. MAFF will determine how each member of the team can best contribute to securing the agreed policy position.

19. In any appropriate cases, the leader of the delegation could agree to Scottish ministers speaking for the UK in Council, and that they would do so with the full weight of the UK behind them, because the policy positions advanced will have been agreed among the UK interests. The same approach will apply in official-level meetings chaired by the Council or Commission.

20. MAFF will inform SE as quickly as possible when meetings referred to in paragraph 16 above, of relevance to the UK's negotiating position, are to take place. MAFF will also copy to SE the records of all such meetings as soon as they are produced. MAFF will take account of the views of SE at all stages in the negotiating process. The SE minister will write to the MAFF minister in advance regarding ministerial attendance at forthcoming Council meetings.

Implementation of European Obligations

21. It will be the responsibility of MAFF formally to notify SE at official level of any new EU obligation which concerns devolved matters and which it will be the responsibility of SE to implement in Scotland. In addition MAFF will, as necessary, liaise closely with SE about the implementation by UK legislation of obligations in non-devolved areas, particularly where these could impact on devolved areas. Both MAFF and SE will identify to the other any mistake which they find, or difficulty arising from the text of the EU legislation. Following consultation and in collaboration with SE, MAFF will notify any such mistakes to the Commission, via UKREP, copying relevant papers to SE.

22. To ensure that consistency of purpose is maintained, as appropriate, and for the avoidance of surprises to either party, MAFF and SE agree to co-operate in the following ways:

- Within four weeks of the notification of a requirement to implement an EU obligation – or sooner if the EU timetable demands – they will consult on the timetable for implementation;
- SE will let MAFF know within the four-week period whether it intends to use the option to implement through use of UK/GB instruments. Where this option is used, or where it has been agreed that SE will use MAFF draft legislation to draw up implementing legislation in Scotland, MAFF will ensure that the draft legislation is forwarded to SE in sufficient time to allow necessary procedures, including consultation, to be completed by the implementation deadline.

23. When it is decided that separate legislation will apply in each territory to implement an EU obligation:

- Both parties agree to consult on draft instructions for lawyers at least five working days before they have to be submitted;
- Both parties will exchange copies of the Statutory Instruments at least five working days before they are finalised. Any changes as a result of examination of the text by senior lawyers will be communicated by each party to the other for consultation;
- Similarly, where SE opts to implement EU obligations separately by Act of the Scottish Parliament, it will have a responsibility to consult MAFF (and other departments as necessary) on its proposals with a view to ensuring consistency of effect and timing, where appropriate;
- Both parties will keep each other informed about developments (e.g. Judicial Reviews) which might have implications for the other.

Enforcement of European Obligations

24. SE is responsible in Scotland as MAFF is in England, for the correct enforcement of EU obligations which concern devolved matters. MAFF and SE recognise that enforcement may have cross-border implications. Where there is a risk of inequality or disallowance, enforcement will need to be tackled with a consistency of purpose and effect, though different circumstances may mean that identical rules are inappropriate. To this end MAFF and SE will consult with and then inform each other of their chosen methods of enforcement, for example by exchanging copies of scheme rules. They also agree to such mutual exchanges of information as are required to assist the good management of schemes and the observance of EU obligations.

25. Where enforcement difficulties arise in Scotland or England, MAFF and SE will consult with each other in advance of any discussion with the European Commission or European Court of Auditors. They will similarly consult on any corrective action demanded by the European Commission or European Court of Auditors.

26. In the interests of good communication and for the avoidance of surprises, MAFF and SE will, wherever possible, inform each other at least one week in advance of bilateral contacts with the Commission or other Member States which are relevant to the enforcement of EU legislation. They also agree to report back to each other about such meetings, copying any records as soon as they are available.

Source: http://www.maff.gov.uk/

Appendix III: Joint Ministerial Committee on the European Union[2]

Composition and Terms of Reference

Note by the Joint Secretariat

By agreement between the UK government, Scottish ministers, the Cabinet of the National Assembly for Wales [and the Northern Ireland Executive Committee] a Ministerial Committee has been constituted with the following Composition and Terms of Reference:

Composition

Secretary of State for Foreign and Commonwealth Affairs (Chair)
Deputy Prime Minister and Secretary of State for the Environment, Transport and the Regions
Chancellor of the Exchequer
Secretary of State for the Home Department
Secretary of State for Education and Employment
President of the Council and Leader of the House of Commons
Minister for the Cabinet Office
Minister of State, Scotland Office
Secretary of State for Defence
Parliamentary Secretary, Treasury and Chief Whip
Secretary of State for Northern Ireland
Secretary of State for Wales
Secretary of State for International Development
Minister of Agriculture, Fisheries and Food
Secretary of State for Trade and Industry
Minister for Energy and Competitiveness in Europe, Trade and Industry
Attorney General
Minister of State, Foreign and Commonwealth Office
Scottish First Minister
Scottish Deputy First Minister
Welsh First Secretary
Welsh Assembly Business Secretary

Other Ministers and Secretaries of the National Assembly for Wales may be invited to attend as necessary.

---

2   This is the composition as of February 2000. At that point Northern Irish devolution was in suspense; hence the membership of the Secretary of State for Northern Ireland.

The United Kingdom's Permanent Representative to the European Union is also in attendance.

Terms of Reference

'To consider the UK government's position on European Union issues which impinge on devolved responsibilities; to consider the implementation of EU law in the different parts of the United Kingdom; to keep the arrangements for liaison between the UK government and the three devolved administrations on EU issues under review; and to consider disputes between the administrations on EU issues'.

Cabinet Office
Scottish Executive Secretariat
Welsh Cabinet Secretariat

Bibliography

Armstrong, K. and Bulmer, S. (1996) 'United Kingdom', in Rometsch, D. and Wessels, W. (eds), *The European Union and Member States* (Manchester: Manchester University Press) 253–90.

Baker, D. and Seawright, D. (eds) (1998) *Britain For and Against Europe: British Politics and the Question of European Integration* (Oxford: Clarendon Press).

Blackburn, R. and Plant, R. (eds) (1999) *Constitutional Reform: The Labour Government's Constitutional Reform Agenda* (London: Longman).

Bogdanor, V. (1998) 'Constitutional Reform in the UK', paper presented to Centre for Public Law conference, University of Cambridge, January 1998.

Bulmer, S. and Burch, M. (1996) 'The British Core Executive and European Integration: A New Institutionalist Research Prospectus', EPRU Working Paper, 4/96 (Manchester: University of Manchester).

Bulmer, S. and Burch, M. (1998) 'Organising for Europe: Whitehall, the British State and the European Union', *Public Administration*, 76: 4, 601–28.

Bulmer, S. and Burch, M. (2000) 'Coming to Terms with Europe: Europeanisation, Whitehall and the Challenge of Devolution, Queen's University Belfast Papers on Europeanization, no 9/2000 (http://www.qub.ac.uk/ies/onlinepapers/poe9.pdf).

Bulmer, S., George, S., and Scott, A. (eds) (1992) *The United Kingdom and EC Membership Evaluated* (London: Pinter Publishers).

Burch, M. and Holliday, I. (1996) *The British Cabinet System* (London: Prentice Hall).

Burch, M. and Holliday, I. (2000) 'New Labour and the Constitution', in Coates, D. and Lawler, P. (eds), *New Labour in Power* (Manchester: Manchester University Press), 80–91.

Cabinet Office (1999) *Memorandum of Understanding and Supplementary Agreements – between the United Kingdom Government, Scottish Ministers and the Cabinet of the National Assembly for Wales* Cm 4444.

Carter, C. (2001) 'The UK Parliament: Scrutiny Unleashed?', in Maurer, A. and Wessels, W. (eds), *The European Parliament and National Parliaments After Amsterdam* (Baden-Baden: Nomos).

Collier, R. and Collier, D. (1991) *Shaping the Political Agenda: Critical Junctures, the Labour Movement, and Regime Dynamics in Latin America* (Princeton: Princeton University Press).

Commission of the European Communities (1998) *The Wales–Europe Report 1998* (Cardiff: Commission of the European Communities).

Constitution Unit Wales Report (1999) 'Devolution in Transition – Monitoring the National Assembly July to December 1999', Institute of Welsh Affairs, May (http://www.ucl.ac.uk/constitution-unit/leverh/index.htm).

Constitution Unit Wales Report (2000) 'Devolution in Transition – Monitoring the National Assembly February to May 2000', Institute of Welsh Affairs, May at (http://www.ucl.ac.uk/constitution-unit/leverh/index.htm).

Consultative Steering Group on the Scottish Parliament (1998) *Shaping Scotland's Parliament* (London: HMSO).

Cortell, P. and Peterson, S. (1999) 'Altered States: Explaining Domestic Institutional Change', *British Journal of Political Science*, 29, 177–203.

Cowley, P. (2000) 'Legislatures and Assemblies', in Dunleavy, P. *et al.* (eds), *Developments in British Politics*, (Basingstoke: Palgrave Macmillan Ltd.), 108–26.

Crick, B. and Millar, D. (1997) *To Make the Parliament of Scotland, a Model for Democracy* (Edinburgh: John Wheatley Centre).

Daugbjerg, C. (1997) 'Policy Networks and Agricultural Policy Reforms', *Governance*, 10: 2, 123–42.

Davies, R. (1998) 'Devolution: A Process Not an Event', *The Gregynog Papers*, Vol. 2 (2), (Cardiff: Institute of Welsh Affairs).

Davies, R. (2000) Speech reproduced in *Agenda*, Winter 2000 (Cardiff: Institute of Welsh Affairs).

DETR/SE Concordat (1999) *Concordat Between the Department of Environment, Transport and the Regions and the Scottish Executive* (http://www.scotland.gov.uk/concordats/).

Dewar, D. (1999) Speech to the Scottish Parliament, 1 July 1999 (www.scottish.parliament.uk/msps/biographies/dewar.htm).

Drucker, H. and Brown, G. (1980) *The Politics of Nationalism and Devolution* (London: Longman).

Dunkerley, D. and Thompson, A. (eds) (1999) *Wales Today* (Cardiff: University of Wales Press).

European Commission (1997) *Agenda 2000: For a Stronger and Wider Union* (Brussels: European Commission).

European Strategy Group Report (1998) *The National Assembly for Wales and the European Union* (Cardiff: Welsh Office).

Government of Wales Act 1998, Chapter 38, *Public Acts*, Session 1997–98.

Gray, J. and Osmond, J. (1997) *Wales in Europe: the Opportunity Presented by a Welsh Assembly* (Cardiff: Institute of Welsh Affairs).

Hall, P. (1993) 'Policy Paradigms, Social Learning and the State: the Case of Economic Policy Making in Britain', *Comparative Politics*, 25: 275–96.

Hall, P. and Taylor, R. (1996) 'Political Science and the Three New Institutionalisms', *Political Studies*, Vol. 44, 936–58.

Hayes-Renshaw, F. and Wallace, H. (1997) *The Council of Ministers* (Basingstoke: Palgrave Macmillan).

Hazell, R. (ed.) (1999) *Constitutional Futures: A History of the Next Ten Years* (Oxford: Oxford University Press).

House of Commons (1999) *The European Scrutiny System in the House of Commons* (mimeo), House of Commons.

House of Commons (1998) Resolution of the House of 17 November, Votes and Proceedings, p. 1250.

House of Commons (1998) Select Committee on Scottish Affairs, 2nd Report, *The Operation of Multi-Layer Democracy*, Session 1997–98, 18 November.

House of Lords (1999) Resolution, 6 December.

Humphreys, J. (1996) *A Way through the Woods: Negotiating in the European Union* (London, Department of the Environment).

Jeffery, C. (ed.) (1997) *The European Dimension of the European Union* (London: Frank Cass).

Jeffery, C. (2000) 'Sub-National Mobilization and European Integration: Does it Make Any Difference?', *Journal of Common Market Studies*, 38: 1, 1–23.

Jones, B. (ed.) (1999) *Political Issues in Britain Today* (Manchester: Manchester University Press).

Jordan, A. (2000) 'The Europeanisation of UK Environmental Policy', ESRC One Europe or Several? Programme Working Paper 11/00 (Brighton: Sussex European Institute).

Keesing's Record of World Events, 1998–2001 (London: Longman).

Kellas, J. (1989) *The Scottish Political System*, 4th edn (Cambridge: Cambridge University Press).

Kerse, C. S. (2000) 'Parliamentary Scrutiny of the Third Pillar', *European Public Law*, 6:1, 81–101.

Kilbrandon, Lord (1973) Royal Commission on the Constitution 1969–73, Vol. 1, Report Cmnd 5460, Session 1972–73 (London: HMSO).

Krasner, S. (1988) 'Sovereignty: an Institutional Perspective', *Comparative Political Studies*, 21: 1, 66–94.

Labour Party (1997) *New Labour: Because Britain Deserves Better* (London: Labour Party).

Leicester, G. (1999) 'Scottish and Welsh Devolution', in Blackburn, R. and Plant, R. (eds), *Constitutional Reform: The Labour Government's Constitutional Reform Agenda* (London: Longman), 251–63.

Loughlin, J. (1997) *Wales in Europe: Welsh Regional Actors and European Integration*, Papers in Planning Research, 157, Cardiff (Department of City and Regional Planning, Cardiff University).

Lowe, P. and Ward, S. (eds) (1998) *British Environmental Policy and Europe: politics and policy in transition* (London: Routledge).

MAFF/SE Concordat (1999) 'Main Concordat Between the Ministry of Agriculture, Fisheries and Food and the Scottish Executive' (http://www.maff.gov.uk/).

Majone, G. (1996) *Regulating Europe* (London: Routledge).

Maurer, A. and Wessels, W. (eds) (2001) *The European Parliament and National Parliaments After Amsterdam* (Baden-Baden: Nomos).

Maurer, A. and Wessels, W. (eds) (2001) *National Parliaments on their Ways to Europe: Losers or Latecomers?* (Baden-Baden: Nomos Verlagsgesellschaft).

Mazey, S. and Richardson, J. (1996) 'EU Policy-Making: a garbage can or an anticipatory and consensual policy style?', in Mény, Y., Muller, P. and Quermonne, J.-L. (eds), *Adjusting to Europe* (London: Routledge), 41–58.

Mény, Y., Muller, P. and Quermonne J.-L. (eds) (1996) *Adjusting to Europe* (London: Routledge).

Mitchell, J. (1996) *Strategies for Self-Government: the Campaigns for a Scottish Parliament* (Edinburgh: Polygon).

Mitchell, J. (1999) 'Devolution', in Jones, B. (ed.), *Political Issues in Britain Today* (Manchester: Manchester University Press).

Morgan, K. and Mungham, G. (2000) *Redesigning Democracy: the Making of the Welsh Assembly* (Bridgend: Seren).

Munro, C. (1999) *Studies in Constitutional Law* (London: Butterworths).

Munro, C. (2000) 'Scottish Devolution: Accommodating a Restless Nation', in Tierney, S. (ed.), *Accommodating National Identity: New Approaches in International and Domestic Law* (The Hague, London, Boston: Kluwer Law International), 133–49.

National Assembly Advisory Group (1998) *Report to the Secretary of State for Wales: Recommendations* (Cardiff: NAAG).

Osmond, J. (1997) *The European Union and the Governance of Wales: A Background Paper* (Cardiff: Institute of Welsh Affairs).

Osmond, J. (1999) *Devolution: A dynamic, settled process?* (Cardiff: Institute of Welsh Affairs).

Osmond, J. (2000a) 'Coalition Politics Come to Wales', Constitution Unit Wales Report (Cardiff: Institute of Welsh Affairs).

Osmond, J. (ed.) (2000b) *Devolution in Transition. Monitoring the National Assembly February to May 2000* (Cardiff: Institute of Welsh Affairs).

Paterson, L. (1998) *A Diverse Assembly: the Debate on a Scottish Parliament* (Edinburgh: Edinburgh University Press).

Peters, B. G. (1999) *Institutional Theory in Political Science: the New Institutionalism* (London: Pinter).

Radaelli, C. (2000) 'Whither Europeanization? Concept stretching and substantive change', paper for conference on Europeanization: Concept and Reality (University of Bradford, May).

Raunio, T. and Wiberg, M. (2000a) 'Building Elite Consensus: Parliamentary Accountability in Finland', *Journal of Legislative Studies*, 6: 1, 59–80.

Raunio, T. and Wiberg, M. (2000b) 'Does Support Lead to Ignorance? National Parliaments and the Legitimacy of EU Governance', *Acta Politica*, 35, 146–68.

Richardson, J. (ed.) (1996) *European Union: Power and Policy-Making* (London: Routledge).

Rometsch, D. and Wessels, W. (eds) (1996) *The European Union and Member States* (Manchester: Manchester University Press).

Royal Commission (1998) 'Reform of the House of Lords – A Consultation Paper' March.

Sbragia, A. (1996) 'Environmental Policy: The "Push–Pull" of Policy-Making', in Wallace, H. and Wallace, W. (eds), *Policy-Making in the European Union* (Oxford: Oxford University Press), 235–57.

Scotland Act 1998, Chapter 46, *Public Acts*, Session 1997–98.

Scott, A. (2001) 'The Role of Concordats in the New Governance of Britain', *Edinburgh Law Review*, 5: 1, 21–48.

Scottish Office (1991) *The Scottish Office and the European Community – A Review: summary of the main findings and recommendations* (Edinburgh: Scottish Office Industry Department).

Scottish Office (1997) *Scotland's Parliament – A White Paper*, Cm 3658, 07–97 (Stationery Office: Edinburgh).

Scottish Office (1998a) 'CSG: Scrutiny of European Legislation by the Scottish Parliament' Position Paper, CSG (98) (36), 21 August.

Scottish Office (1998b) 'Scotland's Parliament: Handling of European Business' Draft Consultation Paper, mimeo.

Sharp, R. (1998) 'Responding to Europeanisation: A governmental perspective', in Lowe, P. and Ward, S. (eds), *British Environmental Policy and Europe: politics and policy in transition* (London: Routledge), 33–56.

Smith, J. (2001) 'Cultural Aspects of Europeanisation: The Case of the Scottish Office', *Public Administration*, 79: 1, 147–65.

Steiner, J. (1992) 'Legal System', in Bulmer, S., George, S., and Scott, A. (eds), *The United Kingdom and EC Membership Evaluated* (London: Pinter Publishers), 124–37.

Steinmo, S., Thelen, K. and Longstreth, F. (eds) (1992) *Structuring Politics: Historical Institutionalism in Comparative Politics* (Cambridge: Cambridge University Press).

Thain, C. and Wright, M. (1995) *The Treasury and Whitehall: The Planning and Control of Public Expenditure, 1976–1993* (Oxford: Clarendon Press).

Thelen, K. and Steinmo, S. (1992) 'Historical institutionalism in comparative politics', in Steinmo, S., Thelen, K. and Longstreth, F. (eds), *Structuring Politics: Historical Institutionalism in Comparative Politics* (Cambridge: Cambridge University Press), 1–33.

Thomas, A. (1999) 'Politics in Wales: a New Era?', in Dunkerley, D. and Thompson, A. (eds), *Wales Today* (Cardiff: University of Wales Press), 287–302.

Thompson, A. (1999) 'Wales in Europe' in Dunkerley, D. and Thompson, A. (eds), *Wales Today* (University of Wales Press: Cardiff), 305–18.

Tierney, S. (ed.) (2000) *Accommodating National Identity: New Approaches in International and Domestic Law* (The Hague, London, Boston: Kluwer Law International).

Tratt, J. (1996) *The Macmillan Government and Europe: A Study in the Process of Policy Development* (London: Palgrave Macmillan).

Wallace, H. and Wallace, W. (eds) (1996) *Policy-Making in the European Union* (Oxford: Oxford University Press).

Welsh Affairs Select Committee at Westminster (1995) *Wales in Europe* Vol. 1 (London: HMSO).

Welsh Development Agency (1996) *Gateway Europe*, 20 (Cardiff: Welsh Development Agency).

Welsh Development Agency (1998) *Wales Commercial Centre: Linking Welsh Business to Europe* (Cardiff: Welsh Development Agency).

Welsh Office (1997) *A Voice for Wales: the Government's Proposals for a Welsh Assembly*, Cm 3718, 07–97 (London: Stationery Office).

Welsh Office (1999) *The Standing Orders of the National Assembly for Wales*, (www.wales.gov.uk/assembly).

Westlake, M. (1995) *The Council of the European Union* (London: Cartermill Publishing).

Wright, V. (1996) 'The National Coordination of European Policy-Making: Negotiating the Quagmire', in Richardson, J. (ed.), *European Union: Power and Policy-Making* (London: Routledge), 148–69.

Index